Cultures and Organizations

Software of the mind

Cultures and Organizations

Software of the mind

Geert Hofstede
Institute for Research on Intercultural Cooperation
(IRIC)
University of Limburg at Maastricht,
The Netherlands

McGRAW-HILL

New York · San Francisco · Washington, D.C. · Auckland · Bogotá
Caracas · Lisbon · London · Madrid · Mexico City · Milan
Montreal · New Delhi · San Juan · Singapore
Sydney · Tokyo · Toronto

Library of Congress Cataloging-in-Publication Data
Hofstede, Geert H.
   Cultures and organizations: software of the mind / Geert Hofstede.
     p.   cm.
   Includes bibliographical references and index.
   ISBN 0-07-029307-4
   1. Intercultural communication.   2. Organization—Research.
3. International cooperation.   4. National characteristics.
5. Ethnopsychology.   I. Title.
HM258.H574   1991
306—dc20

91-205
CIP

McGraw-Hill

A Division of The McGraw-Hill Companies

   6 7 8 9 0   DOC/DOC   9 0 1 0 9

ISBN 0-07-029307-4

Printed and bound by R. R. Donnelley & Sons Company.

This book was first published copyright © 1991 by McGraw-Hill International
(UK) Limited

McGraw-Hill books are available at special quantity discounts to use as
premiums and sales promotions, or for use in corporate training
programs. For more information, please write to the Director of Special
Sales, McGraw-Hill, 11 West 19th Street, New York, NY 10011.
Or contact your local bookstore.

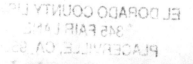

Contents

Preface to the first edition

In the late 1960s I accidentally became interested in cultural differences—and gained access to rich data for studying them. This study resulted in the publication in 1980 of a book on the subject, *Culture's Consequences*. It was written for a scholarly public; it had to be, because it cast doubts on the universal validity of established theories in psychology, organization sociology, and management theory: so I had to show the theoretical reasoning, base data, and statistical treatments used to reach the conclusions. A 1984 paperback edition of the book left out the base data and the statistics but was otherwise identical to the 1980 hardcover version.

Culture's Consequences appeared at a time when interest in cultural differences, both between nations and between organizations, was rapidly rising, and there was a dearth of empirically supported information on the subject. As far as differences among nations were concerned the earlier book certainly provided such information, but maybe too much of it at once. Many readers evidently only read parts of the message. For example, I lost count of the number of people who cited the book claiming that I studied the values of IBM (or 'Hermes') *managers*. The data I used were from IBM *employees* and that, as the book itself showed, makes quite a difference.

The theme of cultural differences is, of course, not only and even not primarily of interest to social scientists or international business students. It concerns anyone who meets people from outside his or her own narrow circle, and in the modern world that is virtually everybody. This new book does what should have been done earlier: it addresses itself to any interested reader. It avoids social scientific jargon where possible and explains it where necessary; a glossary is added for this purpose.

Reformulating the message of *Culture's Consequences* after 10 years has made it possible to include the results of more recent research by others and by myself, including research on differences in organizational cultures. Since 1980 many people have published important studies on cultural differences. The second half of the book is almost entirely based on new material. I am particularly indebted to Michael Bond in Hong Kong and to Michael Hoppe in Chapel Hill NC, USA who through their work stimulated my thinking in fundamental ways. Another debt is to the collaborators in the IRIC research project on organization cultures in Denmark and the Netherlands: the key people were Denise Ohayv in Copenhagen and Geert Sanders and Bram Neuijen in Groningen. The inventive mind of Bob Waisfisz, management consultant in The Hague, was a permanent source of inspiration: he let me share his tremendous experience in ways of teaching practice-oriented people about culture; he also commented on a draft version of the manuscript. John W. Bing, René Olie, Louise Pannenborg-Stutterheim, Hein Schreuder, and Gert Van de Paal also helped me greatly by reading and commenting on draft versions of the book.

In contrast to the earlier books there are no secretaries to be complimented for their conscientious typing. I composed the manuscript on a personal computer, leaving the secretaries to more important tasks. Both the secretaries and I enjoy the new technology and I even suspect that it increases my creativity.

In the panel of informants, discussion partners, and benevolent critics for new ideas during the book's gestation period the members of the Hofstede tribe: Maaike, Josephie, Gert-Jan, Rokus, Bart, and Gideon have all contributed. Since the discussions at the family dinner table at the time of *Culture's Consequences*, they have all become professionals in their own varied fields. Our common interest in cultural differences has remained, and it has again been a source of support both at the intellectual and at the emotional level. I think of them all with love and gratitude.

This book is dedicated to our grandchildren Liesbeth and Bregje Hofstede and others that may yet be born. The world we are now passing on to their generation is full of clashes between differently programmed minds. Liesbeth and Bregje will not like the book now because it has no nice pictures. I am sorry about that; but I hope it will contribute a little bit to mutual understanding across cultures in tomorrow's world which is theirs.

GEERT HOFSTEDE
Maastricht/Velp, the Netherlands

Preface to the revised edition

Since this book first appeared in 1991, the worlds of politics, of business and of ideas have kept changing fast. For example, the text has been amended to refer to the *former* Soviet Union and to the *former* Yugoslavia. The disgusting term 'ethnic cleansing' has been coined for what used to be called 'genocide'. South Africa has become a politically correct place to visit and to do business with, and turned from an international pariah into the only hope for a continent that trails all statistics of development. In several poor countries, first-ever democratic elections have been held under international pressure and control. Even if these have been successful, few countries have known what to do with the results, except shoot at the opposition. Nevertheless, in business literature 'globalization' has become the new buzzword. More multinationals are flocking to China in a unusual mood of charity, spending money without any guarantee of return. And Eastern Europe has seen herds of economic and business consultants flying in and out again, often in despair. Electronic highways have been built overnight, and individuals at monitor screens have tried to make sense out of communications with people whose computers may be programmed the same, but whose minds are most certainly not.

Other trends from the previous decade have continued. In wealthy countries, minorities have stepped up their claims for a fair share of opportunities, and have often been disappointed. The economies of East Asia have continued to outperform the rest of the world. Japan's per capita Gross National Product has exceeded the corresponding figure for the USA by twenty per cent. Singapore, Hong Kong, Taiwan and South Korea have all moved into the category of high-income economies along with Western Europe and the Anglo countries. The Chinese have further developed their brand of authoritarian market socialism with very little regard for Western style Human Rights. World-wide migration for political and economic reasons, legal or illegal, has reached the highest level ever and led to immense suffering and exploitation, and a surge of xenophobia. Yet in spite of this, some migrants have adapted quite successfully to their new homeland. Migrants' children have had to bridge the culture gap between the old and the new life style, and have often fought with their parents. Religious groups have continued to decide that they—and nobody else—happen to possess the Absolute Truth or Absolute Virtue, which justifies imposing their laws on others, even killing those who disagree with them. The numbers of AIDS-infected cases and prospective cases have multiplied, and consequent drives for behavioral change have tried to break century-old taboos, often in vain. No doubt this list could be continued.

This book is about the human constants in all these changes. It argues, on the basis of hard research, that all human societies share some basic problems that have always existed and will continue to exist as long as Mankind. They are the problems of (in)equality, of group solidarity, of gender roles, of an uncertain future, and of need gratification. Over millennia, different societies have developed their own solutions to these problems which have been transferred from generation to generation. To those within a society its own solution is natural, rational, and morally right—but from one society to another, solutions differ in ways that are not always obvious. This is the domain of basic values that are the core of national cultures, and one only discovers this when in contact with another culture; like a fish only discovers water after it has been caught.

This book is also a cultural atlas: it is explicit about what research has shown about the differences in culture-based values among more than fifty countries. Thus it allows a reader from country X to position himself or herself vis-à-vis country Y. I have tried to avoid language which implies that X is better than Y or vice versa. Deciding what is better is a choice made within each culture. I do not defend absolute cultural relativism, but I do try to show where the sense of what is good and evil differs between one culture and another. This has made the book internationally appealing—so far, it has appeared in eleven languages (besides the original English, this book has appeared in Chinese, Danish, Dutch, Finnish, French, German, Japanese, Korean, Norwegian and Swedish).

On a trip around the world some years ago, I bought three world maps. All three maps were of the flat kind, projecting the surface of the globe on a plane. The first was the classic type, with Europe and Africa in the middle, the Americas to the West and Asia to the East; thus showing how the terms 'the West' and 'the East' were products of a Euro-centered world view. The second map, which I bought in Hawaii, showed the Pacific Ocean in the center, with Asia and Africa on the left, and Europe—tiny—in the far upper left-hand corner, and the Americas to the right. From Hawaii, the East lies West and the West lies East! My third map, bought in New Zealand, was like the second but upside-down: South on top and North at the bottom. Now Europe appeared in the far lower right-hand corner. Which of these maps was right? All three, of course! The Earth is round and any place on the surface is as much the center as any other. All peoples have considered their country the center of the world; the Chinese call China the 'Middle Kingdom' (*zhongguo*), and the ancient Scandinavians called their country by a similar name (*midgaard*). I believe that even today most citizens, politicians and academics in any country in their heart feel that their country is the Middle one; and they act correspondingly.

These feelings are so powerful that it is almost always possible, when reading a book, to determine the nationality of the author, even if it has not been mentioned. The same, of course, applies to this book—its author is from The Netherlands, and even when I write in English, as I did, the Dutch software of my mind will remain evident to the careful reader. This makes reading the book by people who are not my compatriots in itself a cross-cultural experience—maybe even a culture shock to some. That is okay; studying culture without experiencing culture shock is like practising to swim without water. In Asterix, the famous French cartoon, the oldest villager expresses his dislike of visiting foreigners as follows: 'I don't have anything against foreigners. Some of my best friends are foreigners. But these foreigners are not from here!'

In the booming market for cross-cultural training, there are courses and books that show only the sunny side: cultural synergy, no cultural conflict. Maybe that is the message some business-minded people like to hear, but it is false. Studying culture without culture shock is only listening to the foreigners who are from here. Max Pagès, a leading French social psychologist, wrote about a training course in the USA: 'they treated me as another American who had this peculiarity of being a Frenchman!' Culture is more often a source of conflict than of synergy. Cultural differences are a nuisance at best and often a disaster. But if we really want to globalize, there is no way around them so we better take them for what they are.

One part of this book deals with organizational (or corporate) cultures, an immensely popular subject about which a lot of nonsense has been written. Its treatment in this book is based on careful research, not on wishful thinking. This has led to some surprises: contrary to national cultures, corporate cultures are not a matter of shared values as some authors want it. They are rooted in the values of the founders and significant leaders, but their values have been converted into the practices, the rules of the game, for all other members of the corporation. And this explains what would otherwise be a riddle: how multinationals can function productively, if the national cultures of their personnel in different countries are as different as they are. Effective multinationals have created practices that bridge the national value differences.

In bridging their internal national value differences, multinationals are setting a mode of operation for the world at large: our common world-wide problems demand concerted action, but if we have to wait until all peoples share the same cultural values we will wait forever. Common practices, not common values are what solve practical problems. The differences in values should be understood, the differences in practices should be resolved. These two steps are what this book is about.

GEERT HOFSTEDE
Velp, the Netherlands

A guide through this book

This book consists of four parts. Part I lays the foundation for a good understanding of the remainder of the book by explaining what we mean when we talk about 'culture', and by providing a small vocabulary of essential terms to be used in the following parts.

Part II, by far the largest part, consists of Chapters 2 to 7 and deals with differences among cultures at *national level*. Chapters 2 to 5 describe the four dimensions empirically found in research across more than 50 countries: to wit power distance, collectivism versus individualism, femininity versus masculinity, and uncertainty avoidance. Each of these chapters is composed in the same way: the dimension is described, the scores of the various countries are shown, and the consequences of the dimension for family life, school, workplace, organization, state, and the development of ideas are discussed. Speculatively, something is said about the origins and the possible future of differences along each dimension. Differences according to gender, generation, and social class are brought in wherever they are relevant.

Chapter 6 looks at the consequences of national culture differences in the way people in a country organize themselves, combining the dimensions described in the four previous chapters. It shows that organizational practices and theories are culturally dependent.

Chapter 7 brings in the fifth cross-national dimension: long-term versus short-term orientation. It also explores the implications of the fact that this dimension could only be detected with a questionnaire designed by the Chinese; it reveals deep differences between Eastern and Western thinking related to the importance of 'virtue' versus 'truth'.

Part III deals with *organizational culture differences*, and consists of one single chapter: Chapter 8. It describes the new insights collected in IRIC's research project across 20 organizational units in Denmark and the Netherlands conducted in the period 1985–1987. These are complementary to the national culture differences illustrated in the earlier chapters.

Part IV deals with the *practical implications* of the culture differences and similarities described so far. Chapter 9 looks at what happens when people from different cultures meet. It treats phenomena such as culture shock, ethnocentrism, stereotyping, differences in language and in humor. It refers to intercultural encounters in tourism, schools, development cooperation, international negotiations, and joint business ventures. It discusses how intercultural communication skills can be developed. Chapter 10 summarizes the message of the book and translates it into suggestions for parents, managers, and the media. It also speculates about political developments in the coming years, on the basis of cultural processes.

Practitioners can stop reading the book here. A final section entitled *Reading Mental Programs* is mainly addressed at research colleagues and is added as an appendix. It deals with how to collect reliable information about cultural differences. It also refers to controversies within the social sciences around the subject of culture, and explains the methodological choices behind the approach followed.

Practitioners may benefit, however, from the glossary which follows the appendix, in which the scientific terms used in the book are listed each with a brief explanation. Finally, there is a literature reference list, a name index, and a subject index; the latter includes references to the glossary.

Part I

Introduction

1

Levels of culture

11th juror: (*rising*) 'I beg pardon, in discussing . . '
10th juror: (*interrupting and mimicking*) 'I beg pardon. What are you so goddam polite about?'
11th juror: (*looking straight at the 10th juror*) 'For the same reason you're not. It's the way I was brought up.'

From Reginald Rose, *Twelve Angry Men*

Twelve Angry Men is an American theatre piece which became a famous motion picture, starring Henry Fonda. The play was written in 1955. The scene consists of the jury room of a New York court of law. Twelve jury members who have never met before have to decide unanimously on the guilt or innocence of a boy from a slum area, accused of murder. The quote above is from the second and final act when emotions have reached boiling point. It is a confrontation between the tenth juror, a garage owner, and the eleventh juror, a European-born, probably Austrian, watchmaker. The tenth juror is irritated by what he sees as the excessively polite manners of the other man. But the watchmaker cannot behave otherwise. After many years in his new home country, he still behaves the way he was raised. He carries within himself an indelible pattern of behavior.

Different minds but common problems

The world is full of confrontations between people, groups, and nations who think, feel, and act differently. At the same time these people, groups, and nations, just like our twelve angry men are exposed to common problems which demand cooperation for their solution. Ecological, economical, military, hygienic, and meteorological developments do not stop at national or regional borders. Coping with the threats of nuclear warfare, acid rain, ocean pollution, extinction of animals, AIDS, or a worldwide recession demands cooperation of opinion leaders from many countries. They in their turn need the support of broad groups of followers in order to implement the decisions taken.

3

Understanding the differences in the ways these leaders and their followers think, feel, and act is a condition for bringing about worldwide solutions that work. Questions of economic, technological, medical, or biological cooperation have too often been considered as merely technical. One of the reasons why so many solutions do not work or cannot be implemented is because differences in thinking among the partners have been ignored. Understanding such differences is at least as essential as understanding the technical factors.

The objective of this book is to help in dealing with the differences in thinking, feeling, and acting of people around the globe. It will show that although the variety in people's minds is enormous, there is a structure in this variety which can serve as a basis for mutual understanding.

Culture as mental programming

Every person carries within him or herself patterns of thinking, feeling, and potential acting which were learned throughout their lifetime. Much of it has been acquired in early childhood, because at that time a person is most susceptible to learning and assimilating. As soon as certain patterns of thinking, feeling and acting have established themselves within a person's mind, (s)he must unlearn these before being able to learn something different, and unlearning is more difficult than learning for the first time.

Using the analogy of the way in which computers are programmed, this book will call such patterns of thinking, feeling, and acting *mental programs*, or, as the sub-title goes: *'software of the mind'*. This does not mean, of course, that people are programmed the way computers are. A person's behavior is only partially predetermined by her or his mental programs: (s)he has a basic ability to deviate from them, and to react in ways which are new, creative, destructive, or unexpected. The *'software of the mind'* this book is about only indicates what reactions are likely and understandable, given one's past.

The sources of one's mental programs lie within the social environments in which one grew up and collected one's life experiences. The programming starts within the family; it continues within the neighborhood, at school, in youth groups, at the work place, and in the living community. The European watchmaker from the quote at the beginning of this chapter came from a country and a social class in which polite behavior is still at a premium today. Most people from that environment would have reacted as he did. The American garage owner, who worked himself up from the slums, acquired quite different mental programs. Mental programs vary as much as the social environments in which they were acquired.

A customary term for such mental software is *culture*. This word has several meanings, all derived from its Latin source, which refers to the tilling of the soil. In most Western languages 'culture' commonly means 'civilization' or 'refinement of the mind' and in particular the results of such refinement, like education, art, and literature. This is 'culture in the narrow sense'; I sometimes call it 'culture one'. Culture as mental software, however, corresponds to a much broader use of the word which is common among social anthropologists: this is 'culture two', and it is the concept which will be used throughout this book.

Social (or cultural) anthropology is the science of human societies, in particular (although not only) traditional or 'primitive' ones. In social anthropology, 'culture' is a catchword for all those patterns of thinking, feeling, and acting referred to in the previous paragraphs. Not only those activities supposed to refine the mind are included in 'culture two', but also the ordinary and menial things in life: greeting, eating, showing or not showing feelings, keeping a certain physical distance from others, making love, or maintaining body hygiene. Politicians and journalists sometimes confuse culture two and culture one without being aware of it: the adaptation problems of immigrants to their new host country are discussed in terms of promoting folk dance groups. But culture two deals with much more fundamental human processes than culture one; it deals with the things that hurt.

Culture (two) is always a collective phenomenon, because it is at least partly shared with people who live or lived within the same social environment, which is where it was learned. It is *the collective programming of the mind which distinguishes the members of one group or category*[1] *of people from another.*[2]

Culture is learned, not inherited. It derives from one's social environment, not from one's genes. Culture should be distinguished from human nature on one side, and from an individual's personality on the other (see Fig. 1.1), although exactly where the borders lie between human nature and culture, and between culture and personality, is a matter of discussion among social scientists.

Human nature is what all human beings, from the Russian professor to the Australian aborigine, have in common: it represents the universal level in one's mental software. It is inherited with one's genes; within the computer analogy it is the 'operating system' which determines one's physical and basic psychological functioning. The human ability to feel fear, anger, love, joy, sadness, the need to associate with others, to play and exercise oneself, the facility to observe the environment and to talk about it with other humans all belong to this level of mental programming. However, what one does with these feelings, how one expresses fear, joy, observations, and so on, is modified by culture. Human nature is not as 'human' as the term

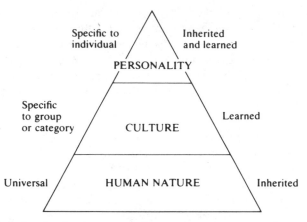

Fig. 1.1 Three levels of uniqueness in human mental programming

suggests, because certain aspects of it are shared with parts of the animal world.[3]

The *personality* of an individual, on the other hand, is her/his unique personal set of mental programs which (s)he does not share with any other human being. It is based upon traits which are partly inherited with the individual's unique set of genes and partly learned. 'Learned' means: modified by the influence of collective programming (culture) *as well as* unique personal experiences.

Cultural traits have often been attributed to heredity, because philosophers and other scholars in the past did not know how to explain otherwise the remarkable stability of differences in culture patterns among human groups. They underestimated the impact of learning from previous generations and of teaching to a future generation what one has learned oneself. The role of heredity is exaggerated in the pseudo-theories of *race*, which have been responsible, among other things, for the Holocaust organized by the Nazis during the Second World War. Racial and ethnic strife is often justified by unfounded arguments of cultural superiority and inferiority.

In the USA, a heated scientific discussion erupted in the late 1960s on whether blacks were genetically less intelligent than whites.[4] The issue became less popular in the 1970s, after some researchers had demonstrated that using the same logic and tests, Asians in the USA on average scored *more* in intelligence than whites. It is extremely difficult, if not impossible, to find tests that are culture free. This means that they reflect only ability, not the differences in, for example, social opportunity. There is little doubt that, on average, blacks in the USA (and other minority and even majority groups in other countries) have fewer *opportunities* than whites.

Cultural relativism

The student of culture finds human groups and categories thinking, feeling, and acting differently, but there are no scientific standards for considering one group as intrinsically superior or inferior to another. Studying differences in culture among groups and societies presupposes a position of cultural relativism.[5] Claude Lévi-Strauss, the grand old man of French anthropology, has expressed it as follows:

> 'Cultural relativism affirms that one culture has no absolute criteria for judging the activities of another culture as "low" or "noble". However, every culture can and should apply such judgment to its own activities, because its members are actors as well as observers.'[6]

Cultural relativism does not imply normlessness for oneself, nor for one's society. It does call for suspending judgment when dealing with groups or societies different from one's own. One should think twice before applying the norms of one person, group or society to another. Information about the nature of the cultural differences between societies, their roots, and their consequences should precede judgment and action.

Even after having been informed, the foreign observer is still likely to deplore certain ways of the other society. If (s)he is professionally involved in the other society , for example as an expatriate manager or development assistance expert, (s)he may very well want to induce changes. In colonial days, foreigners often wielded absolute power in other societies and they could impose their rules on it. In these postcolonial days, foreigners who want to change something in another society will have to negotiate their interventions. Again, negotiation is more likely to succeed when the parties concerned understand the reasons for the differences in viewpoints.

Symbols, heroes, rituals, and values

Cultural differences manifest themselves in several ways. From the many terms used to describe manifestations of culture the following four together cover the total concept rather neatly: symbols, heroes, rituals, and values. In Fig. 1.2 these are illustrated as the skins of an onion, indicating that symbols represent the most superficial and values the deepest manifestations of culture, with heroes and rituals in between.

Symbols are words, gestures, pictures or objects that carry a particular meaning which is only recognized by those who share the culture. The words in a language or jargon belong to this category, as do dress, hairstyles, Coca-Cola, flags, and status symbols. New symbols are easily developed and old ones disappear: symbols from one cultural group are regularly copied by others. This is why symbols have been put into the outer, most superficial layer of Fig. 1.2.

Heroes are persons, alive or dead, real or imaginary, who possess characteristics which are highly prized in a culture, and who thus serve as models for behavior. Even phantasy or cartoon figures, like Batman or, as a contrast, Snoopy in the USA, Asterix in France, or Ollie B. Bommel (Mr Bumble) in the Netherlands can serve as cultural heroes. In this age of television, outward appearances have become more important in the choice of heroes than they were before.

Rituals are collective activities, technically superfluous in reaching desired ends, but which, within a culture, are considered as socially essential: they are therefore carried out for their own sake. Ways of greeting and paying respect to others, social and religious ceremonies are examples. Business and political meetings organized for seemingly rational reasons often serve mainly ritual purposes, like allowing the leaders to assert themselves.

In Fig. 1.2 symbols, heroes, and rituals have been subsumed under the term *practices*. As such, they are visible to an outside observer; their cultural meaning, however, is invisible and lies precisely and only in the way these practices are interpreted by the insiders.

The core of culture according to Fig. 1.2 is formed by *values*. Values are broad tendencies to prefer certain states of affairs over others. Values are feelings with an arrow to it: they have a plus and a minus side. They deal with:

> evil vs. good
> dirty vs. clean
> ugly vs. beautiful
> unnatural vs. natural
> abnormal vs. normal
> paradoxical vs. logical
> irrational vs. rational

Values are among the first things children learn—not consciously, but implicitly. Development psychologists believe that by the age of 10, most children have their basic value system firmly in place, and after that age, changes are difficult to make. Because they were acquired so early in our lives, many values remain unconscious to those who hold them. Therefore they cannot be discussed, nor can they be directly observed by outsiders. They can only be inferred from the way people act under various circumstances.

For systematic research on values, inferring them from people's actions is cumbersome and ambiguous. Various paper-and-pencil questionnaires have been developed which ask for people's preferences among alternatives. The answers should not be taken too literally: in practice, people will

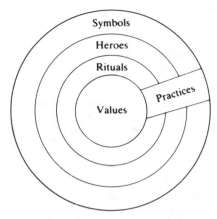

Fig. 1.2 The 'onion diagram': manifestations of culture at different levels of depth

not always act as they have scored on the questionnaire. Still the question-naires provide useful information, because they show differences in answers between groups or categories of respondents. For example, suppose a question asks for one's preference for time off from work versus more pay. An individual employee who states (s)he prefers time off may in fact choose the money if presented with the actual choice, but if in group A more people claim preferring time off than in group B, this does indicate a cultural difference between these groups in the relative value of free time versus money.

In interpreting people's statements about their values it is important to distinguish between the *desirable* and the *desired*: how people think the world ought to be versus what people want for themselves. Questions about the desirable refer to people in general and are worded in terms of right/wrong, agree/disagree or something similar. In the abstract, everybody is in favor of virtue and opposed to sin, and answers about the desirable express people's views about what represents virtue and what corresponds to sin. The desired, on the contrary, is worded in terms of 'you' or 'me' and what we consider important, what we want for ourselves, including our less virtuous desires. The desirable bears only a faint resemblance to actual behavior, but even statements about the desired, although closer to actual behavior, should not necessarily correspond to the way people really behave when they have to choose.

What distinguishes the desirable from the desired is the nature of the *norms* involved. Norms are the standards for values that exist within a group or category of people.[7] In the case of the desirable, the norm is absolute, pertaining to what is ethically right. In the case of the desired, the norm is statistical: it indicates the choices actually made by the majority. The desirable relates more to ideology, the desired to practical matters.

Interpretations of value studies which neglect the difference between the desirable and the desired may lead to paradoxical results. A case in which the two produced diametrically opposed answers was found in the IBM studies (see later in this chapter). Employees in different countries were asked for their agreement or disagreement with the statement 'Employees in industry should participate more in the decisions made by management'. This is a statement about the desirable. In another question people were asked whether they personally preferred a manager who 'usually consults with subordinates before reaching a decision'. This is a statement about the desired. A comparison between the answers to these two questions revealed that employees in countries where the manager who consults was less popular, agreed more with the general statement that employees should participate more, and vice versa; maybe the ideology served as a compensation for the day-to-day relationship with the boss (Hofstede, 1980, p. 109; 1984, p. 82).

Layers of culture

As almost everyone belongs to a number of different groups and categories of people at the same time, people unavoidably carry several layers of mental programming within themselves, corresponding to different levels of culture. For example:

- a national level according to one's country (or count*ries* for people who migrated during their lifetime);
- a regional and/or ethnic and/or religious and/or linguistic affiliation level, as most nations are composed of culturally different regions and/or ethnic and/or religious and/or language groups;
- a gender level, according to whether a person was born as a girl or as a boy;
- a generation level, which separates grandparents from parents from children;
- a social class level, associated with educational opportunities and with a person's occupation or profession;
- for those who are employed, an organizational or corporate level according to the way employees have been socialized by their work organization.

Additions to this list are easy to make. The mental programs from these various levels are not necessarily in harmony. In modern society they are often partly conflicting: for example, religious values may conflict with generation values; gender values with organizational practices. Conflicting mental programs within people make it difficult to anticipate their behavior in a new situation.

National culture differences

Human societies have existed for at least 10 000 years, possibly much longer. Archaeologists believe that the first humans led a nomadic existence as hunter–gatherers. After many thousands of years, some of them settled down as farmers. Gradually some farming communities grew into larger settlements, which became towns, cities, and finally modern megalopolises like Mexico City with over 25 million inhabitants.

Different human societies have followed this development to different extents, so that hunter–gatherers survive even today (according to some, the modern urban yuppy has reverted to a hunting–gathering state). As the world became more and more populated, an amazing variety of answers was found to the basic question of how people can live together and form some kind of a structured society.

In the fertile areas of the world large empires had already been built several thousand years ago, usually because the rulers of one part succeeded in conquering other parts. The oldest empire in existence within living memory is China. Although it had not always been unified, the Chinese empire possessed a continuous history of about 4000 years. Other empires disintegrated: in the eastern Mediterranean and southwestern part of Asia empires grew, flourished, and fell, only to be succeeded by others: the Sumerian, Babylonian, Assyrian, Egyptian, Persian, Greek, Roman, and Turkish states, to mention only a few. The South Asian subcontinent and the Indonesian archipelago had their empires, like the Maurya, the Gupta, and later the Moghul in India and the Majapahit on Java; in Central and South America the Aztec, Maya, and Inca empires have left their monuments. In Africa, Ethiopia and Benin are examples of ancient states.

Next to and often within the territory of these larger empires, smaller units survived in the form of tribes or independent small 'kingdoms'. Even now, in New Guinea most of the population lives in small and relatively isolated tribes, each with its own language, and hardly integrated into the larger society.

The invention of 'nations', political units into which the entire world is divided and to one of which every human being is supposed to belong—as manifested by her or his passport—is a recent phenomenon in human history. Earlier, there were states, but not everybody belonged to one of these or identified with one. The nation system was only introduced worldwide in the mid-twentieth century. It followed the colonial system which had developed during the preceding three centuries. In this colonial period the technologically advanced countries of Western Europe divided among themselves virtually all the territories of the globe which were not held by another strong political power. The borders between the ex-colonial nations still reflect the colonial legacy. In Africa, particularly, national borders correspond more to the logic of the colonial powers than to the cultural dividing lines of the local populations.

Nations, therefore, should not be equated to *societies*. Historically, societies are organically developed forms of social organization, and the concept of a common culture applies strictly speaking, more to societies than to nations. Nevertheless, many nations do form historically developed wholes even if they consist of clearly different groups and even if they contain less integrated minorities.

Within nations that have existed for some time there are strong forces towards further integration: (usually) one dominant national language, common mass media, a national education system, a national army, a national political system, national representation in sports events with a strong symbolic and emotional appeal, a national market for certain skills, products, and services. Today's nations do not attain the degree of internal homogeneity of the isolated, usually nonliterate societies studied by field anthropologists, but they are the source of a considerable amount of common mental programming of their citizens.[8]

On the other hand there remains a tendency for ethnic, linguistic, and religious groups to fight for recognition of their own identity, if not for national independence; this tendency has been increasing rather than decreasing in the latter part of the twentieth century. Examples are the Ulster Roman Catholics, the Belgian Flemish, the Basques in Spain and France, the Kurds in Iran, Iraq, Syria, and Turkey, and many of the ethnic groups in the former Soviet Union.

In research on cultural differences nationality—the passport one holds— should therefore be used with care. Yet it is often the only feasible criterion for classification. Rightly or wrongly, collective properties are ascribed to the citizens of certain countries: people refer to 'typically American', 'typically German', or 'typically Japanese' behavior. Using nationality as a criterion is a matter of expediency, because it is immensely easier to obtain data for nations than for organic homogeneous societies. Nations as political bodies supply all kinds of statistics about their populations. Survey data, i.e., the answers of people on paper-and-pencil questionnaires related to their culture, are also mostly collected through national networks. Where it *is* possible to separate results by regional, ethnic or linguistic group, this should be done.

A strong reason for collecting data at the level of nations is that one of the purposes of the research is to promote cooperation among nations. As was argued at the beginning of this chapter, the (over 200) nations that exist today populate one single world and we either survive or perish together. So it makes practical sense to focus on cultural factors separating or uniting nations.

Dimensions of national cultures

In the first half of the twentieth century, social anthropology has developed the conviction that all societies, modern or traditional, face the same basic problems; only the answers differ. American anthropologists, in particular Ruth Benedict (1887–1948) and Margaret Mead (1901–1978), played an important role in popularizing this message for a wide audience.

The logical next step was that social scientists attempted to identify *what* problems were common to all societies, through conceptual reasoning and reflection upon field experiences, as well as through statistical studies. In 1954 two Americans, the sociologist Alex Inkeles and the psychologist Daniel Levinson, published a broad survey of the English-language literature on national culture. They suggested that the following issues qualify as common basic problems worldwide, with consequences for the functioning of societies, of groups within those societies, and of individuals within those groups:

1. Relation to authority
2. Conception of self, in particular:
   a.   the relationship between individual and society, and
   b.   the individual's concept of masculinity and femininity
3. Ways of dealing with conflicts, including the control of aggression and the expression of feelings. (Inkeles and Levinson, 1969, pp. 447ff.)

Twenty years later I was given the opportunity of studying a large body of survey data about the values of people in over 50 countries around the world. These people worked in the local subsidiaries of one large multinational corporation—IBM. At first sight it may seem surprising that employees of a multinational—a very special kind of people—could serve for identifying differences in *national* value systems. However, from one country to another they represent almost perfectly matched samples: they are similar in all respects except nationality, which makes the effect of nationality differences in their answers stand out unusually clearly.

A statistical analysis of the answers on questions about the values of similar IBM employees in different countries revealed common problems, but with solutions differing from country to country, in the following areas:

1. Social inequality, including the relationship with authority;
2. The relationship between the individual and the group;

3. Concepts of masculinity and femininity: the social implications of having been born as a boy or a girl;
4. Ways of dealing with uncertainty, relating to the control of aggression and the expression of emotions.

These empirical results covered amazingly well the areas predicted by Inkeles and Levinson 20 years before. The discovery of their prediction provided strong support for the theoretical importance of the empirical findings. Problems which are basic to all human societies should turn up in different studies regardless of the approaches followed. The Inkeles and Levinson study is not the only one whose conclusions overlap with mine, but it is the one that most strikingly predicts what I found.[9]

The four basic problem areas defined by Inkeles and Levinson and empirically found in the IBM data represent *dimensions* of cultures. A dimension is an aspect of a culture that can be measured relative to other cultures. The basic problem areas correspond to dimensions which I named *power distance* (from small to large), *collectivism* versus *individualism*, *femininity* versus *masculinity*, and *uncertainty avoidance* (from weak to strong). Each of these terms existed already in some part of the social sciences, and they seemed to apply reasonably well to the basic problem area each dimension stands for. Together they form a four-dimensional (4-D) model of differences among national cultures. Each country in this model is characterized by a score on each of the four dimensions.

A dimension groups together a number of phenomena in a society which were empirically found to occur in combination, even if at first sight there does not always seem to be a logical necessity for their going together. The logic of societies, however, is not the same as the logic of the individuals looking at them. The grouping of the different aspects of a dimension is always based on statistical relationships, that is, on *trends* for these phenomena to occur in combination, not on iron links. Some aspects in some societies may go against a general trend found across most other societies. Because they are found with the help of statistical methods dimensions can only be detected on the basis of information about a certain number of countries—say, at least 10. In the case of the IBM research I was fortunate to obtain comparable data about culturally determined values from 50 countries and three multicountry regions, which made the dimensions within their differences stand out quite clearly.

More recently, a fifth dimension of differences among national cultures was identified, opposing a *long-term orientation* in life to a *short-term orientation*. The fact that it had not been encountered earlier can be attributed to a cultural bias in the minds of the various scholars studying culture, including myself. We all shared a 'Western' way of thinking. The new dimension was discovered when Michael Harris Bond, a Canadian located in the Far East for many years, studied people's values around the world using a questionnaire composed by 'Eastern', in this case Chinese, minds. Besides adding this highly relevant new dimension, Bond's work showed the all-pervading impact of culture: even the minds of the researchers studying it are programmed according to their own particular cultural framework.

The scores for each country on one dimension can be pictured as points along a line. For two dimensions at a time, they become points in a diagram. For three dimensions, they could, with some imagination be seen as points in space. For four or five dimensions they become difficult to envisage. This is a disadvantage of the dimensional model. Another way of picturing differences among countries (or other social systems) is through *typologies* instead of dimensions. A typology describes a number of ideal types, each of them easy to imagine. Dividing countries into the First, Second, and Third World is such a typology. A more sophisticated example is found in the work of the French political historian Emmanuel Todd who divides the cultures of the world according to the family structure traditionally prevailing in that culture. He arrives at eight types, four of which occur in Europe. Todd's thesis is that these historically preserved family structures explain the success of a particular type of political ideology in a country (Todd, 1983).

Whereas typologies are easier to grasp than dimensions, they are still problematic in empirical research. Real cases seldom fully correspond to one single ideal type. Most cases are hybrids, and arbitrary rules have to be made for classifying them as belonging to one of the types. With a dimensional model, on the contrary, cases can always be scored unambiguously. On the basis of their dimension scores cases can *afterwards* empirically be sorted into clusters with similar scores. These clusters then form an empirical typology. More than 50 countries in the IBM study could, on the basis of their 4-D scores, be sorted into 13 such clusters.[10]

In practice, typologies and dimensional models can be considered as complementary. Dimensional models are preferable for research but typologies for teaching purposes. This book will use a kind of typology approach for explaining each of the five dimensions. For every separate dimension it describes the two opposite extremes, which can be seen as ideal types. Some of the dimensions are subsequently taken two by two, which creates four ideal types. However, the country scores on the dimensions will show that most real cases are somewhere in between the extremes pictured.

Cultural differences according to region, religion, gender, generation, and class

Regional, ethnic, and religious cultures account for differences within countries; ethnic and religious groups often transcend political country

borders. Such groups form minorities at the crossroads between the dominant culture of the nation and their own traditional group culture. Some
assimilate into the mainstream, although this may take a generation or
more; others continue to stick to their own ways. The USA, as the world's
most prominent example of a people composed of immigrants, shows
examples of both assimilation (the 'melting pot') and retention of group
identities over generations (an example are the Pennsylvania Dutch).
Discrimination according to ethnic origin delays assimilation and represents
a problem in many countries. Regional, ethnic, and religious cultures can be
described in the same terms as national cultures: basically, the same
dimensions which were found to differentiate among national cultures apply
to these differences within countries.

Religious affiliation by itself is less culturally relevant than is often assumed.
If we trace the religious history of countries, then the religion a population
has embraced along with the version of that religion seem to have been a
result of previously existing cultural value patterns as much as a *cause* of
cultural differences. The great religions of the world, at some time in their
history, have all undergone profound schisms: between Roman Catholics,
Eastern Orthodox, and various Protestant groups in Christianity; between
Sunni and Shia in Islam; between liberals and various fundamentalist groups
in Jewry; between Hinayana and Mahayana in Buddhism. Cultural differences among groups of believers have always played a major role in such
schisms. For example, the Reformation movement within the Roman
Catholic Church in the sixteenth century initially affected all of Europe.
However, in countries which more than a thousand years earlier had
belonged to the Roman Empire, a Counter-Reformation reinstated the
authority of the Roman church. In the end, the Reformation only succeeded
in countries without a Roman tradition. Although today most of Northern
Europe is Protestant and most of Southern Europe Roman Catholic, it is not
this religious split which is at the origin of the cultural differences between
North and South but the inheritance of the Roman Empire. This does not
exclude that once a religion has settled, it does reinforce the value patterns
on the basis of which it was adopted, by making these into core elements in
its teachings.

Gender differences are not usually described in terms of cultures. It can be
revealing to do so. If we recognize that within each society there is a men's
culture which differs from a women's culture, this helps to explain why it is
so difficult to change traditional gender roles. Women are not considered
suitable for jobs traditionally filled by men, not because they are technically
unable to perform these jobs, but because women do not carry the symbols,
do not correspond to the hero images, do not participate in the rituals or
foster the values dominant in the men's culture; and vice versa. Feelings and

fears about behaviors by the opposite sex are of the same order of intensity as the reactions of people exposed to foreign cultures.

Generation differences in symbols, heroes, rituals, and values are evident to most people. They are often overestimated. Complaints about youth having lost respect for the values of their elders have been found on Egyptian papyrus scrolls dating from 2000 BC and in the writings of Hesiod, a Greek author from the end of the eighth century BC. Many differences in practices and values between generations will be just normal attributes of age which repeat themselves for each successive pair of generations. Historical events, however, do affect some generations in a special way. The Chinese who were of student age during the Cultural Revolution stand witness to this. The development of technology also leads to a difference between generations which is unique.

Not all values and practices in a society, however, are affected by technology or its products. If young Turks drink Coca-Cola this does not necessarily affect their attitudes toward authority. In some respects, young Turks differ from old Turks; just as young Americans differ from old Americans. Such differences often involve the relatively superficial spheres of symbols and heroes, of fashion and consumption. In the sphere of values, i.e., fundamental attitudes towards life and towards other people, young Turks differ from young Americans just as much as old Turks differed from old Americans. There is no evidence that the cultures of present-day generations from different countries are converging.

Social classes carry different class cultures. Social class is associated with educational opportunities and with a person's occupation or profession; this even applies in countries which their governments call socialist, preaching a classless society. Education and occupation are in themselves powerful sources of cultural learning. There is no standard definition of social class which applies across all countries, and people in different countries distinguish different types and numbers of class. The criteria for allocating a person to a class are often cultural: symbols play an important role, such as accents in speaking the national language, the use and nonuse of certain words, and manners. The confrontation between the two jurors in *Twelve Angry Men* also contains a class component.

Gender, generation, and class cultures can only partly be classified by the four dimensions found for national cultures. This is because they are not *groups* but *categories* of people. Countries (and ethnic groups too) are integrated social systems. The four dimensions apply to the basic problems of such systems. Categories like gender, generation, or class are only parts of social systems and therefore not all dimensions apply to them. Gender, generation, and class cultures should be described in their own terms, based on special studies of such cultures.

Organizational cultures

Organizational or corporate cultures have been a fashionable topic since the early 1980s. At that time, the management literature began to popularize the claim that the 'excellence' of an organization is contained in the common ways by which its members have learned to think, feel and act. 'Corporate culture' is a soft, holistic concept with, however, presumed hard consequences. I once called it 'the psychological assets of an organization, which can be used to predict what will happen to its financial assets in five years' time.'

Organization sociologists have stressed the role of the soft factor in organizations for more than half a century. Using the label 'culture' for the shared mental software of the people in an organization is a convenient way of re-popularizing these sociological views. Yet organizational 'cultures' are a phenomenon *per se*, different in many respects from national cultures. An organization is a social system of a different nature than a nation; if only because the organization's members usually had a certain influence in their decision to join it, are only involved in it during working hours, and may one day leave it again.

Research results about national cultures and their dimensions proved to be only partly useful for the understanding of organizational cultures. The part of this book which deals with organizational culture differences (Chapter 8) is not based on the IBM studies but on a special research project carried out by IRIC, the Institute for Research on Intercultural Cooperation, within 20 organizational units in Denmark and the Netherlands.

Notes

1   A *group* means a number of people in contact with each other. A *category* consists of people who, without necessarily having contact, have something in common: e.g., all women managers, or all people born before 1940.

2   The concept of a 'collective programming of the mind' resembles the concept of '*habitus*' proposed by the French sociologist Pierre Bourdieu: 'Certain conditions of existence produce a *habitus*, a system of permanent and transferable dispositions. A habitus . . . functions as the basis for practices and images . . . which can be collectively orchestrated without an actual conductor.' (Bourdieu, 1980, pp. 88–89, translation by GH).

3   'Sociobiology' is an area of study which tries to illustrate how some human social behaviors have analogies in the animal world. From these analogies sociobiology infers that these social behaviors are biologically (i.e. genetically) determined. See Wilson (1975); for criticisms see Gregory *et al.* (eds.) (1978).

4   The name of Professor A.R. Jensen is linked with the genetic inferiority thesis.

5   US professor Allan Bloom warns against a cultural relativism in American universities which he calls 'nihilism', but he uses the word 'culture' in the sense of 'culture one'. (Bloom, 1988, first published in the USA in 1987.)

6   Translation by GH from Lévi-Strauss and Eribon (1988, p. 229).

7   In popular parlance, the words 'norm' and 'value' are often used indiscriminately, or the twin expression 'values and norms' is handled as an inseparable

pair, like Laurel and Hardy. In this latter case, one of the two words is redundant.

[8] Some nations are less culturally integrated than others. Examples are some of the ex-colonies and multilingual, multiethnic countries like ex-Yugoslavia, Belgium or Malaysia. Yet even in these countries ethnic and/or linguistic groups which consider themselves as very different from each other may have common traits in comparison to the populations of other countries. I have shown this to be the case for the two language groups of Belgium (1980, pp. 335 ff; 1984, pp. 228 ff).

[9] See Hofstede (1980 or 1984) for the first analysis covering 40 countries, and Hofstede (1983, pp. 335–355) for a later extension.

[10] Hofstede (1980, p. 334; 1984, p. 229) shows 11 clusters among the first 40 countries studied, and the later article in Hofstede (1983, p. 346) extends this to 13 clusters among 50 countries and three regions.

Part II

National Cultures

2

More equal than others

In a peaceful revolution—the last revolution in Swedish history—the nobles of Sweden in 1809 deposed King Gustav IV whom they considered incompetent, and surprisingly invited Jean Baptiste Bernadotte, a French general who served under their enemy Napoleon, to become King of Sweden. Bernadotte accepted and he became King Charles XIV; his descendants occupy the Swedish throne to this day. When the new King was installed he addressed the Swedish Parliament in their language. His broken Swedish amused the Swedes, and they roared with laughter. The Frenchman who had become King was so upset that he never tried to speak Swedish again.

In this incident Bernadotte was a victim of culture shock: never in his French upbringing and military career had he experienced subordinates who laughed at the mistakes of their superior. Historians tell us he had more problems adapting to the egalitarian Swedish and Norwegian mentality (he later became King of Norway as well) and to his subordinates' constitutional rights. He was a good learner, however (except for language), and he ruled the country as a highly respected constitutional monarch until 1844.

Inequality in society

One of the aspects in which Sweden differs from France is the way its society handles *inequality*. There is inequality in any society. Even in the most simple hunter–gatherer band, some people are bigger, stronger, or smarter than others. The next thing is that some people have more power than others: they are more able to determine the behavior of others than vice versa. Some people acquire more wealth than others. Some people are given more status and respect than others.

Physical and intellectual capacities, power, wealth, and status may or may not go together. Successful athletes, artists, or scientists usually enjoy status, but only in some societies do they enjoy wealth as well, and rarely do they have political power. Politicians in some countries can enjoy status and power without wealth; businessmen, wealth and power without status. Such inconsistencies between the various areas of inequality are often felt to be problematic. In some societies, people try to resolve them by making the areas more consistent. Sportsmen become professionals to become wealthy; politicians may exploit their power in order to do the same; successful businessmen enter public office in order to acquire status. This trend obviously increases the overall inequalities in these societies.

In other societies the dominant feeling is that it is a good thing, rather than a problem, if a person's rank in one area does not match his/her rank in another. A high rank in one area should partly be offset by a low rank in another. This process increases the size of the middle class in between those who come out top in all respects, and those who lack any kind of opportunity. The laws in many countries have been conceived to serve this ideal of equality by treating everybody as equal regardless of status, wealth, or power; but there are few societies in which reality matches the ideal. The praise of poverty in the Christian Bible can be seen as a manifestation of a desire for equality; the same is true for Karl Marx's plea for a 'dictatorship of the proletariat'.

Measuring the degree of inequality in society: the power distance index

Not only Sweden and France, but also other nations can be distinguished by the way they are accustomed to deal with inequalities. The research among IBM employees in similar positions but different countries has allowed us to assign to each of these countries a score indicating its level of *power distance*. Power distance is one of the 'dimensions' of national cultures suggested in Chapter 1. It reflects the range of answers found in the various countries to the basic question of how to handle the fact that people are unequal. It derives its name from the research by a Dutch experimental social psychologist, Mauk Mulder, into the emotional distance that separates subordinates from their bosses (Mulder, 1976, 1977).

Scores on power distance for 50 countries and 3 multicountry regions have been calculated from the answers by IBM employees in the same kind of positions on the same survey questions. All questions were of the pre-coded answer type so that answers could be represented by a score number: usually 1, 2, 3, 4, or 5. A mean score was computed for the answers of an equally composed sample of people from each country (say, 2.53 as the mean score for the sample from country X and 3.43 for country Y) or the percentage was computed of people choosing particular answers (say, 45 percent of the sample choosing answer 1 or 2 in country X and 33 percent in country Y). Thus a table was composed of mean scores or percentages for each question and for all countries.

A statistical procedure (factor analysis) was used to sort the survey questions into groups, called *factors* or *clusters*, for which the mean scores or percentages appeared to vary together.[1] This meant that if a country scored high on one of the questions from the cluster, it also could be expected to score high on the others, or not high but *low* for questions carrying the opposite meaning. If, on the other hand, a country scored low on one question from the cluster, it also would most likely score low on the others, or *high* on questions formulated the other way round. If a country scored average on one question from the cluster, it probably would score average on all of them.

One of the clusters found was composed of questions which all seemed to have something to do with power and (in)equality. From the questions in this cluster I selected the three which were most strongly related.[2] From the mean scores of the standard sample of IBM employees in a country on these three questions, a *power distance index* (PDI) for the country was calculated. The formula developed for this purpose uses simple mathematics (adding or subtracting the three scores after multiplying each with a fixed number, and finally adding another fixed number). The purposes of the formula were: (1) to ensure that each of the three questions would carry equal weight in arriving at the final index and (2) to arrive at index values ranging from about 0 for a small power distance country to about 100 for a large power distance country. In fact one country scored above 100, because it was added to the list after the formula had been fixed and it would have been cumbersome to keep changing the formula.

The three survey questions used for composing the power distance index were:

1. Answers by nonmanagerial employees on the question: 'How frequently, in your experience, does the following problem occur: employees being afraid to express disagreement with their managers?' (mean score on a 1–5 scale from 'very frequently' to 'very seldom').
2. Subordinates' perception of their boss's *actual* decision-making style (percentage choosing either the description of an autocratic or of a paternalistic style, out of four possible styles plus a 'none of these' alternative).
3. Subordinates' *preference* for their boss's decision-making style (percentage preferring an autocratic or a paternalistic style, or, on the contrary, a style based on majority vote, but *not* a consultative style).

The PDI scores thus composed can be read from Table 2.1. Because of the way they were calculated the scores represent *relative*, not absolute positions of countries: they are measures of differences only. Although all of them are based on answers by IBM employees, the scores paradoxically contain no information about the corporate culture of IBM: they only show to what

Table 2.1 Power distance index (PDI) values for 50 countries and 3 regions

Score rank	Country or region	PDI score	Score rank	Country or region	PDI score
1	Malaysia	104	27/28	South Korea	60
2/3	Guatemala	95	29/30	Iran	58
2/3	Panama	95	29/30	Taiwan	58
4	Philippines	94	31	Spain	57
5/6	Mexico	81	32	Pakistan	55
5/6	Venezuela	81	33	Japan	54
7	Arab countries	80	34	Italy	50
8/9	Equador	78	35/36	Argentina	49
8/9	Indonesia	78	35/36	South Africa	49
10/11	India	77	37	Jamaica	45
10/11	West Africa	77	38	USA	40
12	Yugoslavia	76	39	Canada	39
13	Singapore	74	40	Netherlands	38
14	Brazil	69	41	Australia	36
15/16	France	68	42/44	Costa Rica	35
15/16	Hong Kong	68	42/44	Germany FR	35
17	Colombia	67	42/44	Great Britain	35
18/19	Salvador	66	45	Switzerland	34
18/19	Turkey	66	46	Finland	33
20	Belgium	65	47/48	Norway	31
21/23	East Africa	64	47/48	Sweden	31
21/23	Peru	64	49	Ireland (Republic of)	28
21/23	Thailand	64	50	New Zealand	22
24/25	Chile	63	51	Denmark	18
24/25	Portugal	63	52	Israel	13
26	Uruguay	61	53	Austria	11
27/28	Greece	60			

extent people from an IBM subsidiary in country X answered the same questions differently from similar people in country Y. They tell something about the mental software that comes with having one nationality as compared to another. Because we found the same type of differences in populations *outside* IBM the differences must be due to the effect of growing up inside one national culture as opposed to another.

Table 2.1 shows high power distance values for Latin countries (both Latin European, like France and Spain, and Latin American), and for Asian and African countries; lower values for the USA, Great Britain and its former Dominions, and for the remaining non-Latin part of Europe (to the extent it was covered by the data; Eastern European countries are missing in the data set, except the former Yugoslavia which scored high on the PDI). Sweden scores 31 and France 68. If such a difference existed 200 years ago—for which, as will be argued below, there is a good case—this explains

Bernadotte's culture shock. The first column in Table 2.1 lists the *rank numbers* of the countries from high to low (1 for the largest, 53 for the smallest power distance): in this case, France has rank 15 to 16, and Sweden rank 47 to 48, which accentuates their difference even more.

Power distance defined

Looking at the three questions used to compose the PDI, you may notice something surprising: questions (1) (employees afraid) and (2) (boss autocratic or paternalistic), indicate the way the respondents perceive their daily work environment. Question (3), however, indicates what the respondents express as their *preference*: how they would like their work environment to be.

The fact that the three questions are part of the same cluster shows that from one country to another there is a close relationship between the reality one perceives and the reality one desires.[3] In countries in which employees are not seen as very afraid and bosses as not often autocratic or paternalistic, employees express a preference for a *consultative* style of decision making: a boss who, as the questionnaire expressed it: 'usually consults with his/her subordinates before reaching a decision.'

In countries on the opposite side of the power distance scale, where employees are seen as frequently afraid of disagreeing with their bosses and bosses as autocratic or paternalistic, employees in similar jobs are less likely to prefer a consultative boss. Instead, many among them express a preference for a boss who decides autocratically or paternalistically; but some switch to the other extreme, i.e., preferring a boss who governs by majority vote, which means he/she does not decide him/herself at all. In practice, in most organizations the majority vote is difficult to handle, and few people actually perceived their boss as using this style (bosses who pretend to do it are often accused of manipulation).

In summary: PDI scores inform us about *dependence* relationships in a country. In small power distance countries there is limited dependence of subordinates on bosses, and a preference for consultation, that is, *interdependence* between boss and subordinate. The emotional distance between them is relatively small: subordinates will quite readily approach and contradict their bosses. In large power distance countries there is considerable dependence of subordinates on bosses. Subordinates respond by either *preferring* such dependence (in the form of an autocratic or paternalistic boss), or rejecting it entirely, which in psychology is known as *counterdependence*: that is dependence, but with a negative sign. Large power distance countries thus show a pattern of polarization between dependence and counterdependence. In these cases, the emotional distance between subordinates and their bosses is large: subordinates are unlikely to approach and contradict their bosses directly.

Power distance can therefore be defined as *the extent to which the less powerful members of institutions and organizations within a country expect and accept that power is distributed unequally*. 'Institutions' are the basic elements of society like the family, school, and the community; 'organizations' are the places where people work.

Power distance is thus explained from the value systems of the *less* powerful members. The way power is distributed is usually explained from the behavior of the *more* powerful members, the leaders rather than those led. Popular management literature on 'leadership' often forgets that leadership can only exist as a complement to 'subordinateship'. Authority survives only where it is matched by obedience. Bernadotte's problem was not a lack of leadership on his side; the Swedes had a different conception of the deference due to a ruler from the French—and Bernadotte was a Frenchman. Comparative research projects on leadership values from one country to another show that the differences observed exist in the minds of both the leaders *and* of those led, but often the statements obtained from those who are led are a better reflection of the differences than those obtained from the leaders. This is because we are all better observers of the leadership behavior of our bosses, than we are of ourselves. Besides the questions on perceived and preferred leadership style of the boss—(2) and (3) in the PDI—the IBM surveys also asked managers to rate their *own* style. It appeared that self-ratings by managers closely resembled the styles these managers preferred in their own boss; but not at all the styles the subordinates of these managers perceived them to have. In fact, the subordinates saw their managers in just about the same way as the managers saw *their* bosses. The moral for managers is: if you want to know how your subordinates see you, don't try to look in the mirror; that just produces wishful thinking. Turn around 180 degrees and face your own boss (Sadler and Hofstede, 1976).

Power distance differences within countries: social class, education level, and occupation

Inequality within a society is visible in the existence of different social classes: upper, middle, and lower, or however one wants to divide them—this varies by country. Classes differ in their access to and their opportunities for benefiting from the advantages of society, one of them being education. A higher education automatically makes one at least middle class. Education, in turn, is one of the main determinants of the occupations one can aspire to: so that, in practice, in most societies, social class, education level, and occupation are closely linked. In Chapter 1 all three have been listed as sources of our mental software: there are class, education and occupation levels in our culture, but they are mutually dependent.

The data used for the computation of the PDIs in Table 2.1 were from IBM employees in various occupations and, therefore, from different education levels and social classes. However, the mix of occupations studied was kept constant for all countries. Comparisons of countries or regions should always be based on people in the same set of occupations. One should not compare Spanish engineers to Swedish secretaries. The mix of occupations to be compared across all the subsidiaries was taken from the sales and service offices: these were the only activities that could be found in *all* countries. IBM's product development laboratories were located in only 10 of the larger subsidiaries, and its manufacturing plants in 13.

The sales and service people had all followed secondary or higher education, and could be considered largely middle class. The PDI scores in Table 2.1, therefore, are really expressing differences among *middle-class* persons in these countries. Middle-class values affect the institutions of a country, like governments and education systems, more than lower-class values. This is because the people who control the institutions usually belong to the middle class. Even representatives of lower class groups, like union leaders, tend to be better educated or self-educated, and by this fact alone they have adopted some middle-class values. Lower-class parents often have middle-class ambitions for their children.

For three large countries (France, Germany, and Great Britain), in which the IBM subsidiaries contained the fullest possible range of industrial activities, PDI scores were computed for all the different occupations in the corporation, including those demanding only a lower level of education and therefore usually taken by lower or 'working'-class persons.[4] Altogether, 38 different occupations within these three countries could be compared.

It was possible to calculate PDI scores by occupation, because the three questions used for calculating the PDI across the 53 countries and regions were also suitable for a comparison of the 38 occupations. The way survey questions cluster together depends on the way respondents are grouped. Questions that form a cluster for countries need not do so for occupations. Exceptionally, the three PDI questions, as it appeared, could form an index at the occupation level as well as at the country level. This is because what the PDI measures across countries is social inequality. Differences in social status leading to inequality are also the prime criterion by which occupations can be distinguished. Among the other three dimensions derived from the IBM data masculinity–femininity is the only one for which the country index can also be used for occupations.

Table 2.2   PDI values for six categories of occupation (based on IBM data from Great Britain, France, and Germany)

Category of occupations	Number of occupations in this category	PDI range		
		From	To	Mean
Unskilled and semiskilled workers	3	85	97	90
Clerical workers and nonprofessional salesmen	8	57	84	71
Skilled workers and technicians	6	33	90	65
Managers of the previous categories	8	22	62	42
Professional workers	8	−22*	36	22
Managers of professional workers	5	−19*	21	8
Total	38	−22*	97	47

*The negative values exceed the 0 to 100 range originally established for differences among countries.

The result of the comparison across 38 occupations is summarized in Table 2.2. It demonstrates that the occupations with the lowest status and education level (unskilled and semiskilled workers) show the highest PDI values, and those with the highest status and education level (managers of professional workers, such as engineers and scientists) show the lowest PDI values. Between the extremes in terms of occupation the range of PDI scores is about 100 score points, that is, of the same order of magnitude as across 53 countries and regions from the highest scoring country to the lowest (see Table 2.1; but the country differences were based on samples of people with equal jobs and equal levels of education!).

The next question is whether the differences in power distance between occupations are equally strong within all countries. In order to test this a comparison was done of 4 occupations of widely different status, from each of 11 country subsidiaries of widely different power distance levels. A table crossing the 4 occupations against the 11 countries, thus producing 44 (4 x 11) PDI values, showed that the occupation differences were largest in the countries with the lowest PDI scores, and relatively small in the countries with high PDI scores (Hofstede, 1980, p. 106; 1984, p. 79). In other words, if the country as a whole scored large power distance in Table 2.1, this applied to all employees, those in high-status as well as those in low-status occupations. If the country scored smaller power distance, this applied most to the middle and higher status employees: the lower status, lower educated employees produced power distance scores nearly as high as their colleagues in the large PDI countries. The values of high-status employees with regard to inequality seem to depend strongly on nationality; those of low-status employees much less.[5]

The fact that less educated, low-status employees in various Western countries hold more 'authoritarian' values than their higher status compatriots has been discovered and described by quite a few sociologists already. These authoritarian values are not only manifested at work, but are also found in their home situation. A study in the USA and Italy (Kohn, 1969) showed that working-class parents demanded more obedience from their children than middle-class parents, but that the difference was larger in the USA than in Italy.

Measures associated with power distance: the use of correlations
In the next part of this chapter the differences in power distance scores for countries will be associated with differences in family, school, workplace, state, and in ideas prevailing within the countries. Chapters 3 to 5, which deal with the other three IBM dimensions, will also be structured in this way. The associations described are mostly based on the results of statistical analyses, in which the IBM dimension scores have been *correlated* with the results of other quantitative studies. In addition, use has been made of qualitative information about families, schools, workplaces, and so on, in various countries. In this book the statistical proof will be omitted; interested readers are referred to Hofstede (1980).

For those unfamiliar with the statistical term *correlation* and the meaning of *correlation coefficients*, a brief explanation follows here. Two measures are said to be correlated if they vary together. For example, if we were to measure the height and weight of a hundred people randomly picked from the street, we would find the height and weight measures to be correlated; taller people would usually be heavier, and shorter ones would tend to be lighter. Because some people are tall and skinny and some are short and fat, the correlation would not be perfect.

The coefficient of correlation[6] expresses the strength of the relationship. If the correlation is perfect, so that one measure follows entirely from the other, the coefficient takes the value 1.00. If the correlation is nonexistent— the two measures are completely unrelated—the coefficient is 0.00. The coefficient can become negative if the two measures are each others' opposites: for example, a person's height and the number of times (s)he would meet someone who is still taller. The lowest possible value is −1.00: in this case the two measures are again perfectly correlated, only one is positive when the other is negative, and vice versa. In the example of the height and weight of people, one can expect a coefficient of about 0.80, or even higher if both children and adults were included in the sample (persons extremely small and extremely light and persons very tall and very heavy).

A correlation coefficient is said to be (statistically) significant if it is sufficiently different from zero (to the positive or to the negative side) to rule out the possibility that the similarity between the two measures is due to pure chance. The *significance level*, usually 0.05, 0.01, or 0.001, is the remaining risk that the similarity could still be accidental. If it is 0.05, the odds against an association by chance are 19 to 1.

If one wants to argue for a causal relationship between two measures, one should be able to support this by a significant correlation (or another significant statistical relationship). Most of the distinctions between large and small power distance countries that are described in the remainder of this chapter are based on significant correlations between the PDI and measured data about these countries from other sources. Examples are the degree of inequality in their income distribution and the relative frequency of violence in domestic politics.

Power distance difference among countries: roots in the family
Most people in the world are born into a family. All people start acquiring their mental software immediately after birth from the elders in whose presence they grow up, modelling themselves after the examples set by these elders.

In the large power distance situation children are expected to be obedient towards their parents. Sometimes there is even an order of authority among the children themselves, younger children being expected to yield to older children. Independent behavior on the part of a child is not encouraged. *Respect* for parents and other elders is seen as a basic virtue; children see others showing such respect, and soon acquire it themselves. There is often considerable warmth and care in the way parents and older children treat younger ones, especially when these are very small. But they are looked after; they are not expected to experiment for themselves. Respect for parents and older relatives lasts through adulthood: parental authority continues to play a role in people's life as long as parents are alive. Parents and grandparents are treated with formal deference even after their children have actually taken control of their own lives. There is a pattern of dependence on seniors which pervades all human contacts, and the mental software which people carry contains a strong *need* for such dependence.

In the small power distance situation children are more or less treated as equals as soon as they are able to act, and this may already be visible in the way a baby is handled in its bath.[7] The goal of parental education is to let children take control of their own affairs as soon as they can. Active experimentation by the child is encouraged; a child is allowed to contradict its parents, it learns to say 'no' very early. Relationships with others are not dependent on the other's status; formal respect and deference are seldom shown. Family relations in such societies often strike people from other societies as cold and distant, and lacking intensity. When children grow up they replace the child–parent relationship by one of equals, and there is no question that a grownup person would ask his/her parents' permission or even advice for an important decision. There is an ideal of personal independence in the family. A need for independence is supposed to be a major component of the mental software of adults.

The pictures in the two previous paragraphs have deliberately been polarized. The reality in a given situation will most likely be in between the opposite ends of the power distance continuum: countries will score somewhere along the continuum. We saw that the social class and education levels of the parents, especially in the small power distance countries, play a decisive role. Families develop their own family cultures which may be at variance with the norms of their society, and the personalities of individual parents and children may be strong enough to get away with nontypical behavior. Nevertheless the two pictures indicate the ends of the line along which solutions to the human inequality dilemma vary.

The impact of the family on our mental programming is extremely strong, and programs set at this stage are very difficult to change. Psychoanalysts are aware of this importance of one's family history, but not always of its cultural context. Psychoanalysts deal with the extent to which individual personalities deviate from a societal norm: the extent to which they are 'maladjusted'. This book tries to describe the norm itself as it varies from one society to another. The fact that the norm changes means that psychoanalytic help for a person from another type of society or even from a different sector of the same society is a risky affair. It demands that the helper is aware of his/her own cultural biases versus the client.

Power distance at school

In most societies today children go to school for at least some years. In the more affluent societies the school period may cover more than 20 years of a young person's life. In school, the child further develops its mental programming. Teachers and classmates inculcate additional values, being part of a culture that honors these values. It is an unanswered question to what extent an education system can contribute to changing a society. Can a school create values that were not yet there, or will it unwittingly only be able to reinforce what already exists in a given society? Anyway, in a comparison of schools across societies the same patterns of differences appear that were already found within families. The role pair parent–child is replaced by the role pair teacher–student, but basic values and behaviors are carried forward from one sphere into the other. And of course, most schoolchildren continue to spend most of their time within their families.

In the large power distance situation the parent–child inequality is perpetuated by a teacher–student inequality which caters to the need for dependence well established in the student's mind. Teachers are treated with respect (older teachers even more than younger ones); students may have to stand up when they enter. The educational process is teacher-centered; teachers outline the intellectual paths to be followed. In the classroom there is supposed to be a strict order with the teacher initiating all communication. Students in class speak up only when invited to; teachers are never publicly contradicted or criticized and are treated with deference even outside school. When a child misbehaves teachers involve its parents and expect them to help in putting the child in order. The educational process is highly personalized: especially in more advanced subjects at universities what is transferred is not seen as an impersonal 'truth', but as the personal wisdom of the teacher. The teacher is a 'guru', a term derived from the Sanskrit word for 'weighty' or 'honorable', which in India and Indonesia is, in fact, what a teacher is called. In such a system the quality of one's learning is virtually exclusively dependent on the excellence of one's teachers.

In the small power distance situation teachers are supposed to treat the students as basic equals and expect to be treated as equals by the students. Younger teachers are more equal, and therefore usually more liked than older ones. The educational process is student-centered, with a premium on student initiative; students are expected to find their own intellectual paths. Students make uninvited interventions in class, they are supposed to ask questions when they do not understand something. They argue with teachers, express disagreement and criticisms in front of the teachers, and show no particular respect to teachers outside school. When a child misbehaves parents often side with the child against the teacher. The educational process is rather impersonal; what is transferred comprises 'truths' or 'facts' which exist independently of this particular teacher. Effective learning in such a system depends very much on whether the supposed two-way communication between students and teacher is, indeed, established. The entire system is based on the students' well-developed need for independence; the quality of learning is to a considerable extent determined by the excellence of the students.

Earlier in this chapter it was shown that power distance scores are lower for occupations needing a higher education, at least in countries which, as a whole, score relatively low on power distance. This means that in the latter countries, students will become more independent of teachers as they proceed in their studies: their need for dependence decreases. In large power distance countries, however, students remain dependent on teachers even after reaching high education levels.

Corporal punishment at school, at least for children of pre-pubertal age, is much more acceptable in a large power distance culture than in its opposite. It accentuates and symbolizes the inequality between teacher and student and is often considered good for the development of the child's character. In a small power distance society it will readily be classified as child abuse and may be a reason for parents to complain to the police. There are exceptions, which relate to the dimension of masculinity (versus femininity) to be described in Chapter 4: in some masculine, small power distance cultures like Britain corporal punishment at school is not considered objectionable by everybody.

As in the case of the family discussed in the previous section, reality is somewhere in between these extremes. An important conditioning factor is the ability of the students: less gifted or handicapped children in small power distance situations will not develop the culturally expected sense of independence, and will be handled more in the large power distance way. Able children from working-class families in small power distance societies are at a disadvantage in educational institutions such as universities which assume a small power distance norm: as shown in the previous section, working-class families often have a large power distance subculture.

Power distance in the workplace

Most people start their working lives as young adults, after having gone through learning experiences in the family and at school. The role pairs parent–child and teacher–student are now complemented with the role pair boss–subordinate, and it should not surprise anybody when attitudes towards parents, especially fathers, and towards teachers, which are part of our mental programming, are transferred towards bosses.

In the large power distance situation superiors and subordinates consider each other as existentially unequal; the hierarchical system is felt to be based on this existential inequality. Organizations centralize power as much as possible in a few hands. Subordinates are expected to be told what to do. There are a lot of supervisory personnel, structured into tall hierarchies of people reporting to each other. Salary systems show wide gaps between top and bottom in the organization. Workers are relatively uneducated and manual work has a much lower status than office work. Superiors are entitled to privileges (private laws) and contacts between superiors and subordinates are supposed to be initiated by the superiors only. The ideal boss, in the subordinates' eyes, is a benevolent autocrat or 'good father'. After some experiences with 'bad fathers', they may ideologically reject the boss's authority completely, while in practice they will comply.

Relationships between subordinates and superiors in a large power distance organization are frequently loaded with emotions. Philippe d'Iribarne heads up a French public research center on international management. Through extensive interviews his research team compared manufacturing plants from the same French multinational in France (PDI 68), the USA (PDI 40), and the Netherlands (PDI 38). In his book (d'Iribarne, 1989) on this project, d'Iribarne comments:

> The often strongly emotional character of hierarchical relationships in France is intriguing. There is an extreme diversity of feelings towards superiors: they may be either adored or despised with equal intensity. This situation is not at all universal: we found it neither in the Netherlands nor in the USA. (Translation by Geert Hofstede)

This quote confirms the polarization in France between dependence and counterdependence versus authority persons which I found to be characteristic of large power distance countries in general.

Visible signs of status in large power distance countries contribute to the authority of bosses; it is quite possible that a subordinate feels proud if he can tell his neighbor that *his* boss drives a bigger car than the neighbor's boss. Older superiors are generally more respected than younger ones. Being a victim of power abuse by one's boss is just bad luck; there is no assumption that there should be a means of redress against such a situation. If it gets too bad, people may join forces for a violent revolt. Packaged leadership methods invented in the USA, like management by objectives (MBO),[8] will not work because they presuppose some form of negotiation between subordinate and superior which neither party will feel comfortable with.

In the small power distance situation subordinates and superiors consider each other as existentially equal; the hierarchical system is just an inequality of roles, established for convenience; and roles may be changed, so that someone who today is my subordinate may tomorrow be my boss. Organizations are fairly decentralized, with flat hierarchical pyramids and limited numbers of supervisory personnel. Salary ranges between top and bottom jobs are relatively small; workers are highly qualified, and high-skill manual work has a higher status than low-skill office work. Privileges for higher-ups are basically undesirable, and all should use the same parking lot, toilets, and cafeteria. Superiors should be accessible for subordinates, and the ideal boss is a resourceful (and therefore respected) democrat. Subordinates expect to be consulted before a decision is made that affects their work, but they accept that the boss is the one who finally decides.

Status symbols are suspect, and subordinates will most likely comment negatively to their neighbors if their boss spends company money on an excessive car. Younger bosses are generally more appreciated than older ones. Organizations are supposed to have structured ways of dealing with employee complaints about alleged power abuse. Some packaged leadership methods, like MBO, may work if given sufficient management attention.

Once more, these are extremes, and most work situations will be in between and contain some elements of both. Management theories, however, have rarely recognized that these different models exist and that their occurrence is culturally determined. Chapter 6 will come back to this issue and show how different theories of management and organization reflect the different nationalities of their authors.

Table 2.3 summarizes the key differences between small and large power distance societies discussed so far.

Table 2.3   Key differences between small and large power distance societies. I: general norm, family, school, and workplace

Small power distance	Large power distance
Inequalities among people should be minimized	Inequalities among people are both expected and desired
There should be, and there is to some extent, interdependence between less and more powerful people	Less powerful people should be dependent on the more powerful; in practice, less powerful people are polarized between dependence and counterdependence
Parents treat children as equals	Parents teach children obedience
Children treat parents as equals	Children treat parents with respect
Teachers expect initiatives from students in class	Teachers are expected to take all initiatives in class
Teachers are experts who transfer impersonal truths	Teachers are gurus who transfer personal wisdom
Students treat teachers as equals	Students treat teachers with respect
More educated persons hold less authoritarian values than less educated persons	Both more and less educated persons show almost equally authoritarian values
Hierarchy in organizations means an inequality of roles, established for convenience	Hierarchy in organizations reflects the existential inequality between higher-ups and lower-downs
Decentralization is popular	Centralization is popular
Narrow salary range between top and bottom of organization	Wide salary range between top and bottom of organization
Subordinates expect to be consulted	Subordinates expect to be told what to do
The ideal boss is a resourceful democrat	The ideal boss is a benevolent autocrat or good father
Privileges and status symbols are frowned upon	Privileges and status symbols for managers are both expected and popular

Power distance and the state

The previous sections have looked at the implications of power distance differences among countries for the role pairs of parent–child, teacher–student, and boss–subordinate; one which is obviously equally affected is authority–citizen. It must be immediately evident to anyone who reads any world news at all that some countries handle power differences between authorities and citizens in very different ways from others, and that different convictions dominate as to what ways of handling such power differences are desirable.

In the large power distance situation power is seen as a basic fact of society which precedes the choice between good and evil. Its legitimacy is irrelevant. Might prevails over right. This is a strong statement which may rarely be presented in this form, but which is reflected in the behavior of those in power *and* of ordinary people. There is an unspoken consensus that there should be an order of inequality in this world in which everybody has his or her place. Such an order satisfies people's need for dependence and it gives a sense of security both to those in power and to those lower down.

At the beginning of this chapter, reference was made to the tendency in some societies to achieve consistency in people's positions with regard to power, wealth, and status. A desire for status consistency is typical for large power distance cultures. In such cultures the powerful are entitled to privileges, and are expected to use their power to increase their wealth. Their status is enhanced by symbolic behavior which makes them look as powerful as possible. Their main sources of power are family and friends, charisma, and/or the ability to use force; the latter explains the frequency of military dictatorships in countries on this side of the power distance scale. Scandals involving persons in power are expected, and so is the fact that they will be covered up. If something goes wrong, the blame goes to people lower down the hierarchy. If it gets too bad, the way to change the system is by replacing those in power through a revolution. Most such revolutions fail even if they succeed, because the newly powerful, after some time, repeat the behaviors of their predecessors, in which they are supported by the prevailing values regarding inequality.

Even without revolutions, large power distance countries have more domestic political violence (politically-inspired riots) than small power distance countries. They often have one-party political systems: where elections allow more parties, the same party usually wins, and this is a party not stressing equality (right-wing). The political spectrum of the large power distance countries is characterized by strong right and left wings with a weak center, a political reflection of the polarization between dependence and counterdependence described earlier in this chapter. Incomes in these countries are very unequally distributed, with a few very rich and many very poor people. Moreover, taxation protects the wealthy, so that incomes after taxes can even be more unequal than before. Labor unions tend to be government controlled; where they are not, they are ideologically based and involved in politics.

In the small power distance society a feeling dominates that the use of power should be legitimate and subject to the judgment between good and evil. Inequality is considered basically undesirable; although unavoidable, it should be minimized by political means. The law should guarantee that everybody, regardless of status, has equal rights. Power, wealth, and status need not go together; it is even considered a good thing if they do not. Status symbols for powerful people are suspect, and leaders may enhance their informal status by renouncing formal symbols: the minister taking the streetcar to work. The main sources of power are one's formal position, one's assumed expertise, and one's ability to give rewards. Scandals usually mean the end of a political career. Revolutions are unpopular; the system is changed in evolutionary ways, without necessarily deposing those in power. Violence rarely occurs in domestic politics. Countries with small power distance value systems usually have pluralist governments which can shift peacefully from one party or coalition to another on the basis of election results. The political spectrum in such countries usually shows a powerful center and weaker right and left wings.[9] Incomes are less unequally distributed than in large power distance countries. Taxation serves to redistribute income, making income after taxes less unequal than before. Labor unions are independent and less oriented to ideology and politics than to pragmatic issues on behalf of their members.

The reader will quickly recognize that some elements of both extremes can be found in many countries. A country like Spain, ruled dictatorially until the 1970s, has shifted remarkably smoothly to a pluralist government system. The government in the United Kingdom, an old democracy, tried hard to prevent the publication of unwanted revelations by a former secret agent. *Glasnost* has penetrated the autocratic institutions of the USSR.

Institutions from small power distance countries are sometimes copied in large power distance countries because political ideas travel. Political leaders who studied in other countries may try to emulate these countries' political systems. Governments of smaller power distance countries often eagerly try to export their institutional arrangements in the context of development cooperation. However, just going through the moves of an election will not change the political mores of a country, if these are deeply rooted in the mental software of a large part of the population. In particular, underfed and uneducated masses make poor democrats and ways of government customary in more well-off countries are unlikely to function in poor ones. Actions by foreign governments intended to lead other countries toward democratic ways and respect for human rights are clearly inspired by the mental programming of the foreign helpers, and they are usually more effective in dealing with the opinions of the foreign electorate than with the problems in the countries supposed to be helped.

Power distance and ideas
Parents, teachers, managers, and rulers are all children of their cultures; in a way they are the followers of their followers, and their behavior can only be understood if one also understands the mental software of their children, students, subordinates, and subjects. However, not only the doers in this world but also the thinkers are children of a culture. The authors of management books and the founders of political ideologies generate their ideas from the background of what they learned when they grew up. Thus differences among countries along value dimensions like power distance help not only in understanding differences in thinking, feeling, and behaving by the leaders and those led, but also in appreciating the theories produced or adopted in these countries to explain or prescribe thought, feeling, and behavior.

In world history some philosophers have dealt very explicitly with questions of power and inequality. In China around 500 BC, Kong Ze, whom the Jesuit missionaries 2000 years later latinized as Confucius (from the older name Kong Fu Ze), maintained that the stability of society is based on unequal relationships between people. He distinguished the *wu lun*, the five basic relationships: ruler–subject, father–son, older brother–younger brother, husband–wife, and senior friend–junior friend. These relationships contain mutual and complementary obligations: the junior partner owes the senior respect and obedience; the senior owes the junior partner protection and consideration. Confucius' ideas have survived as guidelines for proper behavior for Chinese people to this day. In the People's Republic of China Mao Tse-Tung tried to wipe out Confucianism but in the meantime his own rule contained Confucian elements.[10] Countries in the IBM study with a Chinese majority or which have undergone Chinese cultural influences are, in the order in which they appear in Table 2.1, Singapore, Hong Kong, South Korea, Taiwan, and Japan; they occupy the upper medium and medium PDI zones. People in these countries accept and appreciate inequality, but feel that the use of power should be moderated by a sense of obligation.

In ancient Greece around 350 BC, Plato recognized a basic need for equality among people but at the same time defended a society in which an élite class, the Guardians, would exercise leadership. He tried to resolve the conflict between these diverging tendencies by playing upon two meanings of the word 'equality', a quantitative and a qualitative one, but to me his arguments resemble the famous quote from George Orwell's *Animal Farm*: 'All animals are equal but some are more equal than others'. Present-day Greece in the IBM data scores about halfway on power distance (rank 27/28, score 60).

Niccolò Machiavelli from Italy (1469–1527) is one of world literature's greatest authorities on the use of political power. He distinguished two models: the model of the fox and the model of the lion. The prudent ruler, Machiavelli writes, uses both models each at the proper time: the cunning of the fox will avoid the snares, and the strength of the lion will scare the wolves (see Machiavelli, 1955, p. 91). Relating Machiavelli's thoughts to national power distance differences one finds small power distance countries to be accustomed to the fox model and large power distance countries to the lion model. Italy, in the twentieth-century IBM research data, scores in the middle zone on power distance (rank 34, score 50). It is likely that, were one to study Italy by region, the North would be more foxy and the South more lion-like. What Machiavelli did not write but what the association between political systems and citizens' mental software suggests is that the animal which the ruler should impersonate depends strongly on which animals the followers are.

Karl Marx (1818–1883) also dealt with power but he wanted to give it to the powerless; he never really dealt with the question of whether the revolution he preached would create a new powerless class or not. In fact, he seemed to assume that the exercise of power can be transferred from persons to a system, a philosophy in which we can recognize the mental software of the small power distance societies to which Marx's mother country, Germany, today belongs. It is a tragedy for the modern world that Marx's ideas have been mainly exported to countries at the large power distance side of the continuum in which, as was argued earlier in this chapter, the assumption that power should yield to law is absent. This absence of a check to power has enabled government systems claiming Marx's inheritance to survive even where these systems would make Marx himself turn in his grave. In Marx's concept of the 'dictatorship of the proletariat' the 'dictatorship' has appealed to rulers in some large power distance countries but the 'proletariat' has been forgotten. In fact the concept is naïve: in view of what we know of the human tendency towards inequality, a dictatorship by a proletariat is a logical contradiction.

The export of ideas to people in other countries without regard for the values context in which these ideas were developed—and the import of such ideas by gullible believers in those other countries—is not only limited to politics, but can also be observed in the domains of education and, in particular, management and organization. The economic success of the USA in the decades before and after the Second World War has made people in other countries believe that US ideas about management must be superior and therefore should be copied. They forget to ask about the kind of society in which these ideas were developed and applied—*if* they were really applied as the books claimed. Since the late 1960s the same has happened with Japanese ideas.

The USA in Table 2.1 scores on the low side, but not extremely low, on power distance (rank 38 out of 53). US leadership theories tend to be based on subordinates with medium-level dependence needs: not too high, not too low. A key idea is 'participative management', i.e., a situation in which subordinates are involved by managers into decisions *at the discretion and initiative of these managers*. Comparing US theories of leadership to 'industrial democracy' experiments in countries like Sweden or Denmark (which score extremely low on PDI) one finds that in these Scandinavian countries initiatives to participate are often taken by the subordinates, which US managers find difficult to digest because it represents an infringement on their 'management prerogatives'. Management prerogatives, however, are less sacred in Scandinavia. On the other hand, US theories of participative management are also unlikely to apply in countries much higher on the power distance scale. One study reports the embarrassment of a Greek subordinate when his expatriate US boss asked his opinion on how much time a job should take: 'He is the boss. Why doesn't he tell me?' (see Triandis, 1973).

Table 2.4 summarizes the key differences between small and large power distance societies from the last two sections; together with Table 2.3 it provides an overview of the essence of power distance differences across all spheres of life discussed in this chapter.

The origins of power distance differences

Countries in which a Romance language is spoken (Spanish, Portuguese, Italian, French) score medium to high (from 35 in Costa Rica to 95 in Guatemala) on the power distance scale in Table 2.1. Countries in which a Germanic language is spoken (German, English, Dutch, Danish, Norwegian, Swedish) score low (from 11 in Austria to 49 in South Africa). There seems to be a relationship between language area and present-day mental software regarding power distance. The fact that a country belongs to a language area is rooted in history: Romance languages all derive from Low Latin, and were adopted in countries once part of the Roman Empire, or, in the case of Latin America, in countries colonized by Spain and Portugal which themselves were former colonies of Rome. Germanic languages are spoken either in countries which remained 'barbaric' in Roman days, or in areas once under Roman rule but reconquered by barbarians (like England). Thus some roots of the mental program called power distance go back at least to Roman times—2000 years ago. Countries with a Chinese

Table 2.4   Key differences between small and large power distance societies.
II: politics and ideas

Small power distance	Large power distance
The use of power should be legitimate and is subject to criteria of good and evil	Might prevails over right: whoever holds the power is right and good
Skills, wealth, power, and status need not go together	Skills, wealth, power, and status should go together
The middle class is large	The middle class is small
All should have equal rights	The powerful have privileges
Powerful people try to look less powerful than they are	Powerful people try to look as impressive as possible
Power is based on formal position, expertise, and ability to give rewards	Power is based on family or friends, charisma, and ability to use force
The way to change a political system is by changing the rules (evolution)	The way to change a political system is by changing the people at the top (revolution)
The use of violence in domestic politics is rare	Domestic political conflicts frequently lead to violence
Pluralist governments based on outcome of majority votes	Autocratic or oligarchic governments based on cooptation
Political spectrum shows strong center and weak right and left wings	Political spectrum, if allowed to be manifested, shows weak center and strong wings
Small income differentials in society, further reduced by the tax system	Large income differentials in society, further increased by the tax system
Prevailing religions and philosophical systems stress equality	Prevailing religions and philosophical systems stress hierarchy and stratification
Prevailing political ideologies stress and practice power sharing	Prevailing political ideologies stress and practice power struggle
Native management theories focus on role of employees	Native management theories focus on role of managers

(Confucian) cultural inheritance also cluster on the medium to high side of
the power distance scale—and here is a culture at least 4000 years old.

None of us was present when culture patterns started to diverge between
peoples: the attribution of causes for these differences is a matter of
educated speculation on the basis of historical and prehistorical sources.
Both the Roman and the Chinese empires were ruled from a single power
center, which presupposes a population prepared to take orders from the
center. The Germanic part of Europe, on the other hand, was divided into
small tribal groups under local lords, not prepared to accept directives from
anybody else. It seems a reasonable assumption that early statehood
experiences helped to develop in these peoples the common mental programs necessary for the survival of their political and social system.

The question remains, of course, why these early statehood experiences deviated. One way of supporting the guesswork for causes was to look for quantitative data about countries which might be correlated with the power distance scores. A number of such quantitative variables were available. A statistical tool called *stepwise multiple regression* allowed us to select from these variables the ones which successively contributed most to explaining the differences in PDI scores in Table 2.1. The result was that a country's PDI score can be fairly accurately predicted from the following (Hofstede, 1980, pp. 121 ff: 1984, pp. 95 ff):

1. The country's geographical latitude (higher latitudes associated with lower PDI)
2. Its population size (larger size associated with higher PDI) and
3. Its wealth (richer countries associated with lower PDI)

For the 40 countries on which the first analysis was done geographical latitude (the distance from the equator of a country's capital city) alone allows us to predict 43 percent of the differences (the variance) in PDI values. Latitude and population size together predict 51 percent of the variance, and latitude, population size, plus national wealth (per capita gross national product in 1970, the middle year of the survey period), predict 58 percent. If one knew nothing else about these countries other than those three hard to fairly hard data one would be able to make a list of predicted PDIs which resembles Table 2.1 pretty closely. On average, the predicted values deviate only 10 scale points from those found in the IBM surveys. The worst fit is for Israel where the prediction is 44 and the actual value 13, a difference of 31 points. Other countries, however, are predicted within 1 point difference: India (78 for 77), Spain (56 for 57), and the Netherlands (38 for 38).

Geographical latitude is an extremely interesting measure to correlate with power distances. It is a rough indication of a country's climate: countries with low latitudes are tropical, with medium latitudes subtropical to moderate, with high latitudes cold. Philosophers and popular wisdom have for centuries ventured climate differences as an explanation for differences in the character of inhabitants. Warm climates, for example, would make people lazy; cold ones would make them industrious. Such assertions are unprovable, and it is not difficult to come up with examples which do not fit them—like the industrious Singaporeans who live almost right upon the equator. However, the relationship with PDI is solid and statistically highly significant. For the reader who has not been trained in probability calculus: the relationship found does not mean that geographical latitude *determines* power distance, but that higher latitude *contributes to* smaller power distances, along with other elements.

Statistical relationships do not indicate the direction of causality: they do not tell which is cause and which is effect, or whether the related elements are maybe both the effects of a common third cause. But in the unique case of a country's geographical position, it is difficult to consider it as anything else than a cause, even an archi-cause unless we assume that in prehistoric times peoples have migrated to climates which fitted their concepts of power distance, which is rather far-fetched.

The logic of the relationship, supported by various research studies (Hofstede, 1980, p. 124; 1984, p. 96) could be as follows: first of all, the societies involved have all developed to the level of sedentary agriculture and urban industry. The more primitive hunter–gatherer societies for which a different logic may apply are not included. At lower latitudes (i.e., more tropical climates), agricultural societies generally meet a more abundant nature. Survival and population growth in these climates demands a relatively limited intervention of man with nature: everything grows. In this situation the major threat to a society is the competition of other human groups for the same territory and resources. The better chances for survival exist for those societies that have organized themselves hierarchically and in dependence on one central authority which keeps order and balance.

At higher latitudes (i.e., moderate and colder climates), nature is less abundant. There is more of a need for people's intervention with nature in order to carve out an existence. There are stronger forces supporting the creation of industry next to agriculture. Nature, rather than other humans, is the first enemy to be resisted. Societies in which people have learned to fend for themselves without being too dependent on more powerful others have a better chance of survival under these circumstances than societies which educate their children towards dependence.

Size of population, the second predictor of power distance, fosters dependence on authority because people in a populous country will have to accept a political power which is more distant and less accessible than people from a small nation. On the other hand, a case can be made for a reversal of causality here because less dependently minded peoples will fight harder to avoid being integrated into a larger nation.

National wealth, the third predictor, in itself stands for a lot of other factors, each of which could be both an effect and a cause of smaller power distances. In fact we are dealing with phenomena for which causality is almost always *circular*, like the causality of the chicken and the egg. Factors associated with more national wealth *and* less dependence on powerful others are:

1. Less traditional agriculture
2. More modern technology
3. More urban living
4. More social mobility

5. A better educational system
6. A larger middle class.

More ex-colonies than ex-colonizing nations show large power distances; but having been either a colony or a colonizer at some time during the past two centuries is also strongly related to present wealth. The data do not allow establishing a one-way causal path among the three factors of poverty, colonization, and large power differences. Assumptions about causality in this respect usually depend on what one likes to prove.

The future of power distance differences

So far the picture of differences among countries with regard to power distance has been a static one. The previous section claimed that some of the differences have historical roots of up to 4000 years or more. So much for the past, but what about the future? We live in an era of unprecedented intensification of international communication: should not this eradicate the differences, and help us to grow towards a world standard? And if so, will this be one of large, small, or medium power distances?

Impressionistically at least, it seems that dependence on the power of others in a large part of our world has been reduced over the past two generations. Most of us feel less dependent than we assume our parents and grandparents to have been. Moreover, independence is a politically attractive topic. Liberation and emancipation movements abound. Educational opportunities have been improved in many countries, and we have seen that power distance scores within countries decrease with increased education level. This does not mean, however, that the *differences* between the countries described in this chapter should necessarily have changed. Countries could all have moved to lower power distance levels without changes in their mutual ranking as shown in Table 2.1.

One may try to develop a prediction about longer-term changes in power distance by looking at what could happen to the underlying forces identified in the previous section of this chapter. Of the factors shown to be most closely associated with power distance (latitude, size, and wealth) the first is immutable. As to the second, size of population, one could argue that small and even large countries will be less and less able to make decisions at their own level, and that we are all becoming more and more dependent on decisions made internationally. This would support a global increase in power distances. The third factor, wealth, increases for some countries but not for others. Where it increases, this supports reductions in power distance; where economic development stagnates, i.e., mainly in countries that are already very poor, no reduction in power distance is to be expected.

The empirical evidence about shifts in power distance in different countries over time is limited to a comparison between the situation in IBM in 1968 and in 1972 (Hofstede, 1980, pp. 346 ff; 1984, pp. 234 ff). This four-year term saw a worldwide increase in the *desire for* independence, no doubt under the influence of the international communication of ideas. But this desire was matched by a shift in the direction of more equality in *perceived* power only in countries in which power distances had already been small. This situation resembles what happened with the distribution of national wealth: most rich countries over the past decades have become richer but only a few of the poor have, and the gap has been widening rather than narrowing. In the case of power distance (which is correlated with national poverty) too, the IBM scores from 1968 to 1972 show that countries at opposite ends of the scale have grown further apart.

The IBM data cover only a short, four-year time span. But nobody (as far as I know) has offered evidence of a convergence of countries towards smaller power distances since 1972, nor towards smaller *differences in* power distance. I believe that the picture of national variety presented in this chapter, with its very old historical roots, is likely to survive for a long time yet, at least for some centuries. A worldwide homogenization of mental programs about power and dependence, independence, and interdependence under the influence of a presumed cultural melting-pot process, is still very far away, if it will ever happen.

In December 1988 the following news item appeared in the press:

> Stockholm, December 23. The Swedish King Carl Gustav this week experienced considerable delay while shopping for Christmas presents for his children, when he wanted to pay by cheque but could not show his cheque card. The salesperson refused to accept the cheque without legitimation. Only when helpful bystanders dug in their pockets for one-crown pieces showing the face of the King, the salesperson decided to accept this for legitimation, not, however, without testing the cheque thoroughly for authenticity and noting the name and address of the holder.[11]

Today's Bernadotte (a direct descendant of the French general) still meets with the same equality norm as his ancestor. How much time will have to pass before the Presidents of the United States, the Soviet Union, and the Philippines, or the Heads of the various African states will be handled in the same way in their countries' shops? Or before the Swedes start treating their king like the Iranians treated their Ayatollah?

Notes

[1] The matrix on which the factor analysis was carried out consisted of 32 questions (variables) and 40 countries (cases). Handbooks on factor analysis do not recommend using the technique for matrices with few cases, because the factors become unstable: they can be affected too much by a single deviant case. This limitation does not apply, however, for *ecological* factor analyses, in which the score for each case is the mean of a large number of independent observations. In this situation, the stability of the factor structure is determined by the number of

individuals whose answers went into the mean scores. Therefore ecological factor analyses give stable results even with fewer cases than variables.

2   In statistical terms: items with high loadings on the factor.

3   Pierre Bourdieu (see Chapter 1, note 2) sees this as one of the key characteristics of a *habitus*. It represents necessity turned into virtue (*nécessité faite vertu*). See Bourdieu (1980, p. 90).

4   The term 'working class' is, of course, curiously archaic. If anything, in many countries it covers more people who are *out of* work than the middle class.

5   The samples of IBM employees upon which the cross-national comparison was based included all categories of Table 2.2 except unskilled workers. The mean score of the cross-national samples for Great Britain, France, and Germany was 46.

6   In *Culture's Consequences* (Hofstede, 1980) I have used both 'product moment' (Pearson) correlation coefficients and 'rank order' (Spearman) correlation coefficients; the first are based on the absolute values of measurements, the second on their relative ranks.

7   A classic motion picture *Four Families*, produced by the National Film Board of Canada in 1959, with expert advice from Margaret Mead, shows the relationships between parents and small children in more-or-less matched farmer families in India, France, Japan, and Canada. Audiences to whom I showed the film, before giving them the power distance scores, were able to rank the four countries correctly on this dimension just on the basis of the parent–child relationships pictured in the film.

8   Management by objectives is a system of periodic meetings between superior and subordinate in which the latter commits him/herself to the achievement of certain objectives. In the next meeting this achievement is assessed and new objectives for the coming period are agreed upon.

9   As part of a large research project called the 'European Value Systems Study' (held after the publication of *Culture's Consequences*, Hofstede, 1980) representative samples of the population in nine European countries were asked to indicate their political position on a 10-point scale from left to right. On the basis of their choices a coefficient of variation of political positions was computed. Across the nine countries the variation of political positions was significantly correlated with the PDI scores from the IBM studies (Spearman rank correlation coefficient 0.71). For the data see Stoetzel (1983, p. 60).

10   More about Confucianism will be written in Chapter 7.

11   Translated by GH from the Dutch newspaper *NRC/Handelsblad*, December 23, 1988.

3

I, we, and they

A medium-size Swedish high-technology corporation was approached by a compatriot, a businessman with good contacts in Saudi Arabia. The company sent one of their engineers—let me call him Johannesson—to Riyadh, where he was introduced to a small Saudi engineering firm, run by two brothers in their mid-thirties, both with British university degrees. Johannesson was to assist in a development project on behalf of the Saudi government. However, after six visits over a period of two years, nothing seemed to happen. Johannesson's meetings with the Saudi brothers were always held in the presence of the Swedish businessman who had established the first contact. This annoyed Johannesson and his superiors, because they were not at all sure that this businessman did not have contacts with their competitors as well—but the Saudis wanted the intermediary to be there. Discussions often dwelt on issues having little to do with the business—like Shakespeare, of whom both brothers were fans.

Just when Johannesson's superiors started to doubt the wisdom of the corporation's investment in these expensive trips, a telex arrived from Riyadh inviting him back for an urgent visit. A contract worth several millions of dollars was ready to be signed. From one day to the next, the Saudis' attitude changed: the presence of the businessman–intermediary was no longer necessary, and for the first time Johannesson saw the Saudis smile, and even make jokes.

So far, so good; but the story goes on. The remarkable order contributed to Johannesson being promoted to a management position in a different division. Thus, he was no longer in charge of the Saudi account. A successor was nominated, another engineer with considerable international experience, whom Johannesson personally introduced to the Saudi brothers. A few weeks later a telex arrived from Riyadh in which the Saudis threatened to cancel the contract over a detail in the delivery conditions. Johannesson's help was asked. When he came to Riyadh it appeared that the conflict was over a minor issue and could easily be resolved—but only, the Saudis felt, with Johannesson as the corporation's representative. So the corporation twisted its structure to allow Johannesson to handle the Saudi account although his main responsibilities were now in a completely different field.

The individual and the collective in society

The Swedes and the Saudis in this true story have different concepts of the role of personal relationships in business. For the Swedes, business is done with a company; for the Saudis, with a person whom one has learned to know and trust. As long as one does not know another person well enough it is convenient to have present an intermediary or go-between, someone who knows and is trusted by both parties. At the root of the difference between these cultures is a fundamental issue in human societies: the role of the individual versus the role of the group.

The vast majority of people in our world live in societies in which the interest of the group prevails over the interest of the individual. I will call these societies *collectivist*, using a word which to some readers may have political connotations, but it is not meant here in any political sense. It does not refer to the power of the state over the individual but to the *power of the group*. The first group in our lives is always the family into which we are born. Family structures, however, differ between societies. In most collectivist societies the 'family' within which the child grows up consists of a number of people living closely together; not just the parents and other children, but, for example, grandparents, uncles, aunts, servants, or other housemates. This is known in cultural anthropology as the *extended family*. When children grow up they learn to think of themselves as part of a 'we' group, a relationship which is not voluntary but given by nature. The 'we' group is distinct from other people in society who belong to 'they' groups, of which there are many. The 'we' group (or ingroup) is the major source of one's identity, and the only secure protection one has against the hardships of life. Therefore one owes lifelong loyalty to one's ingroup, and breaking this loyalty is one of the worst things a person can do. Between the person and the ingroup a dependence relationship develops which is both practical and psychological.

A minority of people in our world live in societies in which the interests of the individual prevail over the interests of the group, societies which I will call *individualist*. In these, most children are born into families consisting of two parents and, possibly, other children; in some societies there is an increasing share of one-parent families. Other relatives live elsewhere and are rarely seen. This type is the *nuclear family* (from the Latin *nucleus* meaning core). Children from such families, as they grow up, soon learn to think of themselves as 'I'. This 'I', their personal identity, is distinct from other people's 'I's, and these others are not classified according to their group membership but to individual characteristics. Playmates, for example, are chosen on the basis of personal preferences. The purpose of education is to enable the child to stand on its own feet. The child is expected to leave the parental home as soon as this has been achieved. Not infrequently, children, after having left home, reduce relationships with their parents to a minimum or break them off altogether. Neither practically nor psychologically is the healthy person in this type of society supposed to be dependent on a group.

Measuring the degree of individualism in society

Extreme collectivism and extreme individualism can be considered as the opposite poles of a second global dimension of national cultures, after power distance which was described in Chapter 2. All countries in the IBM studies could be given an individualism index score which was low for collectivist and high for individualist societies.

The new dimension is defined as follows. *Individualism* pertains to *societies in which the ties between individuals are loose: everyone is expected to look after himself or herself and his or her immediate family. Collectivism* as its opposite pertains to *societies in which people from birth onwards are integrated into strong, cohesive ingroups, which throughout people's lifetime continue to protect them in exchange for unquestioning loyalty.*

Degrees of individualism obviously vary within countries as well as between them, so it is again very important to base the country scores on comparable samples from one country to another. The IBM samples offered this comparability.

The survey questions on which the individualism index is based belong to a set of fourteen 'work goals'. People were asked: 'Try to think of those factors which would be important to you in an ideal job; disregard the extent to which they are contained in your present job. How important is it to you to . . .' followed by 14 items, each to be scored on a scale from 1 (of utmost importance to me) to 5 (of very little or no importance). When the answer patterns for the respondents from 40 countries on the 14 items were analyzed they reflected *two* underlying dimensions. One was individualism versus collectivism. The other came to be labeled masculinity versus femininity (see Chapter 4).

The dimension to be identified with individualism versus collectivism was most strongly associated with the relative importance attached to the following 'work goal' items. For the individualist pole:

1. *Personal time* Have a job which leaves you sufficient time for your personal or family life.
2. *Freedom* Have considerable freedom to adopt your own approach to the job.

3. *Challenge* Have challenging work to do—work from which you can achieve a personal sense of accomplishment.

For the opposite, collectivist pole:

4. *Training* Have training opportunities (to improve your skills or learn new skills).
5. *Physical conditions* Have good physical working conditions (good ventilation and lighting, adequate work space, etc.).
6. *Use of skills* Fully use your skills and abilities on the job.

If the IBM employees in a country scored work goal (1) as relatively important, they generally also scored (2) and (3) as important, but (4), (5), and (6) as unimportant. Such a country was considered individualist. If (1) was scored as relatively unimportant, the same generally held for (2) and (3), but (4), (5), and (6) would be scored as relatively more important. Such a country was considered collectivist.

Obviously, these items from the IBM questionnaire do not totally cover the distinction between individualism and collectivism in a society. They only represent the issues in the IBM research which relate to this distinction. The correlations of the IBM Individualism country scores with non-IBM data about other characteristics of societies confirm (validate) the claim that this dimension from the IBM data does, indeed, measure individualism.

In itself, it is not difficult to identify the importance of personal time, freedom, and (personal) challenge with individualism: they all stress the employee's independence from the organization. The work goals at the opposite pole: training, physical conditions, and skills being used on the job refer to things the organization does for the employee, and in this way stress the employee's dependence on the organization which fits with collectivism. Another link in the relationship is that, as will be shown, individualist countries tend to be rich and collectivist countries poor. In rich countries, training, physical conditions, and the use of skills may be taken for granted, which makes them relatively unimportant as work goals. In poor countries, these things cannot be taken for granted: they are essential in distinguishing a good job from a bad one, which makes them quite important among one's work goals.

The actual calculation of the individualism index is not, as in the case of power distance, based on simply adding or subtracting question scores after multiplying them by a fixed number. The statistical procedure used to identify the Individualism, and, in Chapter 4, the masculinity dimension on the basis of the 14 work goals produces automatically a *factor score* for either dimension for each country. These factor scores are a more accurate measure of that country's position on the dimension than could be obtained

Table 3.1 Individualism index (IDV) values for 50 countries and 3 regions

Score rank	Country or region	IDV score	Score rank	Country or region	IDV score
1	USA	91	28	Turkey	37
2	Australia	90	29	Uruguay	36
3	Great Britain	89	30	Greece	35
4/5	Canada	80	31	Philippines	32
4/5	Netherlands	80	32	Mexico	30
6	New Zealand	79	33/35	East Africa	27
7	Italy	76	33/35	Yugoslavia	27
8	Belgium	75	33/35	Portugal	27
9	Denmark	74	36	Malaysia	26
10/11	Sweden	71	37	Hong Kong	25
10/11	France	71	38	Chile	23
12	Ireland	70	39/41	West Africa	20
	(Republic of)		39/41	Singapore	20
13	Norway	69	39/41	Thailand	20
14	Switzerland	68	42	Salvador	19
15	Germany F.R.	67	43	South Korea	18
16	South Africa	65	44	Taiwan	17
17	Finland	63	45	Peru	16
18	Austria	55	46	Costa Rica	15
19	Israel	54	47/48	Pakistan	14
20	Spain	51	47/48	Indonesia	14
21	India	48	49	Colombia	13
22/23	Japan	46	50	Venezuela	12
22/23	Argentina	46	51	Panama	11
24	Iran	41	52	Equador	8
25	Jamaica	39	53	Guatemala	6
26/27	Brazil	38			
26/27	Arab countries	38			

by adding or subtracting question scores. The factor scores for the individualism dimension were multiplied by 25 and a constant number of 50 points was added. This puts all scores in a range from close to 0 for the most collectivist country to close to 100 for the most individualist one.[1]

The individualism index (IDV) scores can be read from Table 3.1. As in the case of the PDI in Chapter 2 the scores represent the *relative* positions of countries. What can immediately be recognized by inspecting Table 3.1 is that nearly all wealthy countries score high on IDV while nearly all poor countries score low. There is a strong relationship between a country's national wealth and the degree of individualism in its culture; it will be further explored later in this chapter.

Sweden scores 71 on IDV and the group of Arab-speaking countries to which Saudi Arabia belongs scores an average of 38, which demonstrates the cultural roots of Johannesson's dilemma. Of course the Arab countries

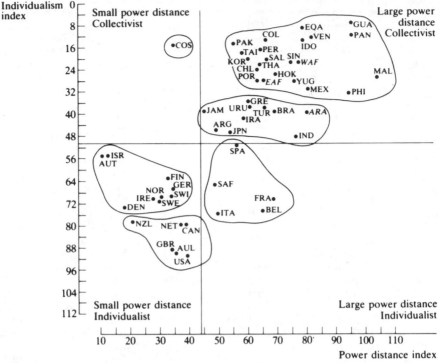

Fig. 3.1   The position of 50 countries and 3 regions on the power distance and individualism–collectivism dimensions (for country name abbreviations see Table 3-2)

differ among themselves, and impressionistically the Saudis within this region are even more collectivist than some other Arabs like Lebanese or Egyptians. In the IBM sample the latter were more strongly represented than the Saudis. Sweden's rank among 53 countries and regions is 10–11 and the Arab countries' rank 26–27, so there are still a lot of countries scoring more than the Arab average. As stated above, collectivism is the rule in our world, and individualism the exception.

Collectivism versus power distance

Many countries which score high on the PDI (Table 2.1) score low on the IDV (Table 3.1) and vice versa. In other words, the two dimensions tend to be negatively correlated: large power distance countries are also likely to be more collectivist, and small power distance countries to be more individualist. The relationship between the two indices is plotted in Fig. 3.1; a list of countries with the abbreviations used is presented in Table 3.2.

In the plot of Fig. 3.1 the countries are grouped around a diagonal from lower left to upper right, reflecting the correlation between power distance and

Table 3.2 Abbreviations for the countries and regions studied

Abbreviation	Country or region	Abbreviation	Country or region
ARA	Arab-speaking countries (Egypt, Iraq, Kuwait, Lebanon, Libya, Saudi Arabia, United Arab Emirates)	ISR	Israel
		ITA	Italy
		JAM	Jamaica
		JPN	Japan
		KOR	South Korea
ARG	Argentina	MAL	Malaysia
AUL	Australia	MEX	Mexico
AUT	Austria	NET	Netherlands
BEL	Belgium	NOR	Norway
BRA	Brazil	NZL	New Zealand
CAN	Canada	PAK	Pakistan
CHL	Chile	PAN	Panama
COL	Colombia	PER	Peru
COS	Costa Rica	PHI	Philippines
DEN	Denmark	POR	Portugal
EAF	East Africa (Ethiopia, Kenya, Tanzania, Zambia)	SAF	South Africa
		SAL	Salvador
		SIN	Singapore
EQA	Equador	SPA	Spain
FIN	Finland	SWE	Sweden
FRA	France	SWI	Switzerland
GBR	Great Britain	TAI	Taiwan
GER	Germany F.R.	THA	Thailand
GRE	Greece	TUR	Turkey
GUA	Guatemala	URU	Uruguay
HOK	Hong Kong	USA	United States
IDO	Indonesia	VEN	Venezuela
IND	India	WAF	West Africa (Ghana, Nigeria, Sierra Leone)
IRA	Iran		
IRE	Ireland (Republic of)	YUG	Yugoslavia

collectivism[2]. In cultures in which people are dependent on ingroups these people are *usually* also dependent on power figures. Most extended families have patriarchal structures with the head of the family exercising strong moral authority. In cultures in which people are relatively independent from ingroups these people are *usually* also less dependent on powerful others.

However, there are exceptions. The Latin European countries, and in particular France and Belgium, combine medium power distances with strong individualism. The French sociologist Michel Crozier has described his country's culture as follows (Crozier, 1964, p. 222):

'Face-to-face dependence relationships are . . . perceived as difficult to bear in the French cultural setting. Yet the prevailing view of authority is still that of . . . absolutism . . . . The two attitudes are contradictory. However, they can be reconciled within a bureaucratic system since impersonal rules and centralization make it possible to reconcile an absolutist conception of authority and the elimination of most direct dependence relationships.'

Crozier's compatriot Philippe d'Iribarne in his comparative study of a French, a US, and a Dutch organization describes the French principle of organizing as 'the rationale of honor' (*la logique de l'honneur*). This principle, which he finds already present in the French kingdom prior to Napoleon, means that everybody has a rank (large power distance), but that the implications of belonging to one's rank are less imposed by the group than determined by tradition. It is 'not so much what one owes to others as what one owes to oneself' (d'Iribarne, 1989, p. 59). It is a stratified form of individualism.

The reverse pattern, small power distance combined with medium individualism, is found in Austria and Israel, and fairly small power distance is combined with outright collectivism in Costa Rica. Costa Rica, one of the six Central American republics, is widely recognized as an exception to the Latin American rule of dependence on powerful leaders, which in Spanish is called *personalismo*. It does not have a formal army. It is described as Latin America's 'most firmly rooted democracy', in spite of its relative poverty as compared to the industrial market economies of the world. In a comparison between Costa Rica and its larger but much poorer neighbor Nicaragua, US development expert Lawrence E. Harrison has written:

'. . . there is ample evidence that Costa Ricans have felt a stronger bond to their countrymen than have Nicaraguans. That bond is reflected in Costa Rica's long-standing emphasis on public education and public health; in its more vigorous cooperative movement; in a judicial system notable by Latin American standards for its impartiality and adherence to fundamental concepts of due process; and above all in the resilience of its politics, its capacity to find peaceful solutions, its appreciation of the need for compromise.'   (Harrison, 1985, pp. 55–56)

In view of the correlation between power distance and Collectivism one could consider them as two manifestations of *one* single dimension of cultural differences. However, one of the reasons for the correlation is that both are associated with a third factor: economic development. If economic development is held constant, i.e., if rich countries are compared to rich ones only and poor to poor ones, the relationship disappears. Among rich countries (the lower left-hand cluster in Fig. 3.1) there is no visible association of power distance and collectivism, neither is there among the poorer countries (the upper right-hand cluster). The fact that different rich and different poor countries make quite different trade-offs between dependence on the ingroup versus dependence on power persons, would become invisible if power distance and collectivism were considered as one single dimension. The uniqueness of cases like France and Costa Rica would be lost.

Comparisons between the results of the IBM and other studies support the distinction between power distance and collectivism. Studies dealing with the distribution of power show results which are more correlated with power distance than with individualism–collectivism and studies dealing with social integration show results more correlated with collectivism than with power distance.

Individualism and collectivism according to occupation

One more argument in favor of distinguishing power distance from collectivism is that while, as Chapter 2 showed, power distance indices could be computed not only for countries but also for occupations, individualism indices can only be calculated for countries, not for occupations. In a comparison of how people in different *occupations* answer the 14 work goals questions from which the IDV was computed, their answers cannot be classified in terms of 'individualist' or 'collectivist'. In distinguishing occupations, for example, the importance of 'challenge' and of 'use of skills' go together, while in distinguishing countries they are opposites. Across occupations, when 'personal time' is rated more important, 'challenge' tends to be less important, while across countries the two reinforce each other.[3]

A pair of terms which can be used to distinguish between occupations is *intrinsic* versus *extrinsic*. These words refer to what motivates people in a job, the work itself (intrinsically motivating jobs) or the conditions and material rewards provided (extrinsically motivating jobs). This distinction was popularized in the late 1950s through the research on work motivation by the American psychologist Frederick Herzberg and his team, who argued that the intrinsic factors are the real 'motivators' while the extrinsic ones represent the psychological 'hygiene' of the job (Herzberg *et al.*, 1959). People in occupations demanding higher education tend to score intrinsic elements as more important, while people in lower status, lower education occupations prefer extrinsic elements. The intrinsic–extrinsic distinction, while useful for distinguishing occupation cultures, is not suitable for comparing countries.

Individualism and collectivism in the family

At the beginning of this chapter individualism was associated with a nuclear family structure and collectivism with an extended family structure, the latter leading to the distinction between ingroup and outgroups. The relationship between the individual and the group, like other basic elements of human culture, is first learned in the family setting. The fact that Japan scores halfway in Table 3.1 (rank 22/23, IDV 46) can at least partly be understood from the fact that in the traditional Japanese family only the oldest son continues to live with his parents, thus creating a 'lineal' structure which is somewhere in between nuclear and extended.

There is a correlation between the degree of collectivism in a society as measured by the IDV and the likelihood that sons will share the occupation of their fathers (Hofstede, 1980, p. 257; 1984, pp. 169–170). In more individualist societies the chances are greater that sons of fathers in manual occupations will move to nonmanual occupations and vice versa. In more collectivist societies this happens more rarely, an obvious outcome of sons staying within the extended family sphere.

The child who grows up among a number of elders, peers, and juniors learns naturally to conceive of itself as part of a 'we'; much more so than the nuclear family child. An extended family child is seldom alone during the day or at night. An African student who came to a Belgian university to study told us that this was the first time in her life she had ever been alone in a room for any sizeable length of time.

In a situation of intense and continuous social contact the maintenance of *harmony* with one's social environment becomes a key virtue which extends to other spheres beyond the family. In most collectivist cultures direct confrontation of another person is considered rude and undesirable. The word 'no' is seldom used, because saying no *is* a confrontation; 'you may be right' or 'we will think about it' are examples of polite ways of turning down a request. In the same vein, the word 'yes' should not necessarily be seen as an approval, but as maintenance of the communication line: 'yes, I heard you' is the meaning it has in Japan.

In individualist cultures, on the other hand, speaking one's mind is a virtue. Telling the truth about how one feels is the characteristic of a sincere and honest person. Confrontation can be salutary; a clash of opinions is believed to lead to a higher truth. The effect of communications on other people should be taken into account, but it does not, as a rule, justify changing the facts. Adult individuals should have learned to take direct feedback constructively. In the family, children are told one should always tell the truth, even if it hurts. Coping with conflict is a normal part of living together as a family.

A former Dutch missionary in Indonesia (a country with IDV 14, rank 47/48) told about his parishioners' unexpected exegesis of the following parable from the Bible: 'A man had two sons. He went to the first and said "Son, go and work in the vineyard today"; he replied "I will go, sir", but he did not go. The man went to the second and said the same to him. He replied "I will not", but afterwards he changed his mind and did go. Which of the two did the will of the father?' (St. Matthew 21: 28–31; Moffatt translation). The biblical answer is 'the last', but the missionary's Indonesian parishioners chose the first; for this son observed the formal harmony and did not contradict his father. Whether he actually went was of secondary importance.

In the collectivist family children learn to take their bearings from others when it comes to opinions. 'Personal opinions' do not exist: they are predetermined by the group. If a new issue comes up on which there is no established group opinion, some kind of family conference is necessary before an opinion can be given. A child who repeatedly voices opinions deviating from what is collectively felt is considered to have a bad character. In the individualist family, on the contrary, children are expected and encouraged to develop opinions of their own, and a child who only ever reflects the opinions of others is considered to have a weak character. The behavior corresponding with a desirable character depends on the cultural environment.

The loyalty to the group which is an essential element of the collectivist family also means that resources are shared. If one member of an extended family of 20 persons has a paid job and the others have not, the earning member is supposed to share his or her income in order to help feed the entire family. On the basis of this principle a family may collectively cover the expenses for sending one member to get a higher education, expecting that when this member subsequently achieves a well-paid job the income will also be shared.

In individualist cultures parents will be proud if children at an early age take small jobs in order to earn pocket-money of their own, which they alone can decide how to spend. In the Netherlands, as in many other individualist Western European countries, the government contributes substantially to the living expenses of students. Recently the system has been changed from an allowance to the parents to an allowance directly to the students themselves, which stresses their independence. From now on the government will consider both boys and girls as independent economic players from age 18 onwards. In the USA it is quite normal for students to pay for their own study by temporary jobs and personal loans; without government support they too are less dependent on their parents and not at all on more distant relatives.

Obligations to the family in a collectivist society are not only financial but also ritual. Family celebrations like baptisms, marriages, and, especially, funerals are extremely important and should not be missed. Expatriate managers from individualist societies are often surprised by the family reasons given by employees from a collectivist host society who apply for a special leave; the expatriates think they are being fooled but most likely the reasons are authentic.

In an individualist culture when people meet they feel a need to communicate verbally. Silence is considered abnormal. Social conversations can be depressingly banal, but they are compulsory. In a collectivist culture the fact of being together is emotionally sufficient; there is no compulsion to talk unless there is information to be transferred. Raden Mas Hadjiwibowo, an Indonesian businessman from a Javanese noble family, recalls the family visits from his youth as follows:

> 'Visits among Javanese family members needed no previous appointment. Actually that could easily be done, for although the telephone had not come into common use yet, one could always send a servant with a letter asking for an appointment. But it was not done, it never occurred to one that a visit would not suit the other party. It was always convenient. Unexpected visitors did not exist. The door was (and still is) always open.

> The visitors were welcomed with joyful courtesy and would be asked to take a seat. The host and hostess hurriedly withdrew to change into more suitable attire than their workaday clothes. Without asking, a servant brought in coffee or tea. Cookies were offered, while in the meantime the host and hostess had joined the party.

> There we sat, but nobody spoke. We were not embarrassed by this silence; nobody felt nervous about it. Every now and then, thoughts and news were exchanged. But this was not really necessary. We enjoyed being together, seeing each other again. After the first exchange of news, any other communication was utterly redundant. If one did not have anything to say, there was no need to recite platitudes. After an hour or so, the guests would ask permission to leave. With mutual feelings of satisfaction, we parted. In smaller towns on the island of Java life is still like this.'[4]

US anthropologist and popular author Edward T. Hall distinguishes cultures on the basis of their way of communicating along a dimension from 'high-context' to 'low context' (Hall, 1976). A high-context communication is one in which little has to be said or written because most of the information is either in the physical environment or within the person, while very little is in the coded, explicit part of the message. This type of communication is frequent in collectivist cultures; Hadjiwibowo's family visit is a case example. A low-context communication is one in which the mass of information is vested in the explicit code, which is typical for individualist cultures. Lots of things which in collectivist cultures are self-evident must be said explicitly in individualist cultures. American business contracts are much longer than Japanese business contracts.

Next to harmony another important concept in connection with the collectivist family is *shame*. Individualist societies have been described as *guilt* cultures: persons who infringe upon the rules of society will often feel guilty, ridden by an individually developed conscience which functions as a private inner pilot. Collectivist societies, on the contrary, are shame cultures: persons belonging to a group from which a member has infringed upon the rules of society will feel ashamed, based upon a sense of collective obligation. Shame is social in nature, guilt individual; whether shame is felt depends on whether the infringement has become known by others. This becoming known is more of a source of shame than the infringement itself.

Such is not the case for guilt, which is felt whether or not the misdeed is known by others.

A last concept bred in the collectivist family is *face*. 'Losing face', in the sense of being humiliated, is an expression which penetrated into the English language from the Chinese; the English had no equivalent for it. David Yau-Fai Ho, a Hong Kong social scientist, defines it as follows: 'Face is lost when the individual, either through his action or that of people closely related to him, fails to meet essential requirements placed upon him by virtue of the social position he occupies.' (Ho, 1976, p. 867). The Chinese also speak of 'giving someone face', in the sense of honor or prestige. Basically, 'face' describes the proper relationship with one's social environment, which is as essential to a person (and that person's family) as the front part of his/her head. The importance of face is the consequence of living in a society that is very conscious of social contexts. The languages of other collectivist cultures have words with more-or-less similar meanings. In Greece, for example, there is a word *philotimo*; Harry Triandis, a Greek–American psychologist, writes:

> 'A person is *philotimos* to the extent in which he conforms to the norms and values of his ingroup. These include a variety of sacrifices that are appropriate for members of one's family, friends, and others who are 'concerned with one's welfare'; for example, for a man to delay marriage until his sisters have married and have been provided with a proper dowry is part of the normative expectations of traditional rural Greeks as well as rural Indians (and many of the people in between).'   (Triandis, 1972, p. 38)

In the individualist society the counterpart characteristic is 'self-respect', but this again is defined from the point of view of the individual, whereas 'face' and 'philotimo' are defined from the point of view of the social environment.

Collectivist societies usually have ways of creating family-like ties with persons who are not biological relatives but who are socially integrated into one's ingroup. In Latin America, for example, this can be done via the institution of *compadres* and *comadres* who are treated as relatives even if they are not. In Japan younger sons in past times became apprentices to craftsmasters through a form of adoption. Similar customs existed in medieval Central Europe.

Individualism and collectivism at school
The relationship between the individual and the group which has been established in a child's consciousness during its early years in the family is further developed and reinforced at school. This is very visible in classroom behavior. In the context of development assistance it often happens that teachers from a more individualist culture move to a more collectivist environment. A typical complaint from such teachers is that students do not speak up in class, not even when the teacher puts a question to the class. For

the student who conceives of him/herself as part of a group, it is illogical to speak up without being sanctioned by the group to do so. If the teacher wants students to speak up, she or he should address a particular student personally.

Collectivist culture students will also hesitate to speak up in larger groups without a teacher present, especially if these are partly composed of relative strangers: outgroup members. This hesitation decreases in smaller groups. Personally I obtained broad participation when teaching a collectivist class by asking students to turn around in their seats so that groups of three were formed. I asked the students to discuss a question for five minutes, and to decide who would report their joint answer to the class. Through this device students had an opportunity to develop a group answer and felt comfortable when speaking up before the class because they acted as the small group's representative. I also noticed that in subsequent exercises the students arranged for the spokespersons to rotate. Taking turns in group activities is a habit which exists in many collectivist cultures.

The desirability of having students speak up in class is more strongly felt in individualist than in collectivist cultures. Because most collectivist cultures also maintain large power distances, their education tends to be teacher-centered with little two-way communication (see Chapter 2).

In the collectivist society ingroup–outgroup distinctions springing from the family sphere will continue at school, so that students from different ethnic or clan backgrounds often form subgroups in class. In an individualist society the assignment of joint tasks leads more easily to the formation of new groups than in the collectivist society. In the latter, students from the same ethnic or family background as the teacher or other school officials will expect preferential treatment on this basis. In an individualist society this would be considered nepotism and intensely immoral, but in a collectivist environment it is immoral *not* to treat one's ingroup members better than others.

In the collectivist classroom the virtues of harmony and the maintenance of 'face' reign supreme. Confrontations and conflicts should be avoided, or at least formulated so as not to hurt anyone; even students should not lose face if this can be avoided. Shaming, that is invoking the group's honor, is an effective way of correcting offenders: they will be put in order by their ingroup members. At all times the teacher is dealing with the student as part of an ingroup, never as an isolated individual.

In the individualist classroom, of course, students expect to be treated as individuals and impartially, regardless of their background. Group formation among students is much more *ad hoc*, according to the task, or to particular friendships and skills. Confrontations and open discussion of conflicts is often considered salutary, and face-consciousness is weak or nonexistent.

The *purpose* of education is perceived differently between the individualist and the collectivist society. In the former it aims at preparing the *individual* for a place in a society of other individuals. This means learning to cope with new, unknown, unforeseen situations. There is a basically positive attitude towards what is new. The purpose of learning is less to know how to do, as to know *how to learn*. The assumption is that learning in life never ends; even after school and university it will continue, for example through recycling courses. The individualist society in its schools tries to provide the skills necessary for 'modern man'.

In the collectivist society there is a stress on adaptation to the skills and virtues necessary to be an acceptable group member. This leads to a premium on the products of *tradition*. Learning is more often seen as a one-time process, reserved for the young only, who have to learn *how to do* things in order to participate in society.

The role of diplomas or certificates as a result of successful completion of study is also different between the two poles of the individualism–collectivism dimension. In the individualist society the diploma not only improves the holder's economic worth but also his or her self-respect: it provides a sense of achievement. In the collectivist society a diploma is an honor to the holder and his or her ingroup which entitles the holder to associate with members of higher-status groups; for example, to obtain a more attractive marriage partner. It is to a certain extent 'a ticket to ride'. The social acceptance that comes with the diploma is more important than the individual self-respect that comes with mastering a subject, so that in collectivist societies the temptation is stronger to obtain diplomas in some irregular way, such as on the black market.

Individualism and collectivism in the workplace
Employed persons in an individualist culture are expected to act according to their own interest, and work should be organized in such a way that this self-interest and the employer's interest coincide. Workers are supposed to act as 'economic men', or as people with a combination of economic and psychological needs, but in either case as individuals with their own needs. In a collectivist culture an employer never hires just an individual, but a person who belongs to an ingroup. The employee will act according to the interest of this ingroup, which may not always coincide with his or her individual interest: self-effacement in the interest of the ingroup belongs to

the normal expectations in such a society. Often earnings have to be shared with relatives.

The hiring process in a collectivist society always takes the ingroup into account. Usually preference is given to hiring relatives, first of all of the employer, but also of other persons already employed by the company. Hiring persons from a family one already knows reduces risks. Also, relatives will be concerned about the reputation of the family and help to correct misbehavior of a family member. In the individualist society family relationships at work are often considered undesirable as they may lead to nepotism and to a conflict of interest. Some companies have a rule that if one employee marries another, one of them has to leave.

The workplace itself in a collectivist society may become an ingroup in the emotional sense of the word. In some countries this is more the case than in others, but the feeling that it should be this way is nearly always present. The relationship between employer and employee is seen in moral terms. It resembles a family relationship with mutual obligations of protection in exchange for loyalty. Poor performance of an employee in this relationship is no reason for dismissal: one does not dismiss one's child. Performance and skills, however, do determine what tasks one assigns to an employee. This pattern of relationships is best known from Japanese organizations. In Japan it applies in a strict sense only to the group of permanent employees which may be less than half of the total work force. Japan scores halfway on the IDV scale. In individualist societies the relationship between employer and employee is primarily conceived as a business transaction, a calculative relationship between buyers and sellers on a 'labor market'. Poor performance on the part of the employee or a better pay offer from another employer are legitimate and socially accepted reasons for terminating a work relationship.

Christopher Earley, a management researcher from the USA, has illustrated the difference in work ethos between an individualist and a collectivist society very neatly with a laboratory experiment. In the experiment, 48 management trainees from southern China and 48 matched management trainees from the USA were given an 'in-basket task'. The task consisted of 40 separate items requiring between two and five minutes each, like writing memos, evaluating plans, and rating job candidates' application forms. Half of the participants in either country were given a group goal of 200 items to be completed in an hour by 10 people; the other half were given each an individual goal of 20 items. Also, half of the participants in either country, both from the group goal and from the individual goal subset, were asked to mark each item completed with their name, the other half turned them in anonymously.

The Chinese, collectivist, participants performed best when operating with a group goal, and anonymously. They performed worst when operating individually and with their name marked on the items produced. The American, individualist, participants performed best when operating individually and with their name marked, and abysmally low when operating as a group and anonymously. All participants were also given a values test to determine their personal individualism or collectivism: a minority of the Chinese scored individualist, and these performed according to the US pattern; a minority of the Americans scored collectivist and these performed like the Chinese (Earley, 1989).

In practice there is a wide range of types of employer–employee relationships *within* collectivist and individualist societies. There are employers in collectivist countries who do not respect the societal norm to treat their employees as ingroup members, but then the employees in turn do not repay them in terms of loyalty. Labor unions in such cases may replace the work organization as an emotional ingroup and there can be violent union–management conflicts, as in parts of India. There are employers in individualist societies who have established a strong group cohesion with their employees, with the same protection-versus-loyalty balance which is the norm in the collectivist society. Organization cultures can to some extent deviate from majority norms and derive a competitive advantage from their originality. Chapter 8 will go into these issues more deeply.

Management in an individualist society is management of individuals. Subordinates can usually be moved around individually; if incentives or bonuses are given, these should be linked to an individual's performance. Management in a collectivist society is management of groups. The extent to which people actually feel emotionally integrated into a work group may differ from one situation to another. Ethnic and other ingroup differences within the work group play a role in the integration process and managers within a collectivist culture will be extremely attentive to such factors. It often makes good sense to put people from the same ethnic background into one crew, although individualistically programmed managers usually consider this dangerous and want to do the opposite. If the work group functions as an emotional ingroup, incentives and bonuses should be given to the group, not to individuals.

Within countries with a dominant individualist middle-class culture, regional rural subcultures have sometimes retained strongly collectivist elements. The same applies to the migrant worker minorities which form majorities among the work force in some industries in some individualist countries. In such cases a culture conflict is likely between managers and regional or minority workers. This conflict expresses itself, among other things in the management's extreme hesitation to use group incentives in cases when they are the only things that really suit the culture of the work force.

Management techniques and training packages have almost exclusively been developed in individualist countries, and they are based on cultural assumptions which may not hold in collectivist cultures. A standard element in the training of first-line managers is how to conduct 'appraisal interviews': periodic discussions in which the subordinate's performance is reviewed. These can form part of MBO (see Chapter 2, note 8), but even where MBO does not exist, conducting performance appraisals and the ability to communicate 'bad news' are considered key skills for a successful manager. In a collectivist society discussing a person's performance openly with him or her is likely to clash head-on with the society's harmony norm and may be felt by the subordinate as an unacceptable loss of face. Such societies have more subtle, indirect ways of communicating feedback: for example by the withdrawal of a normal favor or verbally via an intermediary. I know of a case in which an older relative of the poorly performing employee, also in the service of the employer, played this intermediary role. He communicated the bad news to his nephew, avoiding the loss of face which a formal appraisal interview would have provoked.

The Sensitivity Training (T-Group) fashion of the 1960s, the encounter group fashion of the 1970s, and the transactional analysis fashion of the 1980s have all been developed in the USA, the country with the highest Individualism Index score in Table 3.1. Each of them is based on honest and direct sharing of feelings about other people. Such training methods are unfit for use in collectivist cultures. There, sensitivity training is felt to be training in *in*sensitivity; daily life is filled with encounters so that no special groups have to be formed to this purpose. Relationships between people are never seen as 'transactions' between individuals: they are moral in nature, not calculative.

The distinction between ingroup and outgroups which is so essential in the collectivist culture pattern has far-reaching consequences for business relationships, beyond those between employers and employees. It is the reason behind the cultural embarrassment of Mr Johannesson and his Swedish superiors in Saudi Arabia related at the beginning of this chapter. In individualist societies the norm is that one should treat everybody alike. In sociological jargon this is known as *universalism*. Preferential treatment of one customer over others is considered bad business practice and unethical. In collectivist societies the reverse is true. As the distinction between 'our group' and 'other groups' is at the very root of people's consciousness, treating one's friends better than others is natural and ethical, and sound business practice. Sociologists call this way of thinking *particularism*.

A consequence of particularist thinking is that in a collectivist society a relationship of trust should be established with another person before any business can be done. Through this relationship the other is adopted into one's ingroup and from that moment onwards is entitled to preferential treatment. In Johannesson's case this process of adoption took two years. During this period the presence of the Swedish businessman as an intermediary was essential. After the adoption had taken place it became superfluous. However, the relationship was with Johannesson personally and not with his company. To the collectivist mind only natural persons are worthy of trust, and via these persons their friends and colleagues, but not impersonal legal entities like a company. In summary: in the collectivist society *the personal relationship prevails over the task* and should be established first; in the individualist society *the task is supposed to prevail over any personal relationships*. The naive Western businessman who tries to force quick business in a collectivist culture condemns himself to the role of outgroup member and to negative discrimination.

Table 3.3 summarizes the key differences between collectivist and individualist societies described so far.

Table 3.3 Key differences between collectivist and individualist societies. I: general norm, family, school, and workplace

Collectivist	*Individualist*
People are born into extended families or other ingroups which continue to protect them in exchange for loyalty	Everyone grows up to look after him/herself and his/her immediate (nuclear) family only
Identity is based in the social network to which one belongs	Identity is based in the individual
Children learn to think in terms of 'we'	Children learn to think in terms of 'I'
Harmony should always be maintained and direct confrontations avoided	Speaking one's mind is a characteristic of an honest person
High-context communication	Low-context communication
Trespassing leads to shame and loss of face for self and group	Trespassing leads to guilt and loss of self-respect
Purpose of education is learning how to do	Purpose of education is learning how to learn
Diplomas provide entry to higher status groups	Diplomas increase economic worth and/or self-respect
Relationship employer–employee is perceived in moral terms, like a family link	Relationship employer–employee is a contract supposed to be based on mutual advantage
Hiring and promotion decisions take employees' ingroup into account	Hiring and promotion decisions are supposed to be based on skills and rules only
Management is management of groups	Management is management of individuals
Relationship prevails over task	Task prevails over relationship

Individualism, collectivism, and the state

Alfred Kraemer, an American author in the field of intercultural communication, cites the following comment (Kraemer, 1978) by a Russian poet, Vladimir Korotich, in a Soviet literary journal after a two-month lecturing tour around American universities:

> '. . . attempts to please an American audience are doomed in advance, because out of twenty listeners five may hold one point of view, seven another, and eight may have none at all.'

What strikes the Western reader in this comment is not the described attitudes of American students but the fact that Korotich expected otherwise. He was obviously accustomed to audiences which hold a common point of view, as we argued a characteristic of a collectivist culture. In American parlance the term 'collectivist' is often used to describe political systems like those of the former Soviet Union. Korotich's comment suggests that in Russia, if not in all parts of the former Soviet Union, the collectivist political system is supported by a collectivist cultural system.

Table 3.1 contains no data for the ex-Soviet Union or any of its parts, nor for any other country with a state socialist system, except the former Yugoslavia which scores fairly collectivist. A number of countries in Table 3.1 (from Asia, Africa, the Middle East, and Latin America) have a form of state capitalism and they show medium to low IDV scores, that is, collectivist cultures. The weaker the individualism in the citizens' mental software, the greater the likelihood of the state having a dominating role in the economic system. Political scientists have developed an index of press freedom for a large number of countries (Hofstede, 1980, p. 258; 1984, p. 270). This index is positively correlated with the IDV: the more individualist a country's citizens, the less the likelihood of the freedom of its press being curbed by the authorities.

Because individualism, (small) power distance, and national wealth are correlated across the countries studied in the IBM research, it is sometimes difficult to separate the effects of the three factors on the government of countries. The index of press freedom, for example, is significantly correlated with all three. It is even more strongly correlated with national wealth *per se* than with individualism, but more strongly with individualism than with (small) power distance which is why it is mentioned in this chapter rather than in Chapter 2.

An example of a political phenomenon unrelated to national wealth but strongly related to both power distance and collectivism is the index of 'societal corporatism' developed by the American political scientist Philippe Schmitter (1981, p. 294). Schmitter's research covered 15 developed countries only, which explains why his results are uncorrelated with wealth. Societal corporatism stands for a political system in which interest groups, especially of labor and employers, are represented by formal associations, historically grown rather than established by the state itself, which are given monopoly power by the state to represent those interests. The national labor union (LO) in Sweden and the corresponding employers' confederation (SAF) are examples. The index of societal corporatism is significantly correlated with collectivism but even more with power distance.[5]

However, under closer scrutiny Schmitter's Index is shown to be composed of two separate components. The first, which he labeled 'organizational centralization', is correlated with collectivism but not with power distance. The word 'centralization' could call for an association with power distance, but what is meant by organizational centralization is the degree of institutionalization of the interest associations (large own staff, own strike funds, etc.). The second, 'associational monopoly', is correlated with power distance but not with collectivism.[6] Associational monopoly measures to what extent interests are represented by one single organization, rather than several different ones. What, in short, Schmitter has shown is that in more collectivist wealthy countries more formal political power is given to well-organized interest groups; and that the larger the power distance, the smaller the number of such groups.

If differences in the political systems found in countries are rooted in their citizens' mental software, the possibility of influencing these systems by propaganda, money, or arms from another country is limited. If minds are not receptive to the message, propaganda and money are probably wasted. The ineffectiveness of the millions of dollars spent by the US government helping the Nicaraguan 'contras' is a case in point. If in some poor countries the Soviet Union or China were or still are more popular than the USA this just means that in a collectivist culture, Soviet or Chinese ideas about the role of the state are more in line with the cultural values of the local élites than American ones.

In Chapter 2 the relationship between authority and citizen in a country was shown to be modeled after the relationships between boss and subordinate, teacher and student, and parent and child. An author who developed a grand theory about the link between what happens at the level of the family and what happens at the level of the state is the French social historian Emmanuel Todd. Todd explains the ideological system adopted in a country's government by the family structure historically prevailing in that country. In building his conceptual system he follows a French intellectual tradition going back to Frédéric Le Play (1806–1882). Le Play was one of the most original and most controversial political philosophers of the nineteenth century.

Todd, following Le Play, classifies family structures by two criteria:

1. Whether, after marriage, sons continue to live with their parents (the community family type), or set up their independent home (the nuclear family type). Le Play associated the former with authoritarian relationships, the latter with freedom and individual independence.
2. Whether inheritances are shared among all brothers, or exclude all but one. Le Play associated the former with a preference for equality, the latter with the acceptance of *in*equality.

These two criteria produce four possible combinations of which Le Play identified three in the European countries of his day: he did extensive field research by personally traveling to many countries. Todd recognizes all four in today's Europe. To account for family structures outside Europe he introduces a third criterion, to wit:

3. Whether marriage between first cousins is accepted or not (weak versus strong incest taboo). In Europe the incest taboo is invariably strong, discouraging marriages between first cousins.

With the three criteria Todd arrives at $2 \times 2 \times 2 = 8$ possibilities, of which two can be combined because they always occur together. To the seven remaining he adds 'African systems' as a new eighth category; in these African systems, marriages are unstable and partners change frequently.

Todd has drawn maps of the world and of Europe with the distribution of these eight family types. He relates each type to a particular ideological/ political system or set of systems, arguing that the real reason why a country has adopted a particular way of government is because it fits the way of thinking of the people based upon the family structure in which they or their ancestors grew up. For example, in Russia traditionally the 'exogamous community family structure' prevailed, characterized by cohabitation of married sons with their parents, equality between brothers defined by rules of inheritance, and a taboo on marriage between the children of two brothers. Todd finds a similar traditional structure in Yugoslavia, Slovakia, Bulgaria, Hungary, Finland, Albania, central Italy, China, Vietnam, Cuba, and northern India; these countries, Todd claims, are attracted to communism because 'communism is a transference to the party state of the moral traits and the regulatory mechanisms of the exogamous community family.' (Todd, 1983).

Todd deals with one aspect of the issues covered here and in Chapter 2. His association of the 'community' versus 'nuclear' family structure with ideologies in which the state plays a more or a less important role fits with the distinction between collectivism and individualism. Todd's second criterion, shared versus one-son inheritance, had been recognized by me in Hofstede (1980, p. 128; 1984, p. 101) even with reference to Le Play, and related to power distance. However, curiously, I arrived at attributions of the impact of the inheritance system which are the exact opposite of Todd's and Le Play's. The latter associate divided inheritance with a preference for equality, which would mean *small* power distances. Divided inheritance systems prevail in Latin countries and one-son inheritance systems in Germanic countries, which, according to Chapter 2, means that divided inheritance goes with *large* power distance. My explanation was that divided inheritance led to 'all children remaining on ever-smaller farms, and a need for birth control'; this produced smaller families, which meant that 'parental authority weighs heavier on the children who remain more dependent'. On the other hand, one-son inheritance forces younger sons to move away and develop a career of their own independent of their parents, a theme well known from several of Grimm's fairytales (which were written in Germany where one-son inheritance prevailed). 'The eldest son inherited the mill, the second the donkey, and the youngest the cat'. Thus the link between one-son inheritance and small Power Distance, that is, societal equality rather than inequality, can be explained.

Apart from this difference in interpretation, another major difference between Todd's work and mine is that Todd takes a short cut from the family to the ideology, ignoring all other factors, such as economic development. He uses a typology where I use a dimensional model (see Chapter 1) and applies no statistical significance tests to justify the relationships postulated. Nevertheless, he does provide a wealth of data on family structures around the world and shows once more that in order to understand a country's government one should understand its families.

Individualism, collectivism, and ideas
Individualist societies not only practice individualism but also consider it superior to other forms of mental software. Most Americans feel that individualism is good, and at the root of their country's greatness. On the other hand, the late Chairman Mao Tse Tung of China identified individualism as evil. He found individualism and liberalism reponsible for selfishness and aversion to discipline; they led people to placing personal interests above those of the group, or simply to devoting too much attention to one's own things. Table 3.1 contains no data for the People's Republic of China but the countries with a predominantly Chinese population all score very low on the individualism index (25 for Hong Kong, 20 for Singapore, 17 for Taiwan).

Economics as a discipline was founded in Great Britain in the eighteenth century; among the founding fathers Adam Smith (1723–1790) stands out. Smith assumed that the pursuit of self-interest by individuals through an 'invisible hand' would lead to the maximal wealth of nations. This is a highly individualist idea from a country which even today ranks near the top on individualism. Economics has remained an individualist science and most of its leading contributors have come from strongly individualistic countries like the UK and the USA. However, because of the individualist assumptions on which they are based, economic theories as developed in the West are unlikely to apply in societies in which not individual interest, but group interests prevail. Unfortunately there are few alternative economic theories yet to deal with collectivist economies. The Dutch sociologist Cas Vroom, describing the situation of Indonesia, contrasts the Western orientation towards 'return on investment' with an Indonesian 'return on favors' (Vroom, 1981).

The French Revolution, the bicentennial celebration of which took place in 1989, had as its slogan '*liberté, égalité, fraternité*': freedom, equality, brotherhood. This was the slogan of political idealists who wanted to have their cake and eat it, for it does not recognize that in politics there is an inescapable trade-off between freedom and equality, and very little brotherhood. Not much of the revolutionary ideal was realized in France, as we know: it led to the Reign of Terror and subsequently to the dictatorship and military adventures of Napoleon. In the nineteenth century the ideals of the Revolution were criticized by, among others, Frédéric Le Play. As mentioned in the previous section, Le Play offered his own theories of the origins of preference for 'freedom' versus 'equality'.

In the European value systems study (see Chapter 2, note 14), the data for which were collected among representative samples of the population in nine European countries in 1981 (Harding and Phillips, 1986, p. 86), the following statements were included:

1. I find that both freedom and equality are important. But if I were to make up my mind for one or the other, I would consider personal freedom more important, that is, everyone can live in freedom and develop without hindrance.
2. Certainly both freedom and equality are important. But if I were to make up my mind for one of the two, I would consider equality more important, that is that nobody is underprivileged and that social class differences are not so strong.

In most of the nine European countries respondents on average preferred freedom over equality. The French sociologist Jean Stoetzel who published the first and most informative analysis of the data has computed for each country a ratio: preference for liberty divided by preference for equality. This ratio runs from about 1 in Spain (equal preference) to about 3 in Great Britain (freedom three times as popular as equality). The values of the liberty/equality ratio for the nine countries are significantly correlated with the individualism index from the IBM studies, so the more individualist a country, the stronger its citizens' preference for liberty over equality. The liberty/equality ratio is not at all correlated with the country's PDI.[7]

The degree of individualism or collectivism of a society will affect the conceptions of human nature produced in that society. In the USA the ideas of Abraham Maslow (1908–70) about human motivation have been and are still quite influential, in particular for the training of management students and practitioners. Maslow formulated his famous 'hierarchy of human needs' in 1943. It states that human needs can be ordered in a hierarchy from lower to higher, as follows: physiological, safety, belongingness, esteem, and self-actualization. In order for a higher need to appear it is necessary that the lower needs have been satisfied up to a certain extent. A starving person, that is, one whose physiological needs are not at all satisfied, will not be motivated by anything other than the quest for food, and so forth. At the top of Maslow's hierarchy, which is often pictured as a pyramid, there is the motive of self-actualization: realizing to the fullest possible extent the creative potential present within the individual. This means 'Doing one's own thing', as it was called in the US youth culture of the 1960s. It goes without saying that this can only be the supreme motivation in an individualist society. In a collectivist culture, what will be actualized is the interest and honor of the ingroup which may very well ask for self-effacement from many of the ingroup members. As the interpreter for a group of American visitors to China remarked, the idea of 'doing your own thing' is not translatable into Chinese.

Table 3.4 Key differences between collectivist and individualist societies. II: politics and ideas

Collectivist	Individualist
Collective interests prevail over individual interests	Individual interests prevail over collective interests
Private life is invaded by group(s)	Everyone has a right to privacy
Opinions are predetermined by group membership	Everyone is expected to have a private opinion
Laws and rights differ by group	Laws and rights are supposed to be the same for all
Low per capita GNP	High per capita GNP
Dominant role of the state in the economic system	Restrained role of the state in the economic system
Economy based on collective interests	Economy based on individual interests
Political power exercised by interest groups	Political power exercised by voters
Press controlled by the state	Press freedom
Imported economic theories largely irrelevant because unable to deal with collective and particularist interests	Native economic theories based on pursuit of individual self-interests
Ideologies of equality prevail over ideologies of individual freedom	Ideologies of individual freedom prevail over ideologies of equality
Harmony and consensus in society are ultimate goals	Self-actualization by every individual is an ultimate goal

Maslow's main book in which he explained his theories (Maslow, 1970) is based on a concept of personality which is common in Western thinking, but which is not universal. The Chinese–American anthropologist Francis Hsu has shown that the Chinese language has no equivalent for 'personality' in the Western sense. Personality in the West is a separate entity, distinct from society and culture: an attribute of the individual. The closest translation into Chinese is *jen* (*ren* in the modern transcription), which stands for 'person' as a 'human constant', which includes not only the individual but also his or her intimate societal and cultural environment which makes his or her existence meaningful (Hsu, 1971).

Table 3.4 can be considered as a continuation of Table 3.3: it summarizes the key differences between collectivist and individualist societies from the last two sections.

The origins of individualism–collectivism differences
As in the case of the possible origins of differences in power distance discussed in Chapter 2, the origins of differences on the individualism–collectivism dimension are a matter of conjecture, in which, however, statistical relationships with geographic, economic, and historic variables can support the guesswork.

As mentioned in Chapter 1 it is a common assumption among archaeologists that the development of human societies started with groups of hunter–gatherer nomads; that subsequently, people settled down into a sedentary existence as farmers, and that farming communities grew into larger settlements which became towns, cities, and finally the modern megalopolises. Cultural anthropologists have compared present-day hunter–gatherer tribes, agricultural societies, and urbanized societies. They found that from the most primitive to the most modern society, family complexity first increased and then decreased again. Hunter–gatherers tend to live in nuclear families or small bands. Sedentary agricultural societies mostly show complex extended families or village community ingroups. When farmers migrate to cities the sizes of extended families become reduced and the typical urban family is again nuclear. In most countries today one finds only agricultural and urban subcultures. For these two types, modernization corresponds to individualization.

Table 3.1 and Fig. 3.1 clearly illustrate that the wealthy, urbanized, and industrialized societies score individualist, and the poorer, rural, and traditional societies collectivist. There are some exceptions, especially in east Asia, where Japan and the 'newly industrializing countries' South Korea, Taiwan, Hong Kong, and Singapore seem to have retained considerable collectivism in spite of industrialization.

The relationship between national wealth and individualism is illustrated by Fig. 3.2, in which IDV scores are plotted against the countries' per capita gross national product (GNP) in US dollars, as published by the World Bank for the year 1990. The IBM survey data on which the IDV scores are based date from the period 1967–1973, and in the original study they were related to 1970 per capita GNP data. Figure 3.2 shows that the 1967–1973 IDV scores are still quite strongly related to 1990 wealth.[8]

A statistical relationship as illustrated in Fig. 3.2 does not show which of the two related phenomena is cause and which is effect, or whether both could be caused by a third factor, not shown in the graph. If individualism were the cause of wealth one should find that IDV scores relate not only to national wealth *per se* but also to economic growth. The latter is measured by the World Bank as the average annual percentage increase in per capita GNP during a 23-year period. If individualism leads to wealth, IDV should be positively correlated with economic growth in the period following the

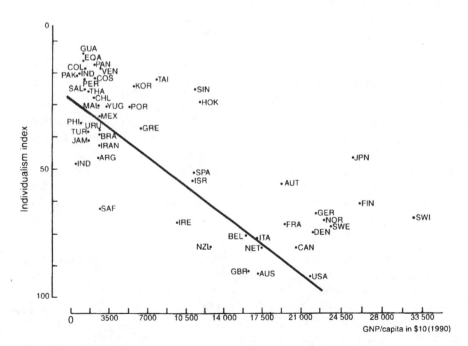

Fig. 3.2 1970 IDV scores versus 1990 GNP/capita for 50 countries. For multicountry regions, GNP/capita data is not a meaningful criterion.) For country name abbreviations see Table 3.2.

collection of the IDV data. However, this is not the case. Across all countries the relationship between IDV and subsequent economic growth is about zero. For the wealthy countries the relationship is even negative: the more individualist wealthy countries showed *less*, not more, economic growth than the less individualist ones. Two extreme examples of this are the USA and Japan: the latter has grown much faster and in 1986 bypassed the USA in per capita GNP.

The reverse causality, national wealth causing individualism, is more plausible and statistically supported in the IBM case.[9] When a country's wealth increases, its citizens have access to resources which allow them to 'do their own thing'. The storyteller in the village market is replaced by TV sets, first one per village, but soon more. In wealthy Western family homes every family member may have his or her own TV set. The caravan through the desert is replaced by a number of buses, and these by a larger number of motor cars, until each adult family member drives a different car. The village hut in which the entire family lives and sleeps together is replaced by a house with a number of private rooms. Collective life is replaced by individual life. However, the negative relationship between individualism and economic growth for the very wealthy countries suggests that this development leads to its own undoing. Where wealth has progressed to a level at which most citizens can afford to do their own thing, this leads to friction losses, and the national economy grows less than in countries where people are still accustomed to doing at least a number of things together—like Japan. However, there are other aspects to the fast economic growth of the East Asian countries which will be discussed in Chapter 7.

After national wealth the next measure statistically related to the IDV scores is geographical latitude: the distance from the equator of a country's capital city. In Chapter 2 latitude was the first predictor of power distance scores. In view of the correlation between collectivism and power distance (Fig. 3.1), it is no surprise that it also plays a role in predicting individualism. Countries with moderate and cold climates tend to show more individualist cultures: in such countries, as we argued already in the case of power distance, people's survival depends more on personal initiative, which supports individualist cultures.

The size of the population of a country which contributes to predicting power distance does not relate to collectivism. However, *population growth* strongly relates to collectivism. Population growth other than by immigration is the result of a large average number of children per family. It should therefore be no surprise that in cultures with higher birth rates collectivist rather than individualist values are bred in the family.

Historical factors, apart from economic ones, can also account for part of the country differences on this dimension, although not as clearly as in the case of the influence of the Roman Empire on power distance. The influence of the teachings of Confucius in the East Asian countries to which most of Chapter 7 will be devoted supports the maintenance of a collectivist value system. On the other hand, in parts of Western Europe, in particular in England, Scotland, and the Netherlands, individualist values could be recognized centuries ago, when the average citizen in these countries was still quite poor and the economics were overwhelmingly rural. The migrants from Europe who populated North America, Australia, and New Zealand were by definition sufficiently individualist to leave their old environment, and they came to countries where, in the frontier spirit, every person had to fend for him/herself.

The future of individualism and collectivism

The deep roots of national cultures make it likely that individualism–collectivism differences, like power distance differences, will survive for a long time. Yet if there is to be any convergence between national cultures it should be on this dimension. The strong relationship between national wealth and individualism is undeniable, with the arrow of causality directed, as shown above, from wealth to individualism. Countries having achieved fast economic development have experienced a shift towards individualism. Japan is an example: the Japanese press regularly publishes stories of breaches of traditional family solidarity. Care for the aged in the past was considered a task for the Japanese family, but provisions by the state have become necessary for cases where the family stops fulfilling its traditional duties.

Nevertheless, even at a level of per capita income equal to or larger than Western countries, Japanese society will very likely conserve distinctive collectivist elements in its family-, school-, and workspheres. The same holds for differences among Western countries themselves. Next to a noticeable convergency towards individualism under the influence of a common economic boom, relationships between the individual and the group continue to differ between, say, the UK, Sweden, and Germany. The cultures shift, but they shift together, so that the differences between them remain intact.

As far as the poor countries of the world are concerned there is no reason why they should become more individualist as long as they remain poor. The IBM data bank allowed for measurement of the shifts in individualism during the four-year period from 1968 to 1972. Out of 20 countries which had been surveyed in both periods, 19 had become richer, and all of these had shifted towards greater individualism. The only country in the set that had become poorer, Pakistan, shifted slightly towards the collectivist end of the scale.

Differences in values associated with the individualism–collectivism dimension will continue to exist and to play a big role in international affairs, for example in negotiations between rich and poor countries. Individualism versus collectivism as a dimension of national cultures is responsible for many misunderstandings in intercultural encounters. In Chapter 9 it will be shown that the problems of such encounters can often be explained by differences on this dimension.

Notes

1 Using factor scores as a basis for country indices was very easy for the initial IBM study but makes it difficult to compute index values in later follow-up studies. The scoring guide for the 1982 values survey module issued by the Institute for Research on Intercultural Cooperation (IRIC) therefore contains an approximation formula, in which the individualism index value can be computed by simple mathematics from four of the 'work goals' mean scores.

2 The (product moment) correlation coefficient between PDI and IDV across the 53 cultures is -0.68.

3 Intellectually, a distinction between occupations in which some occupations demand more individual initiative and others more group loyalty can very well be conceived, but the questions for which the IBM data have answers available across countries and occupations did not permit it to be measured. Someone else with a different set of questions may be able to confirm such a distinction empirically.

4 From a speech by R.M. Hadjiwibowo to Semafor Senior Management College, the Netherlands, September 1983. Translation from the Dutch by GH with suggestions from the author.

5 Spearman rank correlation with IDV -0.58, with PDI 0.67. The first is significant at nearly the 0.01 level, the second well beyond this level. The correlation with national wealth is -0.27, not significant.

6 Spearman rank correlation coefficients of organizational centralization -0.51 with IDV, 0.32 with PDI; of associational monopoly, -0.42 with IDV and 0.71 with PDI. The 0.05 significance limit for 15 cases is at 0.44.

7 (Stoetzel, 1983, p. 78). The ratio values have been read from the diagram. The Spearman rank correlation coefficient between the liberty/equality ratio and IDV is 0.82, significant at the 0.01 level; between l/e ratio and PDI it is 0.02.

8 The product moment correlation coefficient across 50 countries between IDV and per capita GNP is 0.84 for 1970, 0.77 for 1987.

9 Figure 3.2 plots 1970 IDV scores against 1990 GNP/capita but this does not imply that causality is supposed to go from 1970 IDV to 1990 GNP. I just want to show that even with recent GNP/capita data the correlation survives. Note 8 showed that the IDV–GNP correlation is lower for 1987 than for 1970 GNP data; if causality went from IDV to subsequent GNP, the correlation should have increased from 1970 to 1990.

4

He, she, and (s)he

As a young Dutch engineer I once applied for a junior management job with an American engineering company which had recently settled in Flanders, the Dutch-speaking part of Belgium. I felt well qualified: with a degree from the senior technical university of the country, good grades, a record of active participation in student associations, and three years' experience as an engineer with a well-known, although somewhat sleepy Dutch company. I had written a short letter indicating my interest and providing some vital personal data. I was invited to appear in person, and after a long train ride I sat facing the American plant manager. I behaved politely and modestly, as I knew an applicant should, and waited for the other man to ask the usual questions which would enable him to find out how qualified I was. To my surprise he asked very few of the things that I thought should be discussed. Instead he wanted to know some highly detailed facts about my experience in tool design, using English words I did not know, and the relevance of which escaped me. Those were the things I could learn within a week once I worked there. After half an hour of painful misunderstandings he said 'Sorry—we need a first class man.' And I was out in the street.

Assertiveness versus modesty

Years later I was the interviewer and I saw both Dutch and American applicants. Then I understood what had gone wrong in that earlier case. American applicants, to Dutch eyes, oversell themselves. Their CVs are worded in superlatives, mentioning every degree, grade, award, and membership to demonstrate their outstanding qualities. During the interview they try to behave assertively, promising things they are very unlikely to realize—like learning the local language in a few months.

Dutch applicants in American eyes undersell themselves. They write modest and usually short CVs, counting on the interviewer to find out by asking how good they really are. They expect an interest in their social and extra-curricular activities during their studies. They are very careful not to be seen as braggarts and not to make promises they are not absolutely sure they can fulfil.

American interviewers know how to interpret American CVs and interviews and they tend to discount the information provided. Dutch interviewers, accustomed to Dutch applicants, tend to upgrade the information. The scenario for cross-cultural misunderstanding is quite clear. To an uninitiated American interviewer an uninitiated Dutch applicant comes across as a sucker. To an uninitiated Dutch interviewer an uninitiated American applicant comes across as a braggart.

Dutch and American societies are reasonably similar on the dimensions of power distance and individualism described in Chapters 2 and 3 but they differ considerably on a third dimension which opposes among other things the desirability of assertive behavior against the desirability of modest behavior. I will label it: masculinity versus femininity.[1]

Genders and gender roles

All human societies consist of men and women, usually in approximately equal numbers. They are biologically distinct and their respective roles in biological procreation are absolute. Other physical differences between women and men, not directly related to the bearing and begetting of children, are not absolute but statistical. Men are *on average* taller and stronger, but many women are taller and stronger than quite a few men. Women have *on average* greater finger dexterity and, for example, faster metabolism which makes them recover faster from fatigue but some men also excel in these respects.

The absolute and statistical biological differences between men and women are the same the world over, but their social roles are only partly determined by the biological constraints. Every society recognizes many behaviors, not immediately related to procreation, as more suitable for females or more suitable for males; but which behaviors belong to which gender differs from one society to another. Anthropologists having studied nonliterate, relatively isolated societies stress the wide variety of social sex roles that seem to be possible (Mead, 1962). For the biological distinction this chapter will use the terms *male* and *female*; for the social, culturally determined roles *masculine* and *feminine*. The latter terms are *relative*, not absolute: a man can behave in a 'feminine' way and a woman in a 'masculine' way; this only means they deviate from certain conventions in their society.

Which behaviors are considered 'feminine' or 'masculine' differs not only among traditional but also among modern societies. This is most evident in the distribution of men and women over certain professions. Women dominate as doctors in the former Soviet Union, as dentists in Belgium, as shopkeepers in parts of West Africa. Men dominate as typists in Pakistan and form a sizeable share of nurses in the Netherlands. Female managers are virtually nonexistent in Japan but frequent in the Philippines and Thailand.

In spite of the variety found there is a common trend among most societies, both traditional and modern, as to the distribution of social sex roles. From now on this chapter will use the more modern term *gender roles*. Men are supposed to be more concerned with achievements outside the home— hunting and fighting in traditional societies, the same but translated in economic terms in modern societies. Men, in short, are supposed to be assertive, competitive, and tough. Women are supposed to be more concerned with taking care of the home, of the children, and of people in general; to take the tender roles. It is not difficult to see how this role pattern is likely to have developed: women first bore the children and then usually breastfed them, so at least during this period they had to stay close to the children. Men were freer to move around, to the extent that they were not needed to protect women and children against attacks by other men and animals.

Male achievement reinforces masculine assertiveness and competition; female care reinforces feminine nurturance, a concern for relationships and for the living environment. Men, taller, stronger, and free to get out, tend to dominate in social life outside the home: inside the home a variety of role distributions between the genders is possible. The role pattern demonstrated by the father and mother (and possibly other family members) has a profound impact on the mental software of the small child who is programmed with it for life. Therefore it is not surprising that one of the dimensions of national value systems is related to gender role models offered by parents.

Masculinity–femininity as a dimension of societal culture
Chapter 3 referred to the set of 14 work goals in the IBM questionnaire: 'Try to think of those factors which would be important to you in an ideal job; disregard the extent to which they are contained in your present job.' The analysis of the answers to the 14 work goals items produced two underlying dimensions. One was individualism versus collectivism: the importance of 'personal time', 'freedom', and 'challenge' stood for individualism, the importance of 'training', 'physical conditions', and 'use of skills' stood for collectivism.

The second dimension came to be labeled masculinity versus femininity. It was associated most strongly with the importance attached to: for the 'masculine' pole:

1. *Earnings*   Have an opportunity for high earnings.
2. *Recognition*   Get the recognition you deserve when you do a good job.

3. *Advancement*   Have an opportunity for advancement to higher level jobs.
4. *Challenge*   Have challenging work to do—work from which you can get a personal sense of accomplishment.

For the opposite, 'feminine', pole:

5. *Manager*   Have a good working relationship with your direct superior.
6. *Cooperation*   Work with people who cooperate well with one another.
7. *Living area*   Live in an area desirable to you and your family.
8. *Employment security*   Have the security that you will be able to work for your company as long as you want to.

Notice that 'challenge' was also associated with the individualism dimension (Chapter 3). The other seven goals are only associated with masculinity or femininity.

The decisive reason for labeling the second 'work goals' dimension 'masculinity versus femininity' is that *this dimension is the only one on which the men and the women among the IBM employees scored consistently differently* (except, as will be shown, in countries at the extreme feminine pole). Neither power distance nor individualism nor uncertainty avoidance showed a systematic difference in answers between men and women. Only the present dimension produced such a gender difference, with men attaching greater importance to, in particular, the work goals (1) and (3) and women to (5) and (6). The importance of earnings and advancement corresponds to the masculine, assertive, and competitive social role. The importance of relations with the manager and with colleagues corresponds to the feminine, caring, and social-environment oriented role.

As in the case of the individualism versus collectivism dimension, the eight items from the IBM questionnaire do not totally cover the distinction between a masculine and a feminine culture in society. They only represent the aspects of this dimension represented by questions in the IBM research. Again, the correlations of the IBM country scores on masculinity with non-IBM data about other characteristics of societies are needed in order to grasp what the dimension encompasses.

Based on all the information about the distinctions between societies related to this dimension, it can be defined as follows: *masculinity* pertains to societies in which social gender roles are clearly distinct (i.e., men are supposed to be assertive, tough, and focused on material success whereas women are supposed to be more modest, tender, and concerned with the quality of life); *femininity* pertains to societies in which social gender roles overlap i.e., both men and women are supposed to be modest, tender, and concerned with the quality of life).

A *masculinity index* (MAS) score was computed for each of the 50 countries and 3 regions in the IBM data. Like the individualism index, MAS was based on factor scores for each country which were automatically produced by the statistical procedure used (factor analysis). Scores were achieved in a range from about 0 for the most feminine to about 100 for the most masculine country by multiplying the factor scores by 20 and adding 50.[2]

MAS values were computed not only by country but also separately for men and women within each country. Figure 4.1 shows in simplified form the relationship between masculinity by gender and masculinity by country, and reveals that from the most 'feminine' (tender) countries to the most 'masculine' (tough) ones the values of both men and women become tougher but that the difference is larger for men than for women. In the most feminine countries, Sweden and Norway as will soon be shown, there was no difference between the scores of men and women, and both expressed equally tender, nurturing values. In the most masculine countries, Japan and Austria, the men scored very tough but also the women scored fairly tough; nevertheless the gap between men's values and women's values was largest for these countries. From the most feminine to the most masculine country the range of MAS scores for men is about 50 percent larger than the range for women. Women's values differ less between countries than men's values do.

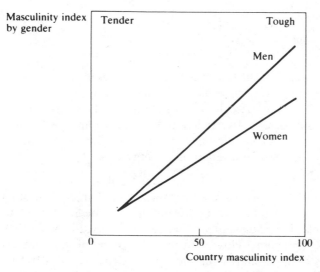

Fig. 4.1 The relationship between masculinity index scores and gender of the respondents

Table 4.1 Masculinity index (MAS) values for 50 countries and 3 regions

Score rank	Country or region	MAS score	Score rank	Country or region	MAS score
1	Japan	95	28	Singapore	48
2	Austria	79	29	Israel	47
3	Venezuela	73	30/31	Indonesia	46
4/5	Italy	70	30/31	West Africa	46
4/5	Switzerland	70	32/33	Turkey	45
6	Mexico	69	32/33	Taiwan	45
7/8	Ireland (Republic of)	68	34	Panama	44
			35/36	Iran	43
7/8	Jamaica	68	35/36	France	43
9/10	Great Britain	66	37/38	Spain	42
9/10	Germany FR	66	37/38	Peru	42
11/12	Philippines	64	39	East Africa	41
11/12	Colombia	64	40	Salvador	40
13/14	South Africa	63	41	South Korea	39
13/14	Equador	63	42	Uruguay	38
15	USA	62	43	Guatemala	37
16	Australia	61	44	Thailand	34
17	New Zealand	58	45	Portugal	31
18/19	Greece	57	46	Chile	28
18/19	Hong Kong	57	47	Finland	26
20/21	Argentina	56	48/49	Yugoslavia	21
20/21	India	56	48/49	Costa Rica	21
22	Belgium	54	50	Denmark	16
23	Arab countries	53	51	Netherlands	14
24	Canada	52	52	Norway	8
25/26	Malaysia	50	53	Sweden	5
25/26	Pakistan	50			
27	Brazil	49			

The MAS scores for the 53 countries and regions (men and women combined) can be read from Table 4.1.[3] Like the scores for power distance and individualism, the masculinity scores represent *relative*, not absolute, positions of countries. Unlike individualism, masculinity is unrelated to a country's degree of economic development: we find both rich and poor masculine and rich and poor feminine countries.

The USA scores 62 on the masculinity index (rank 15) and the Netherlands score 14 (rank 51), so the two countries which appeared in the story at the beginning of this chapter are really far apart. The four most feminine countries (ranks 53 through 50) are Sweden, Norway, the Netherlands, and Denmark; Finland comes close with rank 47. Some of the Latin countries score strongly to moderately feminine: Costa Rica (rank 48/49), Chile (46), Portugal (45), Guatemala (43), Uruguay (42), Salvador (40), Peru (37/38), Spain (37/38), France (35/36), Panama (34). The other countries on the feminine side are Yugoslavia (48/49), Thailand (44), South Korea (41), East and West Africa (ranks 39 and 30/31, respectively), Iran (35/36), Taiwan (32/33), Turkey (32/33), and Indonesia (30/31).

The champions of masculinity are, first, Japan (rank 1) and some continental European countries: Austria (2), Italy (4/5), Switzerland (4/5), and West-Germany (9/10). Also a number of Latin American countries, mainly the larger countries around the Caribbean: Venezuela (3), Mexico (6), Colombia (11/12), Equador (13/14) but, at some distance, also Argentina (20/21). Moderately masculine scores are all Anglo countries: the Republic of Ireland (7/8), Jamaica (7/8), Great Britain (9/10), South Africa (13/14), USA (15), Australia (16), New Zealand (17), Canada (24). Finally the Philippines (11/12), Greece (18/19), Hong Kong (18/19), India (20/21), Belgium (22), and the Arab-speaking countries (23).

Gender cultures

One of the levels of culture introduced in Chapter 1 is the *gender level*. Figure 4.1 clearly illustrates that a particular part of our mental programs depends (in most countries) on whether we were born as a girl or as a boy. Like nationality, gender is an involuntary characteristic: we were not asked before being born, in which country and with what sex we wanted to appear. Because of this the effect of both nationality and gender on our mental programming is largely unconscious. Although both nationality and gender cultures are learned, not inborn, we learned their consequences so early that we never knew anything else, and we are usually unaware of other possibilities.

Figure 4.1 shows that, on average, men have been programmed with tougher values and women with more tender values but that the gap between the sexes varies by country. Even in countries at the feminine extreme of the MAS scale, like Sweden and Norway, men's values and women's values need not be identical in all respects, only they do not differ along a tough–tender dimension. Any country is likely to show cultural differences according to gender. These are again statistical rather than absolute: there is an overlap between the values of men and those of women so that any given value may be found both among men and among women, only with different frequency.

Individual women can learn to function in a masculine way and individual men in a feminine way. Where men are together a masculine culture is likely to dominate; where women are together, a feminine culture. Calling these differences 'cultures' stresses their profound and emotional nature. The feminine culture is alien to most men, as the masculine culture is alien to most women. Exposure to another culture leads initially to culture shock, which is a nonrational 'gut' feeling. We readily experience other cultures as wrong, ridiculous, or frightening, and such feelings can be detected between the genders within the same society. The males in virtually all societies dominate in politics, in the community, and at the workplace; so the subcultures of politics, community affairs, and work are relatively masculine. The subcultures of the family and the school vary more from one society to another. The differences among countries illustrated by Fig. 4.1 have mainly resulted from different gender roles and socialization processes in the family and at school, as described below.

Masculinity and femininity according to occupation

Power distance indices could be used for comparing countries as well as occupations; individualism indices could only be computed for countries. A dimension of masculinity versus femininity, like power distance, *does* appear when we compare occupations, so it makes sense to call some occupations more 'masculine' and some more 'feminine' in terms of the values of those who exercise them. Not surprisingly, the masculine occupations are the ones usually filled by men, and the feminine occupations are the ones usually filled by women. However, the differences in values associated with the occupations are not caused by the gender of the occupants. Men from the IBM population in 'feminine' occupations held more 'feminine' values than women in 'masculine' occupations.

Within IBM 38 occupations could be divided into 6 groups from the most 'masculine' to the most 'feminine' as follows:

1. Salesmen (professional and nonprofessional)
2. Professional workers (engineers/scientists)
3. Skilled workers/technicians
4. Managers of all categories
5. Unskilled and semiskilled workers
6. Office workers

The salesmen (rarely saleswomen) in this case were paid on commission, in a strongly competitive climate. Scientists, engineers, technicians, and skilled workers in IBM focus mostly on individual technical performance which calls for masculine values. Managers deal with both technical *and* human problems, in roles with both assertive *and* nurturing elements. Unskilled and semiskilled workers have no strong achievements to boast but they usually work in teams, so cooperation is important to them. Office workers also have few achievements but their jobs tend to involve even more human contact, also with outsiders.

Masculinity and femininity in the family

The family is the place where most people received their first cultural programming. The family contains two unequal but complementary role pairs: parent–child and husband–wife. The effects of different degrees of inequality in the parent–child relationship were related to the dimension of power distance in Chapter 2. The prevailing role distribution between husband and wife is reflected in a society's position on the masculinity–femininity scale.

Figure 4.2 plots country PDI scores (from Table 2.1) against country MAS scores (from Table 4.1). In the right half of the diagram where PDI values are high, inequality between parents and children is a societal norm. Children are supposed to be controlled by obedience. In the left half, children are controlled by the examples set by parents. In the lower half of the diagram where MAS scores are high, inequality between fathers' and mothers' roles (father tough, mother less tough) is a societal norm. Men are supposed to deal with facts, women with feelings. In the upper half both men and women are allowed to deal with the facts and with the soft things in life.

Thus the lower right-hand quadrant (unequal and tough) stands for a norm of a dominant, tough father and a submissive mother who, although also fairly tough, is at the same time the refuge for consolation and tender

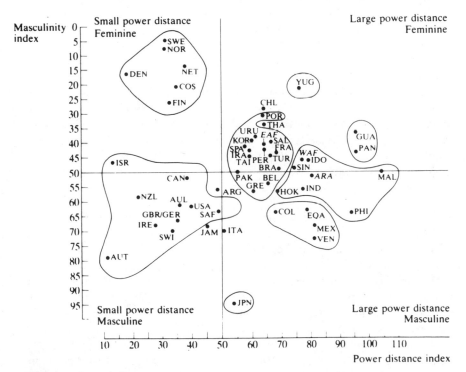

Fig. 4.2 Power distance versus masculinity index scores for 50 countries and 3 regions (for country name abbreviations see Table 3.2)

feelings. In the Latin American countries in this quadrant the internationally understood term 'machismo' has been coined for the attitude expected of men. Less known is the corresponding term 'marianismo' for women, a combination of near-saintliness, submissiveness, and sexual frigidity.

The upper right-hand quadrant (unequal and tender) represents a societal norm of two dominant parents, sharing the same concern for the quality of life and for relationships, both providing at times authority *and* tenderness.

In the countries in the lower left-hand quadrant (equal and tough) the norm is for nondominant parents to set an example in which father is tough and deals with facts and mother is somewhat less tough and deals with feelings. The resulting role model is that boys should assert themselves and girls should please and be pleased. Boys do not cry and should fight back when attacked; girls may cry and do not fight.

Finally, in the upper left-hand quadrant (equal and tender) the norm is for mothers and fathers not to dominate and for both to be concerned with relationships, with the quality of life, with facts *and* feelings, setting an example of a relative equality of gender roles in the family context.

The above typology has the weakness of all typologies that no real-life situation entirely fits its descriptions. Also, what is the 'family' context depends strongly on the country's position on the dimension collectivism–individualism. In a collectivist society, the 'family' is the extended family, and the center of dominant authority could very well be the grandfather as long as he is still alive, with the father as a model of obedience. Ultra-individualist societies contain many one-parent families in which role models are incomplete, or in which outsiders provide the missing roles. The typology serves to stress the importance of a society's role distributions in the family with regard to the values that are transferred from one generation to the next.

Gender-related values and behaviors are programmed into us in subtle ways and from a quite early age. A comparative study (Otaki *et al.*, 1986) of the behaviors of mothers and three-to-four-months-old babies in Japan and the USA showed among other things that the Japanese baby boys were significantly noisier than the Japanese girls while the reverse was true for the US babies. It is extremely unlikely that a difference like this is inborn. It must be due to the mother's conditioning of her child which differs according to the child's sex and to the nationality of the mother. She encourages or soothes the child according to the expectations in her society about the behavior of boys and of girls. Whoever has seen groups of travellers from both countries will have noticed that *adult* Japanese men are also noisier than adult Japanese women and that the reverse holds for adult Americans.

The masculinity–femininity dimension does not just affect how families develop role differences between boys and girls. Figure 4.1 shows that both men *and* women hold tougher values in masculine countries and more tender values in feminine ones. In masculine countries both boys and girls learn to be ambitious and competitive, although the ambition of the girls may be directed towards the achievements of their brothers and later of their husbands and sons. A common image from US motion pictures shows the girls as cheerleaders for the football matches played by the boys. Popular movies are to modern society what religious myths were to traditional ones: they express models for behavior.

In feminine countries both boys and girls learn to be nonambitious and modest. Assertive behavior and attempts at excelling which are appreciated in masculine cultures are easily ridiculed in feminine ones. Excellence is something one keeps to oneself. My own country , the Netherlands, is a case in point; it is the third most feminine in Table 4.1. The Dutch language expresses its feminine stance in an untranslatable expression '*doe maar gewoon, dan doe je al gek genoeg*': something like 'just behave like everybody else, you're ridiculous enough anyway'. This attitude can be called 'leveling': pulling everyone back to a modest average. The Dutch have been described by a visiting French writer as '*un peuple jaloux qui a un curieux penchant pour tout ce qui est terne*': 'a jealous people who are curiously attracted by everything that is dull.' (Baena, 1968, pp. 13, 65).

In masculine cultures children learn to admire the strong; popular fictional heroes created in the USA are 'Batman' and 'Rambo'. In feminine cultures children learn sympathy for the underdog and the anti-hero. Small and friendly 'Rasmus Klump' (called Petzi in translations) is a Danish comic hero; 'Ollie B. Bommel' (Mr Bumble), a clumsy and naive anti-hero, has become a national personality among Dutch intellectuals.[4]

Whereas gender roles in the family strongly affect the values about appropriate behavior for boys and for girls, they do not have immediate implications for the distribution of gender roles in the wider society. As was argued earlier in this chapter, men, being on average taller and stronger and free to get out, have traditionally dominated social life outside the home in virtually all societies. Only exceptional and usually upper-class women had the means to delegate their child-rearing activities to others and to step into a public role. If women entered dominant positions in society at all this was mostly after the age of 45 when their mother status changed into grandmother status. Unmarried women were, and still are, rare in traditional societies and are often ostracized.

The much greater liberty of choice among social roles, beyond those of wife, mother, and housekeeper, which women in many industrialized societies enjoy nowadays is a recent phenomenon. Its impact on the distribution of gender roles *outside* the home is not yet fully felt. Therefore a country's position on the masculinity–femininity scale need not be closely related to women's activities outside the family sphere. Economic possibilities and necessities play a bigger role in this respect than values.

Masculinity and femininity at school

A Dutch management consultant taught part of a course for Indonesian middle managers from a public organization located all over the archipelago. In the discussion following one of his presentations, a Javanese participant came up with a very lucid comment, and the teacher praised him openly. The Javanese said 'You embarrass me. Among us, parents never praise their children to their face.'[5]

This anecdote illustrates two things. Firstly, how strong, at least in Indonesia, is the transfer of behavior models from the family to the school situation, the teacher being identified with the father. Secondly, it expresses the virtue of modesty in the Javanese culture to an extent which even surprised the Dutchman. Indonesia is a multi-ethnic country; one of those about which Chapter 1 warned that national culture scores may be misleading. Indonesians agree that especially on the dimension tough–tender, ethnic groups within the country vary considerably with the Javanese taking an extreme position towards the tender side. The Dutch consultant said that even some of the other Indonesians were surprised by the Javanese's feelings. A Batak from the island of Sumatra said that he now understood why his Javanese boss never praised him when he himself felt that praise should have been due. In fact, the incident became the occasion for an all-out discussion within the group about inter-ethnic differences in values, a topic which so far had never been brought into the open.

Each semester my university offers a program of European studies to students from the USA. To some of the Americans I give the assignment to interview a number of Dutch students about their goals in life. Invariably, the Americans are struck by the fact that the Dutch seem to be much less concerned with grades than they are. Passing is considered enough; excelling is not an openly pronounced goal. Experiences in teaching abroad and discussions with teachers from different countries have led me to conclude that in the more feminine cultures the *average* student is considered the norm, while in more masculine countries like the USA the *best* students are the norm. Parents in these countries expect their children to try to match the best. The 'best boy in class' in the Netherlands is a somewhat ridiculous figure.

This difference is noticeable in classroom behavior. In masculine cultures students try to make themselves visible in class and compete openly with each other (unless collectivist norms put a limit to this, see Chapter 3). In feminine cultures they do not want to appear too eager and mutual solidarity, although not always practised, is seen as a goal.

Interviews with teachers suggest that in masculine countries job choices are strongly guided by perceived career opportunities, while in feminine countries students' intrinsic interest in the subject plays a bigger role.

Failing in school is a disaster in a masculine culture. In strongly masculine countries like Japan and Germany the newspapers report each year about students who killed themselves after failing an examination. In his book *The Gospel According to the Harvard Business School*, Harvard MBA graduate Peter Cohen counts four suicides—one teacher, three students—during his time at this élite American institution (Cohen, 1973). Failure in school in a feminine culture is a relatively minor incident. Some young people in these cultures take their lives too, but for reasons unrelated to performance—like social isolation.

Criteria for evaluating both teachers and students differ between masculine and feminine cultures. On the masculine side teachers' brilliance and academic reputation and students' academic performance are the dominant factors. On the feminine side teachers' friendliness and social skills and students' social adaptation play a bigger role. Corporal punishment in school for children of pre-pubertal age has been associated in Chapter 2 with the power distance between the teacher and the students, but in some schools in masculine cultures with small power distances—like the UK— corporal punishment is considered beneficial for the character development of boys, but less so for girls.

Finally, masculinity–femininity cultural differences affect the subjects chosen by male versus female students at universities. For a range of countries data are available about the distribution of the sexes in each of the following areas of study: education, law, social sciences, engineering, and agriculture. Per country an 'index of segregation (of the sexes) in higher education' has been computed. This index is statistically related to the country's masculinity index, at least for the industrialized countries (in all poor countries, boys are given priority in educational opportunities).[6] In rich and masculine cultures men and women are more segregated at universities than in rich and feminine ones.

One aspect of segregation in job choice is whether teachers themselves are women or men. In masculine societies women mainly teach younger children and men teach at universities. In feminine societies roles are more mixed and men also teach younger children. Paradoxically therefore, in masculine societies children are exposed longer to female teachers. Their status, however, is often low so that the female teachers will be anti-heroines rather than models for behavior.

Masculinity and femininity in the workplace

The Dutch manufacturing plant of a major US corporation had lost three Dutch general managers in a period of 10 years. To the divisional vice-president in the US all these men had come across as 'softies'. They hesitated to implement unpopular measures with their personnel, claiming the resistance of their works council—a body elected by the employees and required by Dutch law which the vice-president did not like anyway. After the third general manager had left, the vice-president stepped in personally and nominated the plant controller as his successor—ignoring strong warnings by the personnel manager. To the vice-president this controller was the only real 'man' in the plant management team. He had always supported the need for drastic action, disregarding its popularity or unpopularity. In his reports he had indicated the weak spots. He should be able to maintain the prerogatives of management, without being sidetracked by this works council nonsense.

The new plant general manager proved the greatest disaster ever. Within six months he was on sick leave and the plant in a state of chaos. Nobody in the plant was surprised. They had known the controller as a congenial but weak personality, who had compensated for his insecurity by using powerful language towards the American bosses. The assertiveness which impressed the vice-president was recognized within the Dutch environment as bragging. As a general manager he received no cooperation from anyone, tried to do everything himself, and suffered a nervous breakdown in the shortest possible time. Thus, the plant lost both a good controller and another general manager. Both the plant and the controller were victims of a culturally induced error of judgment.

This story resembles the one with which this chapter opened. Dutch behavior is often misjudged by Americans and vice versa. Besides the issue of assertiveness versus modesty this second story highlights different ways of handling conflicts in the two countries. In the USA as well as in other masculine cultures like the UK and the Republic of Ireland there is a feeling that conflicts should be resolved by a good fight: 'Let the best man win.' The industrial relations scene in these countries is marked by such fights. If possible, management tries to avoid having to deal with labor unions at all, and labor union behavior justifies their aversion.[7]

In feminine cultures like the Netherlands, Sweden, and Denmark there is a preference for resolving conflicts by compromise and negotiation. The institutional contexts in which this negotiation takes place differ by country. In the Netherlands a works council law makes joint consultation between management and employee representatives compulsory for all but the smallest work organizations. This law gives labor unions a role in submitting candidates for the councils and training them; besides, union representatives deal directly with management representatives at the industry level in order to establish collective wage agreements. In spite of the fact that only about 30 percent of Dutch employed persons are unionized few business leaders would prefer a world without unions. They certainly cause problems but they are indispensable for solutions. In France, which scored moderately feminine in the IBM studies, there is occasionally a lot of verbal insult, both between employers and labor and between bosses and subordinates, but behind this seeming conflict there is a typically French 'sense of moderation', which enables parties to continue working together while agreeing to disagree (see d'Iribarne, 1989, pp. 31, 60–61).

Another issue in which the contrast between masculine and feminine societies manifests itself is the place of work in a person's life. A successful early twentieth century US inventor and businessman, Charles F. Kettering, is reputed to have said:

> 'I often tell my people that I don't want any fellow who has a job working for me; what I want is a fellow whom a job has. I want the job to get the fellow and not the fellow to get the job. And I want that job to get hold of this young man so hard that no matter where he is the job has got him for keeps. I want that job to have him in its clutches when he goes to bed at night, and in the morning I want that same job to be sitting on the foot of his bed telling him it's time to get up and go to work. And when a job gets a fellow that way, he's sure to amount to something.'[8]

Kettering refers to a 'young man' and not to a 'young woman': his is a masculine ideal. It would certainly not be popular in more feminine cultures; there such a young man would be considered a workaholic. In a masculine society the ethos tends more toward 'live in order to work', whereas in a feminine society the work ethos would rather be 'work in order to live'.

The family within a masculine society socializes children towards assertiveness, ambition, and competition; organizations in masculine societies stress results, and want to reward it on the basis of equity, i.e., to everyone according to performance. The family within a feminine society socializes children towards modesty and solidarity, and organizations in such societies are more likely to reward people on the basis of equality (as opposed to equity), i.e., to everyone according to need. Men in masculine societies are expected to aspire to career advancement; research showed remarkable unanimity in this respect among male US students. For female US students career aspirations were *not* socially compulsory; some had them, some not. The research showed a much wider range in women's answers than in men's answers about the need to get ahead on their own (Hofstede, 1980, p. 51). In feminine societies both men and women may or may not be ambitious and there should be no gender difference in the ranges of the answers of both sexes about the need for a career.

Many jobs in business demand few skills and cause a qualitative underemployment of people. This has been recognized as a problem in industrialized masculine and feminine countries. The solutions tried vary according to the type of culture. They have all been labeled as 'humanization of work' but what is considered a humanized job depends on one's model of what it means to be human. In masculine cultures a humanized job should give more opportunities for recognition, advancement, and challenge. This is the principle of 'job enrichment' as defended, among others, by US psychologist Frederick Herzberg (1966). An example is making workers on a simple production task also responsible for the setting up and preventive maintenance of their machines, tasks which had previously been reserved for more highly trained specialists. Job enrichment represents a 'masculinization' of unskilled and semiskilled work which, as shown in one of the earlier sections of this chapter, has a relatively 'feminine' occupation culture.

In feminine cultures a humanized job should give more opportunities for mutual help and social contacts. Famous experiments were conducted in the 1970s by the Swedish car and truck manufacturers Saab and Volvo with assembly by autonomous work groups. These represent a confirmation of the social part of the job: its 'femininization'. In 1974 six US Detroit automobile workers, four men and two women, were invited to work for three weeks in a group assembly system in the Saab-Scania plant in Soedertalje, Sweden. The experiment was covered by journalist Robert B. Goldmann who reported on the Americans' impressions. All four men and one of the women said they continued to prefer the US work system. 'Lynette Stewart chose Detroit. In the Cadillac plant where she works, she is on her own and can make her own challenge, while at Saab-Scania she has to consider people in front and behind her' (Hofstede, 1980, p. 298; 1984, p. 209). Of course this was precisely the rationale of the Swedes for having the group assembly system. A Swedish woman worker whom Goldmann interviewed mentioned the interdependence between workers as one of the system's advantages.

Masculine and feminine cultures create different management hero types. The masculine manager is, of course, assertive, decisive, and 'aggressive' (only in masculine societies does this word carry a positive connotation). He is a lonely decision-maker looking for facts rather than a group discussion leader. It does not hurt if he is slightly macho. J.R. Ewing from the TV show *Dallas* is, of course, a culture hero. The manager in a feminine culture is less visible, intuitive rather than decisive, and accustomed to seeking consensus.[9] Both, however, should be resourceful—believed to be endowed with above average intelligence and drive. A Dutchman who had worked with a prestigious consulting firm in the USA for several years joined the top management team of a manufacturing company in the Netherlands. After a few months he commented on the different function of *meetings* in his present job compared to his previous one. In the Dutch situation, meetings were places where problems were discussed and common solutions were sought; they served for making decisions. In the US situation as he had known it, meetings were opportunities for participants to assert themselves: to show how good they were. Decisions were made by individuals else-where.[10]

Based on their cultural characteristics, masculine versus feminine countries excel in different types of industries. Industrially developed masculine cultures have a competitive advantage in manufacturing, especially in large volume: doing things efficiently, well, and fast. They are good at the production of big and heavy equipment and in bulk chemistry. Feminine cultures have a relative advantage in service industries like consulting and transport, in manufacturing according to customer specification, and in handling live matter such as high-yield agriculture and biochemistry. There is an international division of labor in which countries are relatively more successful in activities which fit their population's cultural preferences than in activities which go against these. Japan is the world leader in high-quality consumer electronics; Denmark and the Netherlands excel in services, in agricultural exports, and they harbor the world's leading companies in biochemistry (enzymes and penicillin).

Although one might expect it, there is no relationship between the mascu-linity or femininity of a society's culture and the distribution of employment over men and women. An immediate relationship between a country's position on this dimension and the roles of men and women exists only within the home. Outside, men have historically dominated, and only recently in history have women in any number been sufficiently freed from other constraints to be able to enter the worlds of work and politics as men's equals. Lower-class women have entered work organizations before but only in low-status, low-paid jobs: not out of a need for self-fulfilment but out of a need for material survival of the family. Statistics therefore show no relationship between a country's percentage of women working outside the home *per se* and its degree of femininity. There is, however, a positive correlation between a country's femininity score and the participation of women in higher-level technical and professional jobs, as a percentage of all working women in a country) (Hofstede, 1980, pp. 292, 306; 1984, p. 203).

All industrial societies over the past decades have shown a gradual increase in female participation in the work force, including professional and man-agement jobs. This development has not been any faster in feminine rather than masculine cultures. The paradox is that in view of the traditional male dominance in the world of work, women have to be very ambitious to beat their male competitors for higher positions. The IBM study showed that female managers, in comparison with a matched group of male managers,

Table 4.2   Key differences between feminine and masculine societies.
I: general norm, family, school, and workplace

Feminine	Masculine
Dominant values in society are caring for others and preservation	Dominant values in society are material success and progress
People and warm relationships are important	Money and things are important
Everybody is supposed to be modest	Men are supposed to be assertive, ambitious, and tough
Both men and women are allowed to be tender and to be concerned with relationships	Women are supposed to be tender and to take care of relationships
In the family, both fathers and mothers deal with facts and feelings	In the family, fathers deal with facts and mothers with feelings
Both boys and girls are allowed to cry but neither should fight	Girls cry, boys don't; boys should fight back when attacked, girls shouldn't fight
Sympathy for the weak	Sympathy for the strong
Average student is the norm	Best student is the norm
Failing in school is a minor accident	Failing in school is a disaster
Friendliness in teachers appreciated	Brilliance in teachers appreciated
Boys and girls study same subjects	Boys and girls study different subjects
Work in order to live	Live in order to work
Managers use intuition and strive for consensus	Managers expected to be decisive and assertive
Stress on equality, solidarity, and quality of work life	Stress on equity, competition among colleagues, and performance
Resolution of conflicts by compromise and negotiation	Resolution of conflicts by fighting them out

held more masculine values than the men (the same was not true for female versus male professionals, however). Ambitious women are more frequently found in masculine rather than feminine societies. In feminine societies the forces of resistance against women entering higher jobs are weaker; on the other hand the candidates are less ambitious. These two influences seem to neutralize each other so that women in feminine societies do not enter higher jobs in much larger numbers than in masculine societies. A notable exception is Finland: since the Second World War, which called virtually all men to the army, women have taken leading roles in Finnish society.

Table 4.2 summarizes the key issues from the past sections on which masculine and feminine societies were shown to differ.

Masculinity, femininity, and the state
National value patterns are present not only in the minds of ordinary citizens but, of course, also in those of political leaders, who also grew up as children

of their society. As a matter of fact people are usually elected or co-opted to political leadership *because* they are supposed to stand for certain values dear to citizens.

Michael Hoppe, a German–American management educator, replicated the IBM study on a population of political and institutional élites. Hoppe obtained scores on the questions used among the IBM employees for the alumni of the Salzburg Seminar in American Studies, an institute in Austria which invites to its courses élites (leaders in politics, business, and labor) from mainly European countries. The project supplied scores on the IBM dimensions for élite samples from 19 countries, 18 of them also represented in the IBM studies. For three out of the four dimensions (all except masculinity–femininity) the scores from the élite populations across the 18 common countries were significantly correlated with the scores of the IBM populations. For masculinity–femininity the correlation was significant across 17 countries, except for the score of Sweden. The Swedish élites scored considerably more masculine than those from the Netherlands and the other Nordic countries, while Swedish IBM employees scored similar to those from Denmark, Norway, Finland, and the Netherlands. The reason is either a split in Swedish society or, more probably, a particular selection of the Swedish participants in Salzburg who were all from the employers' association (Hoppe, 1990).

Politicians translate values dominant in countries into political priorities. The latter are most clearly visible in the composition of national government budgets. The masculinity–femininity dimension affects priorities in the following areas:

1. Reward for the strong versus solidarity with the weak
2. Economic growth versus protection of the environment
3. Arms spending versus aid to poor countries

Masculine culture countries strive for a performance society; feminine countries for a welfare society. In criticisms in the press from masculine countries like the USA and Great Britain (MAS 62 and 66, respectively) versus feminine countries like Sweden and the Netherlands (MAS 5 and 14, respectively), and vice versa, strong and very different value positions appear. There is a common belief, in, for example, the USA, that economic problems in Sweden and the Netherlands are due to high taxes while there is a belief in feminine European countries that economic problems in the USA are due to too much tax relief for the rich. Tax systems, however, do not just happen: they are created by politicians as a consequence of pre-existing value judgments. In Sweden it is considered important to establish a minimum quality of life for everybody and the financial means to that end are collected from those who have them. Even right-wing politicians in Sweden do not basically disagree with this policy, only with the extent to which it can be realized. In the USA and in the UK, many people believe that the miserable fate of the poor is their own fault, that if they would work harder they would not be poor, and that the rich certainly should not pay to support them.

The difference between the two types of ethos does not date from the Thatcher era. Lord Robert Baden Powell (1857–1941), the founder of the international Boy Scouts movement, wrote a book for Rover Scouts (boys over age 16) called *Rovering to Success*. Its translation into Dutch, dating from the 1920s, is called '*Zwervend op de weg naar levensgeluk*': 'Roving on the Road to Happiness.' To the Dutch translators 'success' was not a goal likely to appeal to young men. The word in Dutch has a flavor of quackery. No youth leader would defend it as a purpose in life.

Masculine cultures are less permissive than feminine ones. The European value systems study which used public opinion polls in nine countries in 1981 has produced an index of permissiveness, according to whether a number of debatable acts were justifiable: such as joyriding, using soft drugs, accepting bribes, prostitution, divorce, and suicide. The national permissiveness index is strongly correlated with femininity. Mother is more permissive than father.[11]

'Small is beautiful' is a feminine value. Public opinion survey data from six European countries showed that a preference for working in larger organizations was correlated with the IBM MAS scores (Hofstede, 1980, pp. 186, 302; 1984, p. 198).

The report of the Club of Rome on the *Limits to Growth*, which appeared in 1972, has been the first public recognition that continued economic growth and conservation of our living environment are fundamentally conflicting objectives. The report has been attacked on details, and for a time the issues it raised seemed less urgent. Its basic thesis, however, has never been refuted, and in my view at least, it is irrefutable. Governments will have to make painful choices and, apart from local geographic and ecological constraints, these choices will be made according to the values dominant in a country. Governments in masculine cultures are more likely to give priority to growth and be prepared to sacrifice the living environment for this purpose. Governments in feminine cultures are more likely to choose the reverse priority.

The countries of the European Community show among themselves a range of MAS scores from 70 (Italy) to 14 (Netherlands). Issues of growth versus conservation are already causing considerable conflict within the EC. The establishment of an open internal market requires the unification of regulations with regard to environmental protection. The environment will become one of the major stumbling blocks for the EC.

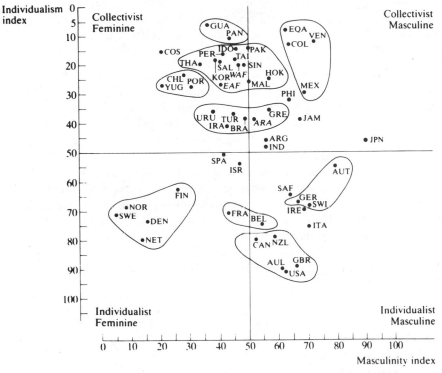

Fig. 4.3 The position of 50 countries and 3 regions on the masculinity–femininity and individualism–collectivism dimensions (for country name abbreviations see Table 3.2)

Figure 4.3 plots the country scores on the two dimensions of masculinity–femininity (from Table 4.1) and of individualism–collectivism (from Table 3.1) against each other. The upper half of the diagram contains the collectivist, that is mostly the poor, countries; the lower half the individualist, that is the rich, countries. Since the late 1950s development assistance money has flown from the rich to the poor countries, that is from bottom to top in our diagram. However, the percentage of the country's gross national product which the governments of the rich countries have decided to allocate to helping the poor ones, varies widely. In 1988, for example, Austria spent 0.24 percent of its GNP, while Norway spent 1.12 percent (*World Development Report 1989*, Table 19), nearly five times as much. This enormous variation in the proportions spent is unrelated to the wealth of the donor countries and also unrelated to their former colonial ties or present trade flows. The only explanation of a high aid quote is a feminine national value system: the statistical correlation between aid in percentage of GNP and a country's masculinity index score is strongly negative (high index, low aid quote).[12] Also, with regard to development aid, many people in masculine countries feel that the fate of the poor is in their own hands, that if they worked harder they would not be poor, and that the rich countries certainly should not pay to support them.

Countries which spend little money on helping the poor in the world tend to spend more on armaments: defense spending as a percentage of GNP is *positively* correlated with masculinity. This even applies for the poor countries which receive help from others. 'Don't give the *boys* their toys' is the slogan of a US woman anti-nuclear armament activist. Mainstream US culture is fairly masculine. Recent data from the former Soviet Union seems to indicate that mainstream Russian culture, at least, is rather feminine. But in the Soviet Union decisions about arms investments were not taken by elected politicians, but by co-opted ones probably selected on masculine values. If the assumption that for both superpowers masculine values prevail is correct, it helps to explain the irrational overkill in the arms race between the two countries during the Cold War period: it is a mutual show of masculine strength like the behavior of male deer in the rutting season.

Masculine countries tend to (try to) resolve international conflicts by fighting; feminine countries by compromise and negotiation (the same distinction was made at the level of work organizations). A striking example is the difference between the handling of the Åland crisis and the handling of the Falkland crisis.

The Åland islands are a small archipelago halfway between Sweden and Finland; as part of Finland they belonged to the Tsarist Russian empire. When Finland declared itself independent from Russia in 1917 the majority of the 30 000 inhabitants of the islands wanted to join Sweden which had ruled them before 1809. The Finns then arrested the leaders of the pro-Swedish movement. After emotional negotiations in which the newly created League of Nations participated, all parties, in 1921, agreed to a solution in which the islands remained Finnish but with a large amount of regional autonomy.

The Falkland islands are also a small archipelago disputed by two nations: the United Kingdom which has colonized the islands since 1833 and nearby Argentina which claims rights on them since 1767 and has tried to get the United Nations to support its claim. The Falklands are about eight times as large as the Ålands but with less than one-fifteenth of the Ålands' number of inhabitants: about 1800 poor sheep farmers. The Argentinian military occupied the islands in April 1982 whereupon the British sent an expeditionary force which chased off the occupiers, at the cost of (officially) 725 Argentinian and 225 British lives and enormous financial expense. Besides, the economy of the islands has been further damaged because it cannot develop without trade relations with the Argentinian hinterland.

What explains the difference in approach and in results between these two remarkably similar international disputes? Finland and Sweden are both feminine cultures; Argentina and the UK are both masculine. The masculine symbolism in the Falkland crisis was evident in the language used on both sides. Unfortunately, the sacrifices have resolved nothing. The Falklands remain a disputed territory needing constant British subsidies and military presence; the Ålands have become a prosperous part of Finland, attracting many Swedish tourists.

One would expect that in countries with a more feminine culture more women would be elected to political office and occupy government posts. This is to some extent true although not as much as reason would suggest. Just as at the workplace, a tradition of male dominance resists the advance of women in more than token numbers to leading political positions. Yet it seems that women advance somewhat more easily in politics than in work organizations. The election processes used in politics react faster to changes in society than the co-optation processes used in business; the latter have to wait for aged gentlemen to retire or die. This presupposes, of course, that the composition of candidate lists for elections is not subject to the same co-optation processes as the composition of boards of management. In some countries candidate lists *are* a matter of co-optation.

Masculinity, femininity, and ideas
In human thinking the issue of the equality or inequality of the sexes is as old as religion, ethics, and philosophy themselves. Genesis, the first book of the Judaeo–Christian Old Testament (which was codified in the fifth century BC), contains two conflicting versions of the creation of the sexes. The first, Genesis 1:27–8, states:

> 'So God created man in his own image, in the image of God created he him; male and female created he them. And God blessed them, and God said to them , "Be fruitful, and multiply, and replenish the earth, and subdue it".'

This text suggests equal partnership between the sexes. The second version, Genesis 2:8ff. (which Old Testament experts suppose to have been derived from a different source document) contains the story of the Garden of Eden, in which God first put 'the man' alone. Then, in Genesis 2:18, it states: 'And the Lord God said "It is not good that the man should be alone: I will make him a help meet for him".'[13] Then follows the story of Woman made from Adam's rib. This text gives clear priority to the male partner and defines the woman as 'a help meet' (that is, appropriate) for him; it justifies a society in which there is male dominance.

In ancient Greece, Plato, in the fourth century BC describes the sexes as equal in principle and (apart from their role in procreation) only statistically different. In *The Republic* he offers a design for an ideal state governed by an élite composed of men as well as women. Of course in actual fact the Greek state was male dominated. So was the Roman state; but at least one Roman writer, C. Musonius Rufus in the first century AD, defended the equality of the sexes and, in particular, the study of philosophy by women and men alike.

Among countries with Christian majorities the percentage of Roman Catholics is correlated with the country's masculinity index.[14] The Roman Catholic church strongly maintains the male prerogative to the priesthood. Plato and Rufus in antiquity came closer to modern feminist positions than the Roman Catholic church does today.

The European value systems study referred to earlier contained a question 'How important is God in your life?' to be answered on a 10-point scale. The mean scores obtained correlate with the countries' masculinity indices: in masculine countries God is felt to be more important. The Christian God is the Father; He is masculine. The importance of God as rated by the respondents to the European value systems study *and* the country masculinity index are both correlated with the claimed observance of the Ten Commandments, but most strongly with the purely religious commandments (no other God, not abusing God's name, and honoring the Sabbath). Masculinity is less correlated with the claimed observance of the sexual commandments (no adultery, do not desire thy neighbor's wife) and least with the claimed observance of the moral commandments (honoring parents, no killing, no stealing, no false witnesses, do not desire thy neighbor's belongings). It is predominantly the emotional meaning of God's name which is more strongly stressed in masculine cultures.

The European value systems study also revealed that women in all countries were more religious than men, but that this applied in particular for women without paid jobs. If the role of the woman changes from a housekeeper to a wage-earner, her attitude to religion moves closer to the attitude of men.[15]

The relationship between the strength of feminism in a country and the position of the country's culture on the masculinity–femininity dimension is complex and ambiguous. Apart from the lunatic fringe that wants to do away with men altogether there is a more 'masculine' and a more 'feminine' form of feminism; the former predictably more frequent in masculine, the latter more frequent in feminine, countries. The masculine form claims that women should have the same possibilities as men have. In terms of Fig. 4.1 it wants to move the female line up towards the male line; this could also be achieved by moving the entire society towards a more masculine value position (more towards the right). The feminine form wants to change society, men included. In Fig. 4.1 this could be achieved by moving the male line downwards towards the female line, or moving the entire society towards a more feminine value position (more towards the left).

The second form, it seems to me, represents a more authentic women's liberation than the first and an innovation over our present society: it allows women to contribute their unique values to society beyond the home—but then I come from a feminine country culture. Simply having women work in the same numbers and jobs as men does not necessarily represent their liberation. It could be a double slavery, at work *and* in the home. Modern Russian stories tell about female engineers or construction workers who after a full working day stand in line at the shops and do the cooking and housekeeping while the husbands watch television. A typical theme in Soviet literature is that mother is overworked and has to be shipped off to a sanatorium. I can see no women's lib which does not permit women to maintain their own gender culture at work and in politics, but this means men's lib at the same time, because gender roles are interdependent.

In May 1989 Zoya Krylova of the Soviet Women's Council spoke to a Women's Council meeting at Delft, the Netherlands. The 150 Dutch women present created quite an uproar when Krylova defended the woman's responsibility for the children's education, for shopping, and for the

Table 4.3   Key differences between feminine and masculine societies. II: politics and ideas

Feminine	Masculine
Welfare society ideal	Performance society ideal
The needy should be helped	The strong should be supported
Permissive society	Corrective society
Small and slow are beautiful	Big and fast are beautiful
Preservation of the environment should have highest priority	Maintence of economic growth should have highest priority
Government spends relatively large proportion of budget on development assistance to poor countries	Government spends relatively small proportion of budget on development assistance to poor countries
Government spends relatively small proportion of budget on armaments	Government spends relatively large proportion of budget on armaments
International conflicts should be resolved by negotiation and compromise	International conflicts should be resolved by a show of strength or by fighting
A relatively large number of women in elected political positions	A relatively small number of women in elected political positions
Dominant religions stress the complementarity of the sexes	Dominant religions stress the male prerogative
Women's liberation means that men and women should take equal shares both at home and at work	Women's liberation means that women will be admitted to positions hitherto only occupied by men

household. The Dutch women claimed this to be as much a task for the husband and said the wife should, if necessary, force the husband to take these responsibilities (*De Volkskrant*, May 10, 1989). The difference in opinion between the Russian and the Dutch women is remarkable because in Russia many more women have full-time jobs than in the Netherlands. Russian women's organizations have claimed more part-time jobs for women. But behind the two points of view there are two different conceptions of gender roles in society.

Table 4.3 complements Table 4.2 by summarizing the key differences between feminine and masculine societies from the last two sections.

The origins of masculinity–femininity differences

Anthropologist Margaret Mead found in New Guinea very different gender role distributions among adjacent tribal groups. She showed that history and tradition allow the survival of a considerable variety in gender roles. I have not found strong correlations with outside factors which could explain why some countries have dominant masculine and others dominant feminine culture. Feminine cultures are somewhat more likely in colder climates, suggesting that an equal partnership between men and women improves the chances of survival and population growth in these climates.

The concentration of feminine cultures in north-western Europe (Denmark, Finland, Netherlands, Norway, Sweden) points to common historical factors. The élites in these countries consisted to a large extent of traders and seafarers. In trading and sailing, maintaining good interpersonal relationships and caring for the ships and merchandise are essential virtues. The Viking period in the Scandinavian countries (AD 800–1000) also meant that the women had to manage the villages while the men were away on their long trips; but Vikings did not settle in the Netherlands for any length of time. The Hanseatic League (AD 1200–1500) covered all north-western European countries including the free cities of Hamburg, Bremen, and Lübeck in Northern Germany and the Baltic states. The Hansa was a free association of trading towns and, for the maintenance of such a system, values associated with femininity were functional. Women played an important role in the Hansa:

> 'Although the wife did not share her husband's legal status, they usually formed a business team. Even in merchant circles, the family was the smallest functional cell of society, where the women and the children had a role to play. This meant that women had a certain degree of emancipation, and their independence and business skills increased. Indeed, some women managed to win the "battle for the trousers" even while their husbands were still alive.'[16]

Latin American countries differ considerably among themselves on the masculinity–femininity scale. The small Central American countries—to the extent scores for them are available from the IBM data—are feminine;

Mexico, Venezuela, Colombia, and Equador very masculine; Peru and Chile again more feminine. One speculative explanation is that these differences reflect the inheritance of the different Indian civilizations dominant prior to the Spanish conquest. Most of Mexico would have inherited the tough Aztec culture, but the southern Mexican peninsula of Yucatan and the adjacent Central American republics would have inherited from the much more sensitive Maya culture. Peru and northern Chile would reflect the Inca inheritance, resembling the Maya.

One of the interesting statistical associations of country masculinity scores is with population growth. The relationship between MAS and the number of children per family (leading to population growth) is negative for the wealthier countries and positive for the poorer countries. In other words, *femininity* stands for larger families in wealthier countries and smaller families in poorer countries. This may be a consequence rather than a cause of feminine values. My interpretation of it is that in feminine cultures the mother has a stronger say in the number of children she will bear and that she adapts this number to the available resources: fewer if the country is poor, more if it is richer. In masculine countries the father determines the family size, begetting (too) large families in poor countries and too small ones in wealthy ones (Hofstede, 1980, p. 292; 1984, p. 203).

The future of differences in masculinity and femininity

At the level of countries no evidence at all exists for convergence on the masculinity–femininity dimension. If at all, research comparing value shifts over a number of years shows masculine countries to have become more masculine and feminine countries more feminine, but this should not be generalized. More interesting is considering how universal developments in population age structure, in technological developments, and in the state of the environment might affect the values related to this dimension.

The relationship between masculinity and age is quite clear and seems to be universal. It resembles Fig. 4.1 if we write 'older' at the left and 'younger' at the right. Young men (age bracket 20–29) hold strongly masculine (assertive, tough) values. Young women (20–29) hold moderately masculine values. Older men (50–59) hold pronouncedly *feminine* values and so do older women (50–59). From age 25 to 55 both men and women lose their masculine values but the men lose them much faster than the women so that at age 55 no more gender difference in values is noticeable. There seems to be a straight relationship between masculine values and sexual productivity (Hofstede, 1980, p. 367; 1984, p. 248).

This trend, which most of us will follow during our lifetime, fits with the observation that young men and women foster more technical interests (which could be considered masculine), and older men and women more social interests. In terms of values (but not necessarily in terms of energy and vitality), older persons are better people managers than younger ones; younger persons are better technical managers.

The demographic development in the industrialized world is towards lower birth rates, so there will be relatively fewer young people.[17] An ageing population will cause a shift towards more feminine values. When birthrates fall, this implies that more women will be both available for and needed in the work force (as there will be fewer young men). In many poor countries birthrates are still very high but in the longer term even these countries will have to follow the above pattern.

Technological and social developments enable even women with young children to participate in society outside the home, along with men. Nowhere is this a fast and undisputed process, but it looks irreversible. In virtually all industrialized countries the number of women in higher level jobs will increase. As their number increases these women will be more able to maintain their own feminine values. They will no longer have to acculture themselves to the male majority. This increase in the number of women in positions in society hitherto held by men should therefore also shift societies as a whole towards more feminine values.

Technology imposes change on work itself. The information revolution is still going on, eliminating many old jobs and creating new ones. The future is bound to show a further reduction of the jobs that can be sufficiently structured to be subject to automation. What will remain are jobs that, by their very nature, cannot be automated. These are in the first place the jobs that deal with the setting of human and social goals, with defining the purpose of life for individuals and societies. These include all political and organizational top leadership functions. In the second place they are the creative jobs, those concerned with inventing new things and subjecting them to criteria of usefulness, beauty, and ethics. A third and very large category of jobs that cannot be automated are those that deal with the unforeseeable: safety, security, defense, maintenance. Finally, there is a large category of jobs whose essence is human contact: supervision, entertainment, keeping people company, listening to them, helping them materially and spiritually, motivating them to learn. In some of these nonautomatable jobs, computers can be introduced as resources, but they can never take over the job itself.

What strikes one about these nonautomatable jobs is that feminine values are as necessary in performing them as are masculine ones (regardless of whether the job incumbents themselves are women or men). For the last category, in which human contact is the core of the task, feminine values are even superior. Tasks related with achievement can more easily be automated than nurturing tasks. On balance, technological developments are more likely to support a need for feminine rather than for masculine values in society.

Finally, the environment poses very serious threats to the survival of mankind. If one species after another of fungi, plants, and animals becomes extinct we should start to worry when it is the turn of the species *Homo sapiens*. Whether we like it or not, we will all be forced to become more conservation-conscious. This development encourages more feminine values and reinforces the other shifts mentioned.

These forecasts may be seen as the wishful thinking of a citizen from a feminine culture country. Possibly I have overlooked important factors which will reinforce a masculinization. I hope not.

Notes

1 Some reviewers, especially from business administration and from countries which in the IBM data score masculine, have criticized my choice of these terms and called them a misnomer. I believe that these critics hold a shallow view of the roots of human behavior. Sexes and sex roles are one of the most profound facts of human existence. Managers in business are not exempt from the effects of social norms about gender-related behavior. Other reviewers, while recognizing the importance of gender roles, have criticized my calling the soft role feminine and the hard role masculine. They do not like roles to be that way. My choice of the terms is based on what *is* in virtually all societies, not on what anybody thinks should be.

2 The same applies here as in note 1 of Chapter 3. For computing MAS index values in later follow-up studies an approximation formula has been composed in which the masculinity index value can be computed by simple mathematics from four of the 'work goals' mean scores.

3 The percentage of women in the IBM survey population varied from 4.0 in Pakistan to 16.2 in Finland. In Hofstede (1980, p. 279; 1984, p. 189), the MAS scores have been recalculated keeping the percentage of women constant for all countries. The effect on the scores is minimal, also because the percentage of women itself is correlated with the country's femininity.

4 The author is Marten Toonder. He started the series in the 1930s as a children's cartoon. Over a period of 40 years the stress in his work has slowly shifted from the drawings to the text, and now the adventures of Ollie B. Bommel and his young friend Tom Poes have become a gem in Dutch adult literature.

5 Dr Jan A.C. de Kock van Leeuwen, personal communication.

6 (Hofstede, 1980, pp. 307–309; 1984, pp. 203–204) The data on segregation are derived from Boulding *et al.* (1976).

7 Especially in the USA the relationships between labor unions and enterprises are governed by extensive contracts serving as peace treaties between both parties. The French researcher Philippe d'Iribarne who compared a French, a US and a Dutch manufacturing plant describes these contracts as a unique feature of the US industrial relations scene (d'Iribarne, 1989, p. 144).

8 From *Coronet*, September 1949, p. 72, quoted by William F. Whyte in Webber (1969, p. 31).

9 Philippe d'Iribarne considers the need for consensus the key characteristic of management in the Dutch manufacturing plant he studied. See d'Iribarne (1989, p. 234ff).

[10] Personal communication.

[11] (Stoetzel, 1983, p. 37). The Spearman rank correlation coefficient between the permissiveness index and the masculinity index is 0.83, significant at the 0.01 level.

[12] The Spearman rank correlation between MAS and average percentage aid over 1967–1976 is −0.81 (Hofstede, 1980, p. 308); between MAS and percentage aid in 1986, −0.82. Both are significant at the 0.001 level.

[13] The quotations are from the Authorized Version of the British and Foreign Bible Society (1954).

[14] The first correlation is with uncertainty avoidance; see Chapter 5 and Hofstede (1980, pp. 209, 293; 1984, p. 204).

[15] (Stoetzel, 1983, pp. 92, 98–101) The Spearman rank correlation coefficient between the ratings for the importance of God and the masculinity index is 0.70, significant at the 0.05 level.

[16] From H. Samsonowicz, 'Die Bedeutung des Grosshandels für die Entwicklung der polnischen Kultur bis zum Beginn des 16. Jahrhunderts', in *Studia Historiae Economica*, 5 (1970), 92ff., cited by Schildhauer (1985, p. 107).

[17] From 1987 to 2000 the population of the high-income countries in the world is expected to grow by about 7 percent, the middle- and low-income countries by 28 percent (*World Development Report 1989*, Table 26).

5

What is different, is dangerous

In the 1960s Arndt Sorge did his military service in the West German army. Near his home town, where he spent his free weekends, were the barracks of the British 'Army on the Rhine'. Sorge was keen on watching British motion pictures with the original sound track which were shown in the British barracks, and he walked up to the sentry to ask whether he, as a German soldier, could attend. The sentry referred him to the sergeant-of-the-guard who called the second-in-command on the telephone, and then tore a page out of a notebook, on which he wrote 'Mr Arndt Sorge has permission to attend film shows' and signed it, adding that permission was granted by the second-in-command.

Sorge used his privilege not only on that occasion, but several other times, and the notebook page always opened the gate for him, in conjunction with his German army identity card. After he was demobilized, he asked the British sentry whether he, now a civilian, could continue to come. The sentry looked at the notebook page, said 'This is for you personally', and let him in.

Arndt Sorge became an organization sociologist, and he remembers this experience as an example of how differently the British seemed to handle such an unplanned request, from what he was accustomed to in the German army. The Germans would have taken more time and would have needed the permission of more authorities; they would have asked more information about the applicant, and issued a more formal document. Finally, the document would have been issued to him as a member of the armed forces, and there would have been no question of his using it after his demobilization.[1]

The avoidance of uncertainty
Germany and the UK have a lot in common. Both are West European countries, both speak a Germanic language, their populations before the German reunification were of roughly equal size (around 60 million each),

and the British royal family is of German descent. Yet it does not take a very experienced traveller to notice the considerable cultural difference between the two countries.

Peter Lawrence is a British sociologist who has written about Germany (Lawrence, 1980, p. 133):

> 'What strikes a foreigner travelling in Germany is the importance attached to the idea of punctuality, whether or not the standard is realised. Punctuality, not the weather, is the standard topic of conversation for strangers in railway compartments. Long distance trains in Germany have a pamphlet laid out in each compartment called a *Zugbegleiter* (literally, 'train accompanier') which lists all the stops with arrival and departure times and all the possible connections *en route*. It is almost a national sport in Germany, as a train pulls into a station, for hands to reach out for the *Zugbegleiter* so that the train's progress may be checked against the digital watch. When trains are late and it happens, the loudspeaker announcements relay this fact in a tone which falls between the stoic and the tragic. The worst category of lateness which figures in these announcements is *unbestimmte Verspätung* (indeterminable lateness: we don't know how late it is going to be!) and this is pronounced as a funeral oration.'

Sorge's surprise at the easy-going approach of the British sentry and Lawrence's at the punctual German travellers suggest that the two countries differ in their tolerance of the unpredictable. In the IBM research, Great Britain and Germany score exactly alike on the two dimensions of power distance (both 35) and masculinity (both 66). On individualism, the British score considerably higher (89 versus 67). The largest difference between the two countries, however, is on a fourth dimension labeled *uncertainty avoidance*.

The term uncertainty avoidance has been borrowed from American organization sociology, in particular from the work of James G. March.[2] March and his colleagues recognized it in American organizations. Ways of handling uncertainty, however, are part and parcel of any human institution in any country. As human beings, we all have to face the fact that we do not know what will happen tomorrow: the future is uncertain but we have to live with it anyway.

Extreme uncertainty creates intolerable anxiety. Every human society has developed ways to alleviate this anxiety. These ways belong to the domains of technology, law, and religion. Technology, from the most primitive to the most advanced, helps to avoid uncertainties caused by nature. Laws and rules try to prevent uncertainties in the behavior of other people. Religion is a way of relating to the transcendental forces that are assumed to control man's personal future. Religion helps in the acceptance of the uncertainties one cannot defend oneself against, and some religions offer the ultimate certainty of a life after death or of victory over one's opponents.

Anthropologists studying traditional societies have spent a good deal of their time on technology, law, and religion. They have illustrated the enormous variety of ways in which human societies deal with uncertainty. Modern societies do not differ essentially from traditional ones in this respect. In spite of the availability of the same information virtually anywhere around the globe, technologies, laws, and religions continue to vary. Moreover, there are no signs of spontaneous convergence.

The essence of uncertainty is that it is a subjective experience, a feeling. A lion-tamer may feel reasonably comfortable when surrounded by his animals, a situation which would make most of us almost die from fear. You may feel reasonably comfortable when driving on a crowded freeway at 55 miles per hour or more, a situation statistically probably as equally risky as the lion-tamer's.

Feelings of uncertainty are not only personal, but may also be partly shared with other members of one's society. Like the values discussed in the last three chapters, feelings of uncertainty are acquired and learned. Those feelings and the ways of coping with them belong to the cultural heritage of societies and are transferred and reinforced through basic institutions like the family, school, and state. They are reflected in the collectively held values of the members of a particular society. Their roots are nonrational. They lead to collective patterns of behavior in one society which may seem aberrant and incomprehensible to members of other societies.

Measuring the (in)tolerance of ambiguity in society: the uncertainty avoidance index

After power distance, individualism–collectivism and masculinity–femininity, uncertainty avoidance (from strong to weak) is the fourth dimension found in the IBM research project. Each country and region in this project could be assigned an *uncertainty avoidance index* (UAI) score.

Differences among countries on uncertainty avoidance were originally discovered as a byproduct of power distance. It all started with a question about job stress. This question runs: 'How often do you feel nervous or tense at work?' with answers ranging from (1) 'I always feel this way' to (5) 'I never feel this way'. I had been struck by the regularity of answer patterns on this question from country to country. For example, British employees always scored less nervous than German employees, be they managers, engineers, secretaries, or unskilled factory workers. However, the country differences found were unrelated to power distance differences.

Close scrutiny of all the questions which produced stable country differences revealed that the country mean scores on three questions were strongly correlated:

1. Job stress, as described above (mean score on the 1–5 scale).

2. Agreement with the statement: 'Company rules should not be broken—even when the employee thinks it is in the company's best interest' (mean score on a 1–5 scale). This question was labeled 'rule orientation'.

3. The percentage of employees expressing their intent to stay with the company for a long-term career. The question was: 'How long do you think you will continue working for IBM?' and the answers ran: (1) 'Two years at the most'; (2) 'From two to five years'; (3) 'More than five years (but I probably will leave before I retire)' and (4) 'Until I retire'. The percentage in a country answering (3) or (4) is correlated with the mean answers on questions (1) and (2).

At first the combination of these three questions did not make sense. Why should someone who feels under stress also want rules to be respected, and his or her career to be long term? But this is a false interpretation. The data do not suggest that 'someone' shares these three attitudes. When one looks at the answers of individual 'someones', the answers to the three questions are not correlated. What the analysis did was to look at *the differences in mean answers by country* of the three questions. Those mean answers were correlated across the countries and regions studied. So if in a country more people feel under stress at work, in the same country more people want rules to be respected, and more people want to have a long-term career. However, the individuals within each country who foster these feelings need not be the same people.

The *culture* of a country—or other category of people—is not a combination of properties of the 'average citizen', nor a 'modal personality'. It is, among other things, a set of likely reactions of citizens with a common mental programming. One person may react in one way (such as, feeling more nervous), another in another way (such as, wanting rules to be respected). Such reactions need not be found within the same *persons*, but only statistically more often in the same *society*. Confusing the level of the individual with the level of the society is known in the social sciences as the *ecological fallacy*. It amounts to a confusion between personality and culture.

The interpretation of the association between questions 1–3 *at the country level* does make sense. We assume that all three are expressions of the level of anxiety that exists in a particular society in the face of an uncertain future. This level of anxiety forms part and parcel of the shared mental programming of people in that society in the family, at school, and in adult life. Because of this anxiety level, a relatively larger number of persons will feel nervous or tense at work (question 1). The idea of breaking a company rule—for whatever good reason—is rejected by more people (question 2), because it introduces ambiguity: what if everybody would just start doing as they pleased? Finally, changing employers is less popular in such a country (question 3), for it means venturing into the unknown.

Uncertainty avoidance can therefore be defined as *the extent to which the members of a culture feel threatened by uncertain or unknown situations.* This feeling is, among other things, expressed through nervous stress and in a need for predictability: a need for written and unwritten rules.

The Uncertainty Avoidance Index (UAI) values for 50 countries and 3 regions are listed in Table 5.1. In a way similar to the computation of the PDI (Chapter 2), the index value for each country was computed from the mean scores of questions (1) and (2) and the percentage score for question (3). The formula used is based on simple mathematics: adding or subtracting the three scores after multiplying each by a fixed number, and finally adding another fixed number. The formula was developed such that (1) each of the three questions would contribute equally to the final index and (2) index values would range from around 0 for the country with the weakest

Table 5.1 Uncertainty avoidance index (UAI) values for 50 countries and 3 regions

Score rank	Country or region	UAI score	Score rank	Country or region	UAI score
1	Greece	112	28	Equador	67
2	Portugal	104	29	Germany FR	65
3	Guatemala	101	30	Thailand	64
4	Uruguay	100	31/32	Iran	59
5/6	Belgium	94	31/32	Finland	59
5/6	Salvador	94	33	Switzerland	58
7	Japan	92	34	West Africa	54
8	Yugoslavia	88	35	Netherlands	53
9	Peru	87	36	East Africa	52
10/15	France	86	37	Australia	51
10/15	Chile	86	38	Norway	50
10/15	Spain	86	39/40	South Africa	49
10/15	Costa Rica	86	39/40	New Zealand	49
10/15	Panama	86	41/42	Indonesia	48
10/15	Argentina	86	41/42	Canada	48
16/17	Turkey	85	43	USA	46
16/17	South Korea	85	44	Philippines	44
18	Mexico	82	45	India	40
19	Israel	81	46	Malaysia	36
20	Colombia	80	47/48	Great Britain	35
21/22	Venezuela	76	47/48	Ireland (Republic of)	35
21/22	Brazil	76	49/50	Hong Kong	29
23	Italy	75	49/50	Sweden	29
24/25	Pakistan	70	51	Denmark	23
24/25	Austria	70	52	Jamaica	13
26	Taiwan	69	53	Singapore	8
27	Arab countries	68			

uncertainty avoidance to around 100 for the strongest. The latter objective was not completely attained, because after the formula had been developed, some more countries were added which produced scores over 100.

Table 5.1 shows a new grouping of countries, unlike the ones found for any of the previous three dimensions. High scores occur for Latin American, Latin European, and Mediterranean countries (from 112 for Greece to 67 for Equador). Also high are the scores of Japan and South Korea (92 and 85). Medium high are the scores of the German-speaking countries Austria, Germany (Federal Republic), and Switzerland (70, 65, and 58, respectively). Medium to low are the scores of all Asian countries other than Japan and Korea (from 69 for Taiwan to 8 for Singapore), for the African countries, and for the Anglo and Nordic countries plus the Netherlands (from 59 for Finland to 23 for Denmark). West Germany scores 65 (rank 29) and Great Britain 35 (rank 47/48). This confirms a culture gap between these otherwise similar countries with regard to the avoidance of uncertainty, as illustrated in the story with which this chapter opened.

Uncertainty avoidance and anxiety

Anxiety is a term taken from psychology and psychiatry, and expressing a diffuse 'state of being uneasy or worried about what may happen' (*Webster's New World Dictionary*). It should not be confused with *fear* which has an object. We are afraid of something: anxiety has no object. The idea that levels of anxiety may differ between countries has been supported by various studies. These go back to the French sociologist Emile Durkheim, who as early as 1897 published a study on the phenomenon of suicide. Durkheim showed that suicide rates in different countries and regions were surprisingly stable from year to year. He used this stability as proof that a highly individual act like taking one's life could nevertheless be influenced by social forces which differed among countries and remained largely the same over time.

High suicide rates are one, but only one, possible outcome of anxiety in a society. In the 1970s the results were published of a large study of anxiety-related phenomena in 18 developed countries by the Irish psychologist Richard Lynn. Lynn used data from official health and related statistics, and showed that a number of indicators were correlated across countries: the suicide death rate, alcoholism (measured by the death rate due to liver cirrhosis), the accident death rate, and the rate of prisoners per 10 000 population. Together these together formed a factor which he labeled 'anxiety' or 'neuroticism'. Some other indicators were negatively related to the anxiety factor: the consumption of caffeine (in coffee and tea), the average daily intake of calories of food, the death rate due to coronary heart disease, and the occurrence of chronic psychosis (measured through the number of patients per 1000 population). Lynn calculated scores for the strength of the anxiety factor of each of his 18 countries, based on data from 1960. He found Austria, Japan, and France to score highest, and New Zealand, Great Britain, and the Republic of Ireland lowest. There is a strong correlation between Lynn's country anxiety scores and the UAI scores found in the IBM studies and listed in Table 5.1 (Hofstede, 1980, pp. 108–110, 193–195; 1984, pp. 124–126). Because the two studies use completely different sources of data, the agreement between their results is very supportive of the solidity of their conclusions: anxiety levels differ from one country to another. Some cultures are more anxious than others.

The more anxious cultures tend to be the more expressive cultures. They are the places where people talk with their hands, where it is socially acceptable to raise one's voice, to show one's emotions, to pound the table. Japan may seem to be an exception in this respect; like other Asians, Japanese generally behave unemotionally in Western eyes. However, in Japan and to some extent also Korea and Taiwan there is the outlet of getting drunk along with colleagues after working hours. During these parties, men release their pent-up aggression, even towards superiors; but the next day business continues as usual. Such drinking bouts represent one of the major institutionalized places and times for anxiety release.

In weak uncertainty avoidance countries anxiety levels are relatively low. According to Lynn's study, more people in these countries die from coronary heart disease. This can be explained by the lower expressiveness of these cultures. Aggression and emotions are not supposed to be shown: people who behave emotionally or noisily are socially disapproved of. This means that stress cannot be released in activity; it has to be internalized. If this happens again and again, it may cause cardio-vascular damage.

Lynn explains the larger number of chronic psychosis patients in low anxiety countries from a lack of mental stimuli in such societies, a certain gloom or dullness. Coffee and tea are stimulating drugs and these societies show a high consumption of such caffeine carriers. Alcohol has the opposite effect, i.e., it releases stress. Weak uncertainty avoidance societies tend to have low average alcohol consumption figures as manifested by their frequency of liver sclerosis deaths. Many people in the Scandinavian countries show a particular pattern of periodic excessive drinking, in which case the alcohol does act as a stimulus but for a short period only, followed by longer periods of abstention; the average alcohol consumption in the Scandinavian countries is still low compared to the rest of Europe.

In countries with strong uncertainty avoidance people come across as busy, fidgety, emotional, aggressive, active. In countries with weak uncertainty avoidance people give the impression of being quiet, easy-going, indolent, controlled, lazy. These impressions are in the eye of the beholder: they depend on the level of emotionality to which the observer has been accustomed in his or her own culture.

The 1981 study by the European value systems group, covering the values of representative samples of the population in a number of European countries, used, among other measures, Bradburn's affect balance scale, a general indicator of subjective well-being. The results for nine countries were published in 1983 by the French sociologist Jean Stoetzel. There is a strong negative correlation between a country's level of uncertainty avoidance according to the IBM studies and its citizens' level of subjective well-being. In strong uncertainty avoidance countries people on average feel less well: this is another expression of the anxiety component in uncertainty avoidance. The European value systems study also asked about people's state of health, to be scored on a five-point scale. Feelings of health in a country are also negatively correlated with the country's uncertainty avoidance score, even more strongly than their feelings of subjective well-being.[3]

Uncertainty avoidance is not the same as risk avoidance

Uncertainty avoidance should not be confused with risk avoidance: uncertainty is to risk as anxiety is to fear. Fear and risk are both focused on something specific: an object in the case of fear, an event in the case of risk. Risk is often expressed as a percentage of probability that a particular event may happen. Anxiety and uncertainty are both diffuse feelings. Anxiety, as was argued earlier, has no object. Uncertainty has no probability attached to it. It is a situation in which anything can happen and we have no idea what. As soon as uncertainty is expressed as risk, it ceases to be a source of anxiety. It may become a source of fear, but it may also be accepted as routine, like the risks of driving a car or practising a sport.

Even more than reducing risk, uncertainty avoidance leads to a reduction of *ambiguity*. Uncertainty avoiding cultures shun ambiguous situations. People in such cultures look for a structure in their organizations, institutions, and relationships which makes events clearly interpretable and predictable. Paradoxically, they are often prepared to engage in risky behavior in order to reduce ambiguities, like starting a fight with a potential opponent rather than sitting back and waiting.

The analysis of the IBM data shows a relationship between the strength of uncertainty avoidance in a (developed) country and the maximum speeds allowed in freeway traffic in that country. The relationship is positive: stronger uncertainty avoidance means faster driving. Faster driving means more fatal accidents (other things being equal), thus more risk. However, this is a *familiar* risk, which uncertainty avoiding cultures do not mind running. Their emotionality provides them with a sense of stress, of urgency, which in turn leads to wanting to drive faster. The higher speed limits in stronger uncertainty avoidance countries show, in fact, a priority of saving time over saving lives.

In countries with weaker uncertainty avoidance there is less of a prevailing sense of urgency, and therefore a more public acceptance of a lower speed limit. Not only familiar, but also unfamiliar risks are accepted: such as those involved in a change of job or in engaging in activities for which there are no rules.

Uncertainty avoidance according to occupation, sex, and age

It is easy to imagine more and less uncertainty avoiding occupations (such as bank clerk versus journalist). Nevertheless, the analysis of the IBM data across the 38 available occupations does not permit use of the UAI for characterizing occupations. The reason is that the three questions used to compute the index for countries (stress, rule orientation, and intent to stay) vary in different ways for different occupations, so that across occupations, the three are not correlated. If anybody wants to measure the amount of uncertainty avoidance in an occupation, he or she will have to develop another set of questions for this purpose.

The same holds for sex differences. Women and men *in the same countries and occupations* show exactly the same stress levels and rule orientation. Only their intent to stay differs (men on average wanting to stay longer), but this does not express their greater avoidance of uncertainty: it just shows that the IBM population contains a percentage of younger women who plan to stop working for some time when they have young children.

The only aspect of the IBM population other than nationality which does show a close relationship with the UAI is average age. In countries where IBM employees tend to be older, we find higher stress, more rule orientation, and a stronger intent to stay. There is a circular logic in the relationship between the UAI and age: in countries with stronger uncertainty avoidance, people not only intend to but do change employers less frequently. Therefore, the mean length of service of IBM employees in these countries is greater, and therefore they are on average older.

The strong association between the UAI and average age made it desirable to test whether the country differences were not entirely due to age differences. A check was done in which UAI scores per country were computed *controlling for age*, i.e., as it would be if all countries had the same average age (Hofstede, 1980, pp. 165, 167; 1984, pp. 122–123). This check showed that even assuming a constant average age, the country differences remain very similar to those in Table 5.1.

Uncertainty avoidance in the family

An American couple spent two weeks in a small Italian town babysitting their grandchildren, whose American parents, temporarily located in Italy, were away on a trip. The children loved to play in the public *piazza*, among lots of Italian children with their *mammas* or nannies. The American children were allowed to run around; they would fall down, but get up again, and the grandparents felt there was little real danger. The Italians, however, reacted quite differently. They would not for a moment lose sight of their children, and when a child fell down, an adult would immediately pick it up, brush it off, and console it.[4]

Among the first things a child learns are the distinctions between clean and dirty, and between safe and dangerous. What is considered clean and safe, or dirty and dangerous, varies widely from one society to the next, and even among families within a society. The British–American anthropologist Mary Douglas has written a book (Douglas, 1966) in which she argues that dirt— that which pollutes—is a relative concept, which depends entirely on cultural interpretation. Dirt is basically matter out-of-place. 'Dangerous' and 'polluting' are things that do not fit our usual framework of thinking, our normal classifications. What a child has to learn is to classify clean things from dirty things and safe things from dangerous things.

In strongly uncertainty avoiding cultures classifications with regard to what is dirty and dangerous are tight and absolute. The Italian *mammas* and nannies (UAI 75) see dirt and danger in the piazza where the American grandparents (UAI 46) see none. Dirt and danger are not limited to matter. They also refer to people. Racism is bred in families. Children learn that persons from a particular category are dirty and dangerous. We could even claim that cultures with strong uncertainty avoidance *need* categories of dangerous others to defend themselves from.

Ideas too can be considered dirty and dangerous. Children in families learn that some ideas are good and others taboo. In some cultures the distinction between good and evil ideas is very sharp. There is a concern about Truth with a capital 'T'. Ideas which differ from this Truth are dangerous and polluting. Little room is left for doubt or relativism.

Taboos are supposed to be a characteristic of traditional, primitive societies, but modern societies too are full of taboos. The family is the place where these taboos are transmitted from generation to generation. In a part of the Netherlands where fundamentalist Protestant Christianity prevails, a schoolgirl from a modern family we know was told by a classmate 'we are not allowed to ride (our bikes) to school with you, because you live in a combune' (she meant a 'commune' as opposed to a traditional family relationship).

Weak uncertainty avoidance cultures also have their classifications as to dirt and danger, but these are wider and more prepared to give the benefit of the doubt to unknown situations, people, and ideas. Norms are expressed in basic terms, like being honest and being polite, but allowing a wide range of personal interpretation as to what this means in a given case. Deviant behavior is not necessarily felt to be threatening. Norms as to dress, hair style, and speech are loose, and children are expected to treat everyone the same way, regardless of their looks.

The strong uncertainty avoidance sentiment can be summarized by the credo of xenophobia: 'What is different, is dangerous.' The weak uncertainty avoidance sentiment on the contrary is: 'What is different, is curious.' Somewhere in between is the prevailing sentiment in my own country, the Netherlands (UAI 53): 'What is different, is ridiculous.'

If children in a family are taught that other people are dangerous this can turn against the family itself. In the European value systems study cited earlier, respondents were asked for their feelings about their family relationships. These feelings were more frequently negative in strong than in weak uncertainty avoidance countries.[5]

Uncertainty avoidance at school
The International Teachers Program (ITP) around 1980 was a summer refresher course for teachers in management subjects. In a class of 50 there might be 20 or more different nationalities. Such a class offered excellent opportunities to watch the different learning habits of the students (who were teachers themselves at other times) and the different expectations they had of the behavior of those who taught them.

One dilemma I experienced when teaching in the ITP was choosing the proper amount of structure to be put into the various activities. Most Germans, for example, favor structured learning situations with precise objectives, detailed assignments, and strict timetables. They like situations in which there is one correct answer which they can find. They expect to be rewarded for accuracy. Their preferences are typical for strong uncertainty avoidance countries. Most British participants on the other hand despise too much structure. They like open-ended learning situations with vague objectives, broad assignments, and no timetables at all. The suggestion that there could be only one correct answer is taboo with them. They expect to be rewarded for originality. Their reactions are typical for countries with weak uncertainty avoidance.

Students from strong uncertainty avoidance countries expect their teachers to be the experts who have all the answers. Teachers who use cryptic academic language are respected; some of the great gurus from these countries write such difficult prose that one needs commentaries by more ordinary creatures explaining what the guru really meant. 'German students are brought up in the belief that anything which is easy enough for them to understand is dubious and probably unscientific' (Stroebe, 1976). French academic books not infrequently contain phrases half a page long.[6] Students in these countries will not, as a rule, confess to intellectual disagreement with their teachers. A Ph.D candidate who finds him/herself in conflict with a thesis advisor on an important issue has the choice of changing his or her mind or finding another advisor. Intellectual disagreement in academic matters is felt as personal disloyalty.

Students from weak uncertainty avoidance countries accept a teacher who says 'I don't know'. Their respect goes to teachers who use plain language, and to books which explain difficult issues in ordinary terms. Intellectual disagreement in academic matters in these cultures can be seen as a stimulating exercise, and I know of thesis advisors whose evaluation of a Ph.D candidate is positively related to the candidate's amount of well-argued disagreement with the professor's position.

The examples used so far stem from university and post-academic teaching and learning situations, but the behavior and expectations of both students and teachers in these examples were clearly developed during earlier school experiences. One more difference between the two types of culture which operates specifically at the elementary and secondary school level is the expected role of parents versus teachers. In cultures with a strong uncertainty avoidance parents are sometimes brought in by teachers as an audience, but they are rarely consulted. Parents are laypersons and teachers are experts who know. In countries with a weak uncertainty avoidance some teachers try to get parents involved in their children's learning process: they actively seek parents' ideas.[7]

Uncertainty avoidance in the workplace

Coming from Holland I once rode an international train into Belgium. I had a general rail pass for the Netherlands, so that I asked the Belgian train conductor to sell me a connecting ticket from the Dutch–Belgian border via Mechelen to Leuven. The conductor seemed to have considerable problems with the request. He struggled with his instruction booklet for about 15 minutes, and finally said 'I can only find the rate via Brussels. Would you please travel via Brussels?' Travelling via Brussels meant a detour which would make me lose at least half an hour. I would gladly have paid whatever rate the poor offical charged me if he just gave me the ticket I asked for. Such flexibility seemed beyond his competence.

Laws and rules were mentioned at the beginning of this chapter as ways in which a society tries to prevent uncertainties in the behavior of people. This is very noticeable at the workplace. In uncertainty avoiding societies there are many formal laws and/or informal rules controlling the rights and duties of employers and employees. There are also many internal rules and regulations controlling the work process, although in this case the power distance level plays a role too. Where power distances are large, the exercise of discretionary power by superiors replaces, to some extent, the need for internal rules. The need for laws and rules is not based on formal logic but on psycho-logic. The need for rules in a society with a strong uncertainty avoidance culture is emotional. People—members of governments, civil servants, employers, and employees—have been programmed since their early childhood to feel comfortable in structured environments. As little as possible should be left to chance.

The emotional need for laws and rules in a strong uncertainty avoidance society often leads to the establishing of rules or rule-oriented behaviors which are clearly nonsensical, inconsistent, or dysfunctional, as in the example of the Belgian railway conductor. Belgium scores quite high on UAI (94), much higher than the Netherlands (53). Critics from countries with weaker uncertainty avoidance do not realize that even ineffective rules satisfy people's emotional need for formal structure. What happens in reality is less important. Philippe d'Iribarne, in his comparative study of a French, a US, and a Dutch manufacturing plant, remarks that some procedures in the French plant were formally followed but only after having been divested of any practical meaning. He compares this to what has been written about the French *ancien régime* (the pre-Napoleon monarchy): '*une règle rigide, une pratique molle*' (a strict rule but a lenient practice) (d'Iribarne, 1989).

In countries with very weak uncertainty avoidance there rather seems to be an emotional horror of formal rules. Rules are only established in case of absolute necessity, such as to determine whether traffic should keep left or right. People in such societies pride themselves that many problems can be solved without formal rules. Germans, coming from a fairly uncertainty avoiding culture, are impressed by the public discipline shown by the British in forming neat queues (lines) for bus stops and in shops. There is no law in Britain governing queueing behavior; it is based on a public habit continuously reinforced by social control. The paradox is that although rules in countries with weak uncertainty avoidance are less sacred, they are generally more respected.

British queueing behavior is facilitated by the unemotional and patient nature of most British citizens. As argued earlier in this chapter, weak uncertainty avoidance also stands for low anxiety. At the workplace, the anxiety component of uncertainty avoidance leads to noticeable differences between strong and weak uncertainty avoidance societies. In strong uncertainty avoidance societies people like to work hard, or at least to be always busy. Life is hurried, and time is money. In weak uncertainty avoidance societies people are quite able to work hard if there is a need for it, but they are not driven by an inner urge towards constant activity. They like to relax.

Time is a framework to orient oneself in, but not something one is constantly watching.

The emotional need for rules in strong uncertainty avoidance societies can be turned into a talent for precision and punctuality. This is especially the case where power distances are relatively small, so that subordinates' behavior does not depend on whether the boss looks or not. The Swiss watch industry used to be an example; nowadays many Japanese industries benefit from this aspect of the Japanese culture. Precision and punctuality in weak uncertainty avoidance countries do not come naturally to most people, but they can be learned if technically needed.

André Laurent at INSEAD business school, Fontainebleau, France, has used a questionnaire survey with managers from different industrialized countries participating in management courses. The following statements belonged to a factor which across 11 countries was strongly correlated with the UAI (Hofstede, 1980, pp. 199–201):

- Most organizations would be better off if conflict could be eliminated forever.
- It is important for a manager to have at hand precise answers to most of the questions that his subordinates may raise about their work.
- If you want a competent person to do a job properly, it is often best to provide him or her with very precise instructions on how to do it.
- When the respective roles of the members of a department become complex, detailed job descriptions are a useful way of clarifying.
- An organizational structure in which certain subordinates have two direct bosses should be avoided at all costs.

All of these indicate a horror of ambiguity and a need for precision and formalization in countries with strong uncertainty avoidance cultures.

A study of top management control in British, French, and German companies by Jacques Horovitz from France has concluded that in Great Britain top managers occupy themselves more with strategic problems and less with daily operations; in France and Germany the reverse is the case (Horovitz, 1980). Both France and Germany score considerably higher on UAI than Great Britain (86 and 65, respectively, versus 35). Strategic problems, being by definition unstructured, demand a greater tolerance for ambiguity than operational problems. During the period in which Horovitz did his study the French and German economies did better than the British, so weak uncertainty avoidance leading to more strategic planning does not necessarily increase business effectiveness. The economic success of companies and countries depends on many more factors.

Weak uncertainty avoidance countries are more likely to stimulate basic innovations as they maintain a greater tolerance towards deviant ideas. On the other hand they seem to be at a disadvantage in developing these basic innovations towards full-scale implementation, as such implementation usually demands a considerable sense of detail and punctuality. The latter are more likely to be found in strong uncertainty avoidance countries. The UK has produced more Nobel Prize winners than Japan, but Japan has put more new products on the world market. There is a strong case here for synergy between innovating and implementing cultures, the first supplying ideas, the second developing them further.

Uncertainty avoidance, masculinity, and motivation

The motivation of employees is a classic concern of management, and probably even more of management trainers and of the authors of management books. Differences in uncertainty avoidance imply differences in motivation patterns, but the picture becomes clearer when we simultaneously consider the masculinity–femininity dimension described in Chapter 4. Figure 5.1 therefore presents a two-dimensional plot of country scores on uncertainty avoidance (vertically) and masculinity (horizontally).

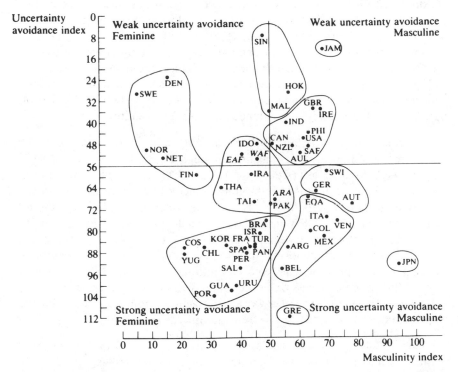

Fig 5.1   The position of 50 countries and 3 regions on the masculinity/femininity and uncertainty avoidance dimensions (for country name abbreviations see Table 3.2)

The usefulness of combining UAI and MAS for studying motivation patterns was suggested by a comparison of the IBM survey results with the work of David McClelland. Harvard University psychologist McClelland in 1961 issued a now classic book *The Achieving Society*. In this book he attempted to trace different dominant motivation patterns in different countries. He distinguished three types of motive: achievement, affiliation (associating with other people), and power. The strength of each motive for each country was measured through a content analysis of the stories appearing in children's readers. McClelland argued that the stories read by second- to fourth-grade schoolchildren, their first readings, are to modern nations what folk tales are to traditional societies. Folk tales have been widely used by field anthropologists to infer motives of nonliterate peoples; McClelland wanted to do the same for nations.

McClelland's research team analyzed children's stories from a large number of countries dating from 1925 and from 1950. For each country and either period, 21 stories were studied. Each story and each country was scored on 'need for achievement', 'need for affiliation', and 'need for power'. McClelland's own objective was to show that the 'need for achievement' in children's stories could serve to predict a country's rate of economic development when these children grew up. On this account, later events have not proven him right (Hofstede, 1980, p. 170–171; 1984, pp. 126–127). A comparison of McClelland's country scores with the IBM dimension scores, however, revealed that the 'need for achievement' as measured from 1925 children's books (the more traditional ones[8]) is strongly correlated with *weak* uncertainty avoidance and even more strongly with the combination of weak uncertainty avoidance and strong masculinity.[9]

This means that McClelland's 1925 ranking of countries on 'need for achievement' follows a diagonal line through Fig. 5.1, from upper right (strong N_{Ach}) to lower left (weak N_{Ach}). Low UAI means willingness to run unfamiliar risks and high MAS the importance of visible results. Both are components of entrepreneurial activity in the American tradition. It should be no surprise that the USA and the other Anglo countries in Fig. 5.1 are to be found in the upper right-hand quadrant, where UAI is low, MAS high, and N_{Ach} strong. In choosing the achievement motive, the American McClelland has promoted a typical Anglo value complex to a *universal* recipe for economic success. A Frenchman, Swede, or Japanese would have been unlikely to conceive of a worldwide achievement motive. Even the word 'achievement' is difficult to translate into other languages.

Leaving McClelland's work aside, the combination of cultural uncertainty avoidance and masculinity–femininity in Fig. 5.1 allows us to recognize different motivation patterns for different clusters of countries. A point of departure is the 'hierarchy of human needs' formulated by Abraham

Maslow and referred to earlier in Chapter 3. Maslow has ordered needs from lower to higher: physiological, safety, belongingness, esteem, self-actualization (Maslow uses the word 'safety', but he includes what in work situations is usually called 'security'). Chapter 3 took issue with the individualistic assumptions in putting *self*-actualization on top. In view of the cultural variety in the world with regard to uncertainty avoidance and masculinity some other provisos should also be made.

Safety or security is likely to prevail over other needs where uncertainty avoidance is strong. Belongingness (human relationships) will prevail over esteem in a feminine culture, but esteem over belongingness in a masculine culture. Thus the supreme motivators—other things like type of work being equal—in Fig. 5.1 will be: achievement (of self or group) and esteem in the upper right-hand corner (USA, etc.); achievement and belongingness in the

Table 5.2   Key differences between weak and strong uncertainty avoidance societies.
I: general norm, family, school, and workplace

Weak uncertainty avoidance	Strong uncertainty avoidance
Uncertainty is a normal feature of life and each day is accepted as it comes	The uncertainty inherent in life is felt as a continuous threat which must be fought
Low stress; subjective feeling of well-being	High stress; subjective feeling of anxiety
Aggression and emotions should not be shown	Aggression and emotions may at proper times and places be ventilated
Comfortable in ambiguous situations and with unfamiliar risks	Acceptance of familiar risks; fear of ambiguous situations and of unfamiliar risks
Lenient rules for children on what is dirty and taboo	Tight rules for children on what is dirty and taboo
What is different, is curious	What is different, is dangerous
Students comfortable with open-ended learning situations and concerned with good discussions	Students comfortable in structured learning situations and concerned with the right answers
Teachers may say 'I don't know'	Teachers supposed to have all the answers
There should not be more rules than is strictly necessary	Emotional need for rules, even if these will never work
Time is a framework for orientation	Time is money
Comfortable feeling when lazy; hard-working only when needed	Emotional need to be busy; inner urge to work hard
Precision and punctuality have to be learned	Precision and punctuality come naturally
Tolerance of deviant and innovative ideas and behavior	Suppression of deviant ideas and behavior; resistance to innovation
Motivation by achievement and esteem or belongingness	Motivation by security and esteem or belongingness

upper left-hand corner (Sweden, etc.); security and esteem in the lower right-hand corner (Japan, Germany, etc.); security and belongingness in the lower left-hand corner (France, etc.).

In this classification, Maslow's five categories have been maintained but they have been reshuffled according to a country's prevailing culture pattern. An additional question is whether other needs should be added, which were missing in Maslow's model because they were not recognized in his mid-twentieth-century US middle-class cultural environment. Candidate needs identified in the previous chapters could be respect, harmony, face, and duty. Chapter 7 will further explore what it means to drop Western assumptions about human values altogether.

The European value systems study in nine countries produced scores for work satisfaction. These appear to be negatively correlated with UAI: in more uncertainty avoiding countries people on average like their jobs less well (earlier in this chapter they were also shown to score lower on general well-being and on satisfaction with health and with family relationships). Jean Stoetzel who analyzed the European Value Systems data also computed a ratio between the work satisfaction of the managers among the respondents, and of the nonmanagers. This ratio appears to be *positively* correlated with UAI, so that in the more uncertainty avoiding countries the gap between the work satisfaction of the leaders and of those led is wider.[10]

Table 5.2 summarizes the key differences between weak and strong uncertainty avoidance societies described so far. Obviously the descriptions refer to the extreme poles of the dimension, and most real countries are somewhere in between, with considerable variation *within* each country.

Uncertainty avoidance and the state
In countries with strong uncertainty avoidance there tend to be more and more precise laws than in those with weak uncertainty avoidance. Germany, for example, has laws for the event that all other laws might become unenforceable (*Notstandsgesetze*), while the UK does not even have a written constitution. Labor–management relations in Germany have been codified in detail, while attempts to pass an Industrial Relations Act in the UK have never succeeded.[11]

Chapter 3 investigated the consequences of large and small power distances for the relationship between a citizen and the authorities. In large power distance countries, authorities have more unchecked power, status, and material rewards than in small power distance countries. Power distance and uncertainty avoidance are two independent dimensions (Chapter 6, Fig. 6.1 will show a diagram in which the two are crossed: countries are found in all quadrants of this diagram). Uncertainty avoidance refers not to differences in *power*, but to differences in *competence* between authorities and citizens.

The term 'citizen competence' was coined in a classic study by the US political scientists Gabriel Almond and Sidney Verba: they showed that the competence attributed to ordinary citizens versus authorities varied strongly among five countries in their research (Almond and Verba, 1963). In *Culture's Consequences* I have shown that Almond and Verba's 'citizen competence' measure correlates strongly negatively with uncertainty avoidance: competence is higher in countries which score lower on uncertainty avoidance. Citizens in strong uncertainty avoidance countries have also been shown to be pessimistic about their possibilities of influencing decisions made by authorities. Few citizens are prepared to protest against decisions made by the authorities, and their means of protest will be relatively conventional, like petitions and demonstrations. In the case of more extreme protest actions, like boycotts and sit-ins, most citizens in strong uncertainty avoidance countries favor that these should be firmly repressed by the government. Citizens in strong uncertainty avoidance countries are not only more dependent on the expertise of the government, but they also seem to feel that this is how things should be. The authorities and the citizens share the same norms about their mutual roles. The authorities tend to think in legal terms: in strong uncertainty avoidance countries higher civil servants more frequently have law degrees than where uncertainty avoidance is weak (65 percent in Germany versus 3 percent in Great Britain).

Citizens from weak uncertainty avoidance countries believe that they can participate in political decisions at the lowest, local level. More than in strong uncertainty avoidance countries are they prepared to protest against government decisions, and they are in favor of strong and unconventional protest actions if the milder actions do not help. They do not think the government should repress such protests (Hofstede, 1980, pp. 173, 178–179; 1984, pp. 129 and 134–135).

The European value systems study contained a question about people's confidence in their country's institutions. Across the nine countries studied this measure is negatively correlated with uncertainty avoidance: the more competent citizens of weak uncertainty avoidance countries are more inclined to trust those institutions.[12] In strong uncertainty avoidance countries, civil servants tend to foster negative feelings towards politics and politicians; in weak uncertainty avoidance countries, positive feelings (Hofstede, 1980, p. 178; 1984, p. 134).

In the strong uncertainty avoidance countries of Europe, citizens are obliged to carry identity cards in order to be able to legitimately identify themselves whenever requested to do so by a person in authority. In the weak uncertainty avoidance countries no such obligation exists, and the burden of proof in identifying the citizen is on the authorities. This identity card obligation splits the 14 countries of Western Europe into two almost exactly equal parts according to UAI.

In strong uncertainty avoidance countries there tends to be more conservatism, even within parties which call themselves progressive, and a stronger need for 'law and order'. Young people are more often considered as suspect (Hofstede, 1980, p. 172; 1984, p. 128). These countries are more likely to harbor extremist minorities within their political landscape than weak uncertainty avoidance countries, and they are also more likely to ban political groups whose ideas are considered dangerous. Banned groups are likely to continue an underground existence, and they may even resort to terrorism. Strong uncertainty avoidance countries have more native terrorists.

Feelings of one country's population towards the populations of other countries (for example, within the European Community) are based on a variety of historical factors, but they also contain a general element of trust or mistrust: strong UAI countries tend to score on the mistrust side, weak UAI countries on the trust side. The xenophobia which is fostered in the strong uncertainty avoidance family is reflected in chauvinism at the national level. Here, too, 'what is different, is dangerous.'

The Axis powers from the Second World War, Germany, Italy, and Japan, are all three characterized by strong uncertainty avoidance plus masculinity (see Fig. 5.1). Under the conditions prior to the war, ethnocentric, xenophobic, aggressive, and assertive tendencies could obtain the upper hand in these countries, more easily than in countries with different culture patterns. Fascism and racism find a fertile ground in cultures with strong uncertainty avoidance and pronounced masculine values. The paradox is that this same complex of values in the postwar period has contributed to the economic miracles leading to the fast recovery of these former Axis powers. For the industrialized countries of the world (not for the poor ones) economic growth since 1960 is positively correlated with the UAI. A culture's weaknesses may, in different circumstances, become its strengths.

The effect of the strength of uncertainty avoidance in a society depends also on its degree of individualism or collectivism. In Fig. 5.2 these two dimensions have been plotted against each other. The combination is relevant for two issues. Firstly, whereas in strong uncertainty avoidance, individualist countries rules will tend to be explicit and written (low-context communication, see Chapter 3), in strong uncertainty avoidance, collectivist countries rules are often implicit and rooted in tradition (high-context communication). This is very clearly the case in Japan, and it represents a bone of contention in the negotiations between Western countries and Japan about the opening of the Japanese markets for Western products. The Japanese rightly argue that there are no formal rules preventing the foreign products from being brought in; but the would-be Western importers find themselves up against the implicit rules of the Japanese distribution system which they do not understand.

A second issue for which Fig. 5.2 is relevant is the way a society deals with intergroup conflict. The presence within the borders of a country of different ethnic, linguistic, or religious groups is a historical fact; some countries are more homogeneous than others. How a population and a government deal with such conflict, however, is a cultural phenomenon. In countries in the upper right-hand corner, strong uncertainty avoidance ('what is different, is dangerous') is combined with collectivist particularism (strong identification with ingroups). Such countries will tend to eliminate intergroup conflict by denying it and either trying to assimilate or repress minorities. The chances of violent intergroup strife within these countries are considerable, as the minorities often hold the same strong uncertainty avoiding, collectivist values. Several countries with severe intergroup conflicts are found inside or near the upper right-hand corner of Fig. 5.2: Arab countries, Iran, Turkey, Yugoslavia, Israel, and the African countries.

Countries in the upper left-hand corner of Fig. 5.2 may contain different groups with strong group identities, but are more likely to find a *modus vivendi* in which groups tolerate and complement each other. Countries in the lower right-hand corner often harbor considerable antagonism against

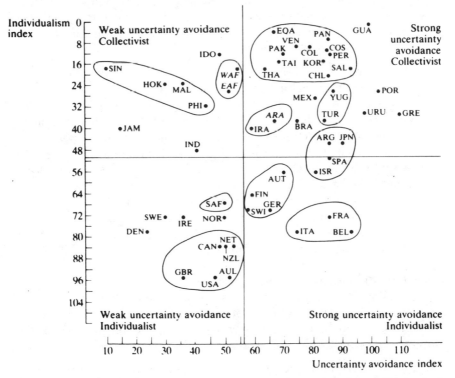

Fig 5.2 The position of 50 countries and 3 regions on the uncertainty avoidance and individualism–collectivism dimensions (for country name abbreviations see Table 3-2)

minorities and ethnic, religious, or linguistic opponent groups, but the universalism of the individualist state at least formally tries to guarantee that everybody's rights are respected; extremism versus others is restricted to the political margin. Finally, countries in the lower left-hand corner are likely to actively try to integrate minorities and guarantee equal rights.

This does not hold, obviously, for South Africa which figures in this quadrant. The IBM data are from whites only, but it is the whites who set the policies. The diagram at least explains why part of the South African whites reject apartheid. The situation in Northern Ireland also does not seem to fit the diagram; the IBM data, however, are from the Republic of Ireland.

Strong uncertainty avoidance leading to the intolerance of deviants and minorities has at times been very costly to countries. The expulsion of the Jews from Spain and Portugal by the Catholic Kings after the *Reconquista* of the Iberian peninsula from the Moors (1492) has deprived these countries of some of their most enterprising citizens, and is supposed to have led to the decadence of the empire in the following centuries. An important group of the Iberian Jews settled in the Netherlands and played a major part in the Dutch colonial expansion in the seventeenth century. Others went to Costa Rica which, even today, is a favorable exception to Latin American *personalismo* and stagnation (see Chapter 3). In recent history, Hitler's expulsion of top scientists, many of whom were Jewish, enabled the Americans to develop the atomic bomb.

Outside the sphere of government, a country's uncertainty avoidance norm is reflected in the way health care resources are spent. For 44 out of the 50 countries in the IBM studies, the *World Development Report 1984* issued by the World Bank lists the number of doctors and the number of nurses. Dividing the latter by the former provides an index of nurses per doctor which is independent of the absolute size of the health budget, i.e., of the country's wealth. There is a strong negative correlation between nurses per doctor and UAI, meaning that uncertainty avoiding countries spend more money on doctors, uncertainty accepting countries on nurses. As in the case of citizens and authorities, the nurse is the lay person who is more respected in weak uncertainty avoidance cultures; the doctor is the expert who is venerated in strong uncertainty avoidance cultures.[13]

Uncertainty avoidance, religion, and ideas
Earlier in this chapter religion was mentioned as one of the ways in which mankind avoids uncertainty. Religious beliefs help us to accept the uncertainties we cannot defend ourselves against. Some religions offer the ultimate certainty of a life after death.

The grouping of countries according to UAI score in Table 5.1 is somewhat associated with their dominant religion. Orthodox and Roman Catholic Christian countries score high (except the Philippines and Ireland). Judaic and Muslim countries tend to score in the middle. Protestant Christian countries score low. Eastern religions score medium to very low, with Japan as an exception.

A problem in classifying countries by religion is that the great religions of the world are all internally heterogeneous. Polish, Peruvian, Italian, and Dutch Roman Catholicism are very different. Indonesian, Iranian, Saudi, and Yugoslav Islam mean totally different things to their believers and to the countries. Thai, Singaporean, and Japanese Buddhism have quite dissimilar affective and practical consequences.

It is evident, as was already suggested in Chapter 1, that religious conversion does not mean a total change in cultural values. The value complexes described by the dimensions of power distance, individualism or collectivism, masculinity or femininity, and uncertainty avoidance seem to have survived religious conversions. These value complexes may even have influenced to what extent a population has been receptive to certain religions, and how the accepted religion has evolved in that country. Indonesian (Javanese) mysticism has survived Hindu, Buddhist, Muslim, and Christian conversions. In the Christian countries the Reformation has separated almost exactly those European countries once under the Roman Empire from the rest. All ex-Roman countries (the ones now speaking Romance languages) refuted the Reformation and remained Roman Catholic; most others became Protestant or mixed. Poland and Ireland were never part of the Roman Empire, but in their case, Roman Catholicism provided them with an identity against non-Catholic oppressors.

In establishing a relationship between uncertainty avoidance and religious belief, it makes sense to distinguish between Western and Eastern religions. This distinction will be taken up again in Chapter 7. The Western religions, Judaism, Christianity, and Islam, are based on divine revelation, and all three originated from what is now called the Middle East. What distinguishes the Western from the Eastern religions is their concern with Truth with a capital 'T'. The Western revelation religions share the assumption that there is an absolute Truth which excludes all other truths and which man can possess. The difference between strong and weak uncertainty avoidance societies adhering to these religions lies in the amount of certainty one needs about having this Truth. In strong uncertainty avoidance cultures the belief is more frequent that 'There is only one Truth and we have it. All others are wrong.' Possessing this Truth is the only road to salvation and the main purpose in a person's life. The consequence of the others being wrong may be trying to convert them, avoiding them, or killing them.

Weak uncertainty avoidance cultures from the West still believe in Truth, but they have less of a need to believe that they alone possess it. 'There is only one Truth and we are looking for it. Others are looking for it as well and we accept as a fact of life that they look in different directions.' Part of this Truth, anyway, is that God wants nobody to be prosecuted for their beliefs.

For centuries, the Roman Catholic church maintained an Inquisition which sent many people with deviant ideas to their deaths, and banned or burned books; some books are banned by the Roman Catholic church even today. In Iran, Ayatollah Khomeini, shortly before his death in 1989, banned the book *The Satanic Verses* by Salman Rushdie and invited all believers to kill the author and his publishers. It is somewhat amazing that many people in Christian countries were so shocked by this in view of their own countries' histories of religious intolerance. With some exceptions, and Khomeini's action is one of them, Islam in history has been more tolerant of other religions than Roman Catholic Christianity. In the Muslim Turkish Empire, 'people of the Book', i.e., Jews and Christians, were tolerated and could exercise their religions, as long as they paid a special tax. On the other hand even Protestant Christians, generally considered as more broadminded, have made victims of religious intolerance, like Michel Servet who was burned to death by John Calvin in Geneva in 1553. Protestant nations have also in past centuries burned supposed witches.

Confession of sins is a practice which fits the strong uncertainty avoidance culture pattern. If a rule cannot be kept, confession is a way to preserve the rule and put the blame on the individual. The Roman Catholic practice of confession is relatively mild and discreet; militant Communism in the Soviet Union in the days of Stalin made it a public show. In weak uncertainty avoidance cultures, there will be more of a tendency to change a rule if it is evident that it cannot be respected.

Eastern religions are less concerned about Truth. The assumption that there is one Truth which man can possess is absent in their thinking. Buddhism instead stresses the acquisition of insight by meditation. Thus in the East, people will easily absorb elements of different religions. Most Japanese perform both Buddhist and Shinto rituals, although by standards of Western logic the two religious traditions are mutually exclusive.

Across all countries with a Christian majority there is a strong correlation between the percentage of Catholics in the population (as opposed to Protestants) and the country's UAI. A second correlation is with masculinity, implying that where Catholicism prevails, masculine values tend to prevail as well, like refusing to admit women to leadership positions (see Chapter 4 and Hofstede (1980, pp. 181–182, 207, 209, 293; 1984, pp. 137, 204)). The correlation with uncertainty avoidance is easy to interpret as the Catholic Church supplies its believers with a certainty which most Protestant groups lack, apart from some of the smaller sects. The Catholic Church appeals to cultures with a need for such certainty. Within the Protestant nations the dominant culture has equipped people with a lesser need for certainty. Those who do need it find a spiritual home in sects and fundamentalist groups.

Both within Judaism and within Islam there is also a clearly visible conflict between more and less uncertainty avoiding factions, the first dogmatic, intolerant, fanatical, and fundamentalist ('There is only one Truth and we have it'), the second pragmatic, tolerant, liberal, and open to the modern world. In recent years the fanatic wings in all three revelation religions have been quite active and vocal. Historically, periods of fanaticism have always alternated with periods of tolerance, so there is some hope that the fanatic excesses will outlive themselves.

What applies to religions applies also to political ideologies, which are often difficult to separate from religious inspiration. Marxism in many places has taken the form of a secular religion. When East Germany was still solidly communist, the facade of the University of Leipzig was decorated with an enormous banner reading *Der Marxismus ist allmächtig, weil er wahr ist !* (Marxism is all-powerful because it is True![14]) In strong uncertainty avoidance cultures we find intolerant political ideologies, in weak uncertainty avoidance cultures, tolerant ones. The respect for what are commonly called 'human rights' assumes a tolerance for people with different political ideas. Violation of human rights in some countries is rooted in the strong uncertainty avoidance which is part and parcel of their culture. In other countries they are just an outcome of a power struggle (and related to power distance) or of collectivist intergroup strife, however.

In the area of philosophy and science,[15] grand theories are more likely to be conceived within strong uncertainty avoidance cultures than in weak ones. The quest for Truth is an essential motivator for a philosopher. In Europe, Germany and France have produced more great philosophers than the UK and Sweden (like Descartes, Kant, Hegel, Marx, Nietzsche, and Sartre). Weak uncertainty avoidance cultures have produced great empiricists, people developing conclusions from observation and experiments rather than from reflection (like Newton, Linnaeus, and Darwin).

As a social scientist I am sometimes asked to review manuscripts submitted to scientific journals. Manuscripts written by German and French authors often present broad conclusions unsupported by data. Manuscripts written by British and American authors usually are based on extensive data analysis but present few conclusions. The Germans and French tend to reason by deduction, the British and Americans by induction.[16]

Scientific disputes sometimes hide cultural assumptions. Famous is the discussion between the German physicist Albert Einstein (1879–1955) and his Danish colleague Niels Bohr (1885–1962) on whether certain processes inside the atom were governed by laws or were random. 'I cannot imagine

God playing dice,' Einstein is supposed to have said. Bohr could; recent research has proven him right, not Einstein. Denmark scores very low on uncertainty avoidance (rank 51, score 23).

A practical consequence of a society's level of uncertainty avoidance is whether people who hold different convictions can be personal friends. From countries with a strong uncertainty avoidance there are many stories of scientists who separated their links of friendship after a scientific disagreement; like the psychiatrists Sigmund Freud (Austria) and Carl Gustav Jung (Switzerland). In countries with a weak uncertainty avoidance it is much more normal that colleagues remain close personal friends in spite of very different scientific opinions. In strong uncertainty avoidance countries it is definitely not advisable for a doctoral candidate to disagree openly with a professor who supervises his thesis. In weak uncertainty avoidance countries this need not be a problem.

Before and during the Second World War many German and Austrian scientists of Jewish descent or otherwise anti-Nazi fled their countries, mostly to the UK and the USA. Examples are Albert Einstein, Sigmund

Table 5.3 Key differences between weak and strong uncertainty avoidance societies. II: politics and ideas

Weak uncertainty avoidance	Strong uncertainty avoidance
Few and general laws and rules	Many and precise laws and rules
If rules cannot be respected, they should be changed	If rules cannot be respected, we are sinners and should repent
Citizen competence versus authorities	Citizen incompetence versus authorities
Citizen protest acceptable	Citizen protest should be repressed
Citizens positive towards institutions	Citizens negative towards institutions
Civil servants positive towards political process	Civil servants negative towards political process
Tolerance, moderation	Conservatism, extremism, law and order
Positive attitudes towards young people	Negative attitudes towards young people
Regionalism, internationalism, attempts at integration of minorities	Nationalism, xenophobia, repression of minorities
Belief in generalists and common sense	Belief in experts and specialization
Many nurses, few doctors	Many doctors, few nurses
One group's truth should not be imposed on others	There is only one Truth and we have it
Human rights: nobody should be persecuted for their beliefs	Religious, political, and ideological fundamentalism and intolerance
In philosophy and science, tendency towards relativism and empiricism	In philosophy and science, tendency towards grand theories
Scientific opponents can be personal friends	Scientific opponents cannot be personal friends

Freud, Karl Popper, Kurt Lewin, and Theodor Adorno. Unintentionally, this 'brain injection' has been very beneficial to the host countries. The younger among the refugees have made substantial contributions to their scientific field in their new country. There has been a lot of synergy between the Middle European taste for theory (rooted in strong uncertainty avoidance) and the Anglo–American sense for empiricism fostered by weak uncertainty avoidance.

Some of the refugees experienced scientific culture shock. Former Frankfurt sociologist Herbert Marcuse, when preaching his critique of modern society in California, met with what he labeled 'repressive tolerance'. This is a nonsensical term because repression and tolerance are mutually exclusive. However, the term reflects Marcuse's embarrassment at trying to provoke and expecting repression in the German style, but meeting with intellectual tolerance American style.

Table 5.3 continues the summary of key differences between weak and strong uncertainty avoidance societies started in Table 5.2, adding issues covered in the last two sections.

The origins of uncertainty avoidance differences

Possible origins of power distance differences were explored in Chapter 2. The grouping of countries suggested that the roots of the differences should go back as far as the Roman Empire 2000 years ago. In East Asia it assumed roots in the even older Chinese Empire. Both empires left a legacy of large power distances.

On uncertainty avoidance we again find the countries with a Romance language together. These heirs of the Roman Empire all score on the strong uncertainty avoidance side. The Chinese-speaking countries Taiwan, Hong Kong, and Singapore score much lower on uncertainty avoidance, as do countries with important minorities of Chinese origin: Thailand, Indonesia, the Philippines, and Malaysia.

The Roman and Chinese Empires were both powerful centralized states, which support a culture pattern in their populations prepared to take orders from the center. The two empires differed, however, in one important respect. The Roman Empire had developed a unique system of codified laws which, in principle, applied to all people with citizen status regardless of origin. The Chinese Empire never knew this concept of law. The main continuous principle of Chinese administration has been described as 'government of man' in contrast to the Roman idea of 'government by law'. Chinese judges were supposed to be guided by broad general principles, like those attributed to Confucius (see Chapter 7).

The contrast between the two intellectual traditions explains the fact that IBM employees from countries with a Roman inheritance score a stronger uncertainty avoidance than their colleagues from countries with a Chinese inheritance. It is another powerful illustration of the deep historical roots of national culture differences. Their long history should make us modest about expectations of fundamental changes in these value differences within our lifetime.

Power distance differences in Chapter 2 were found to be statistically related to geographical latitude, population size, and national wealth. For uncertainty avoidance no such broad relationships could be found, except a weak negative correlation of national wealth with UAI, meaning that on average, weak UAI countries were slightly wealthier than those with strong UAI.

For the wealthy countries only, a strong correlation was found between UAI and economic growth after 1960. This relationship is particular to this period. Nobel Prize laureate Simon Kuznets has calculated economic growth rates for countries since 1865 (Hofstede, 1980, p. 205). Until 1925 no systematic relationship between the UAI scores from the IBM study and Kuznets' figures for economic growth can be found. For the period 1925–1950 the correlation is *negative*, meaning that the weak uncertainty avoidance countries grew faster. This is because the strong uncertainty avoidance countries were more actively belligerent in the Second World War, and their economies suffered badly. Only after 1950 does the relationship reverse. Part of this may be a catching-up operation. All in all, the statistical analysis does not allow us to identify any *general* sources of weak or strong uncertainty avoidance, other than history.

The future of uncertainty avoidance differences
The IBM studies allow a comparison of scores collected around 1968 with those collected around 1972. During this relatively short period scores on the question about job stress had increased in all countries, but most in those which were already highly stressed in 1968, indicating divergence, not convergence among countries. Rule orientation and intent to stay, the other two questions composing the UAI, had not changed systematically.

Earlier in this chapter the correlation was described between IBM uncertainty avoidance scores and the country anxiety factor scores for 1960 developed by Richard Lynn. In a later publication Lynn calculated anxiety scores for different years: 1935, 1950, 1955, 1960, 1965, and 1970. For 1940 and 1945 no data were available because of the Second World War (Hofstede, 1980, p. 356; 1984, p. 239).

Lynn's anxiety scores for 18 countries show an overall high for 1950, shortly after the war, and an overall low for 1965. The five countries with the highest anxiety scores in 1935 were Austria, Finland, Germany, Italy, and Japan: the Second World War Axis powers and two countries which became involved in the war on their side. From 1935 to 1950 all countries defeated or occupied during the Second World War (1939–1945) increased in anxiety level while six out of the nine countries not defeated or occupied decreased. After the overall low of 1965 the anxiety scores for 14 out of the 18 countries increased sharply. The only countries for which the scores decreased from 1965 to 1970 were Finland, France, Japan, and Norway. The 1965–1970 period overlaps partly with the 1968–1972 period for which the IBM data also show an overall increase in stress (and the IBM stress scores are strongly correlated with Lynn's anxiety scores).

Lynn's data from 1935 to 1970 suggest that national anxiety levels fluctuate and that high anxiety levels are associated with wars. It seems a reasonable assumption that a similar wave of anxiety earlier accompanied the First World War and the various wars before it. The process could be as follows: when anxiety levels in a country increase, uncertainty avoidance increases. This is noticeable in intolerance, xenophobia, religious and political fanaticism, and all the other manifestations of uncertainty avoidance described in this chapter. Leadership passes into the hands of fanatics, and these may drive the country towards war. War, of course, involves other countries which did not show the same fanatism, but which will develop increasing anxiety because of the war threat.

In countries experiencing war on their territory the anxiety mounts further as the war rages on. After the war the stress is released, first for the countries not directly touched, some years later for the others which start reconstructing. Anxiety decreases and tolerance increases, but after a number of years the trend is reversed and a new wave of anxiety sets in which could be the prelude of a new war. Very likely, economic processes also play a role; countries doing well economically are less likely to foster increased anxiety than countries severely beaten in international competition or caught in heavy indebtedness.

Since about 1968 we have watched such a new wave of anxiety manifested in forms of uncertainty avoidance like fundamentalism and xenophobia. Unlike earlier waves, however, this one is not likely to be associated with a new world war because this would evidently destroy the entire world civilization, even if some would-be leaders might be sufficiently paranoid to try engaging in it. Instead of one world conflict there is a series of regional conflicts: the Lebanon, Northern Ireland, Salvador, Afghanistan, Kampuchea, Sudan, Angola, and Sri Lanka.

The global anxiety level has probably mounted during the 1970s. Since the mid-1980s there have been signs of détente in some parts of the world, along with signs of continuing fanaticism in others. The future will show whether humanity can find ways to release its anxiety waves without destroying itself.

Notes

1   Personal communication.
2   The term first appeared in Cyert and March (1963, p. 118ff).
3   (Stoetzel, 1983, pp. 178, 195. In English: Harding and Phillips, 1986) The Spearman rank order coefficients are: UAI and Bradburn score -0.69, significant at the 0.05 level; UAI and health -0.78, significant at the 0.01 level.
4   Personal communication.
5   (Stoetzel, 1983, p. 265) Spearman rank order correlation coefficient between UAI and positive feelings about the family -0.79, significant at the 0.01 level.
6   See for example the works of Pierre Bourdieu cited in Chapters 1 and 2.
7   A more extensive description of cultural differences at school can be found in Hofstede (1986).
8   The 1950 ranking of countries does not show any correlation with any of the IBM indexes, *nor* with the 1925 ranking of the same countries. A plausible explanation is that the more traditional 1925 stories were more like the anthropologists' folk tales which McClelland sought to match. In 1950, after the Second World War, international communication had increased dramatically. This affected among other things ideas about modern education. Children's books produced in this period were more likely to reveal the ideas of innovative educators and less of the old traditions. So the equivalents of folk tale themes are more likely to be found in the 1925 stories than in the 1950 ones.
9   (Hofstede, 1980, pp. 170–171, 194, 196–197, 287–288, 303–304; 1984, pp. 126–128, 198–199) The Spearman rank correlation coefficient between UAI and McClelland's need for achievement scores for 1950 is -0.64, significant at the 0.001 level; the multiple correlation coefficient of need for achievement with UAI and MAS is 0.73.
10   (Stoetzel, 1983, pp. 267, 288) Spearman rank correlation coefficient between UAI and work satisfaction -0.81, significant at the 0.001 level; between UAI and the ratio of work satisfaction managers/nonmanagers 0.78, significant at the 0.01 level.
11   Japan, a strong uncertainty avoidance country, does not fit this classification, as it has few formal laws and rules by Western standards. Japanese society is more collectivist than Western societies and therefore 'high context' in Hall's terms: rules are implicit and informal rather than formal. Japan's informal rules are very rigid. When in the nineteenth century Japan started to modernize and needed a law code, it chose the German legal system as its example. About Japan see also Fig. 5.2 and Chapter 7.
12   (Stoetzel, 1983, p. 66) The Spearman rank order correlation coefficient is -0.66, significant at the 0.05 level.
13   (Hofstede, 1980, pp. 180–181, 207–208; 1984, pp. 136–137) Across 15 developed countries the number of nurses per doctor in 1971 and UAI show a product moment correlation coefficient of -0.80, significant at the 0.001 level. In Hofstede (1987a) I have used nurses per doctor ratios for 44 rich *and* poor countries, based on the 1984 World Development Report. These show a Spearman rank correlation coefficient with UAI of -0.40, significant at the 0.001 level.
14   Dutch journalist Paul Schnabel in *NRC Handelsblad*, December 23, 1989.
15   According to the American author on mythology, Joseph Campbell, religion is rooted in science. The present world religions reflect the state of science at the time they were founded, thousands of years ago. See Campbell (1988, p. 90).
16   Deduction: reasoning from a known principle to a logical conclusion. Induction: reaching a general conclusion by inference from particular facts.

6

Pyramids, machines, markets, and families

Somewhere in Western Europe a middle-sized textile printing company struggled for survival. Cloth, usually imported from Asian countries, was printed in multicolored patterns according to the desires of customers, firms producing fashion clothing for the local market. The company was run by a general manager to whom three functional managers reported: one for design and sales, one for manufacturing, and one for finance and personnel. The total work force numbered about 250.

The working climate in the firm was often disturbed by conflicts between the sales and manufacturing managers. The manufacturing manager had an interest, as manufacturing managers have the world over, in smooth production and in minimizing product changes. He preferred grouping customer orders into large batches. Changing color and/or design implied cleaning the machines which took productive time away and also wasted costly dyestuffs. The worst was changing from a dark color set to a light one, because every bit of dark-colored dye left would show on the cloth and spoil the product quality. Therefore the manufacturing planners tried to start on a clean machine with the lightest shades and gradually move towards darker ones, postponing the need for an overall cleaning round as long as possible.

The design and sales manager tried to satisfy his customers in a highly competitive market. These customers, fashion clothing firms, were notorious for short-term planning changes. As their supplier, the printing company often received requests for rush orders. Even when these orders were small and unlikely to be profitable the sales manager hated to say 'no'. The customer might go to a competitor and then the printing firm would miss that big order which the sales manager was sure would come afterwards. The rush orders, however, usually upset the manufacturing manager's schedules and forced him to print short runs of dark color sets on a beautifully clean machine, thus forcing the production operators to start cleaning all over again.

There were frequent hassles between the two managers over whether a certain rush order should or should not be taken into production. The conflict was not limited to the department heads; production personnel publicly expressed doubts about the competence of the sales people and vice versa. In the cafeteria, production and sales people would not sit together, although they had known each other for years.

Implicit models of organizations

This story describes a quite banal problem of a kind which occurs regularly in all kinds of organizations. Like most organizational problems, it has both structural and human aspects. The people involved react according to their mental software. Part of this mental software consists of people's ideas about what an organization should be like.

From the four dimensions of national culture described in the Chapters 2 through 5, power distance and uncertainty avoidance in particular affect our thinking about organizations. Organizing always demands the answering of two questions: (1) who has the power to decide what? and (2) what rules or procedures will be followed to attain the desired ends? The answer to the first question is influenced by cultural norms of power distance; the answer to the second question, by cultural norms about uncertainty avoidance. The remaining two dimensions, individualism and masculinity, affect our thinking about people in organizations, rather than about organizations themselves.

Power distance and uncertainty avoidance have been plotted against each other in Fig. 6.1 and if the above analysis is correct, the position of a country in this diagram should tell us something about the way to solve organizational problems in that country.

There is empirical evidence for the relationship between a country's position within the PDI–UAI matrix, and models of organizations implicit in the minds of people from those countries which affect the way problems are tackled. In the 1970s Owen James Stevens, an American professor at INSEAD business school in Fontainebleau, France, used as an examination assignment for his organizational behavior course a case study very similar to the one presented at the beginning of this chapter. This case, too, dealt with a conflict between two department heads within a company. Among the INSEAD MBA (Master of Business Administration) students taking the exam, the three largest national contingents were French, German, and British. In Fig. 6.1 we find their countries in the lower right, lower left, and upper left quadrants, respectively.

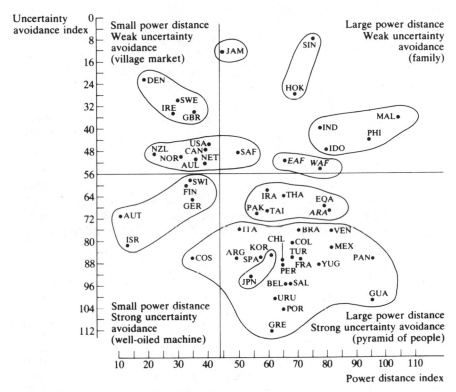

Fig. 6.1   The position of 50 countries and 3 regions on the power distance and uncertainty avoidance dimensions (for country name abbreviations see Table 3-2)

Stevens had noticed earlier that the students' nationality seemed to affect their way of handling this case. He had kept a file of the examination work of about 200 students, in which, with regard to the case in question, the students had written down, individually (1) their diagnosis of the problem and (2) their suggested solution. Stevens had sorted these exams by the nationality of the author, and he went separately through all French, all German, and all British answers.

The results were striking. The French in majority diagnosed the case as negligence by the general manager to whom the two department heads reported. The solution preferred by the French was for the opponents to take the conflict to their common boss, who would issue orders for settling such dilemmas in the future. Stevens interpreted the implicit organization model of the French as a 'pyramid of people': the general manager at the top of the pyramid, and each successive level at its proper place below.

The majority of the Germans diagnosed the case as a lack of structure. The competence of the two conflicting department heads had never been clearly laid down. The solution preferred by the Germans was the establishment of procedures. Ways to develop these could be calling in a consultant, nominating a task force, or asking the common boss. The Germans, Stevens felt, saw an organization ideally as a 'well-oiled machine' in which management intervention is limited to exceptional cases because the rules should settle all daily problems.

The majority of the British diagnosed the case as a human relations problem. The two department heads were poor negotiators, and their skills in this respect should be developed by sending them on a management course, preferably together. 'Transactional analysis' had not yet been invented at that time, but it would be a good term to describe the kind of training recommended. The implicit model of an organization in the minds of the British, Stevens thought, was a 'village market' in which neither hierarchy nor rules, but the demands of the situation, determine what will happen.

Stevens' experience happened to coincide with the discovery, in the context of the IBM research project, of power distance and uncertainty avoidance as dimensions of country cultures. These two dimensions resembled those found a few years earlier through a piece of academic research commonly known as the 'Aston Studies'. From 1961 through 1973 the University of Aston in Birmingham, UK, hosted an 'Industrial Administration Research Unit'. Among the researchers involved were Derek S. Pugh, David J. Hickson, Roy L. Payne, Diana C. Pheysey, and John Child (see Pugh and Hickson, 1976). The Aston Studies represented a large-scale attempt to assess quantitatively, that is to measure, key aspects of the structure of different organizations. At first the research was limited to the UK, but later it was replicated in a number of other countries. The principal conclusion from the Aston Studies was that the two major dimensions along which structures of organizations differ are 'concentration of authority' and 'structuring of activities'. It did not take much imagination to associate the first with power distance, and the second with uncertainty avoidance.

The Aston researchers had tried to measure the 'hard' aspects of organizational structure: objectively assessable characteristics. Power distance and uncertainty avoidance indices measure soft, *subjective* characteristics of the people within a country. A link between the two would mean that organizations are structured in order to meet the subjective cultural needs of their members. Stevens' implicit models of organization in fact provided the proof. French INSEAD MBA students with their 'pyramid of people' model, coming from a country with large power distance *and* strong uncertainty avoidance, advocated measures to concentrate the authority *and* structure the activities. Germans with their 'well-oiled machine' model, coming from a country with strong uncertainty avoidance but small power distance, wanted to structure the activities *without* concentrating the authority. British INSEAD MBA students with a 'village market' model and a national culture characterized by small power distance and weak uncertainty avoidance, advocated neither concentrating authority nor structuring activities—and all of them were dealing with the same case study. People with international business experience have confirmed many times over that, other things being equal, French organizations *do* concentrate authority more, German ones *do* need more structure, and people in British ones *do* believe more in resolving problems *ad hoc*.

Stevens' three implicit models leave one quadrant in Fig. 6.1 unexplained. The upper right-hand corner contains no European countries, only Asian and African ones. People from these countries were rare at INSEAD, so that there were insufficient data from this group. A discussion of Stevens' models with Indian and Indonesian colleagues led to the suggestion that the equivalent implicit model of an organization in these countries is the (extended) 'family', in which the owner–manager is the omnipotent (grand)-father. It corresponds to large power distance but weak uncertainty avoidance, a situation in which people would resolve the conflict described by permanent referral to the boss: concentration of authority without structuring of activities. Negandhi and Prasad, two Americans originally from India, quote a senior Indian executive with a Ph.D from a prestigious American university:

> 'What is most important for me and my department is not what I do or achieve for the company, but whether the Master's favor is bestowed on me. . . . This I have achieved by saying "yes" to everything the Master says or does. . . . To contradict him is to look for another job. . . . I left my freedom of thought in Boston.'
> (Negandhi and Prasad, 1971, p. 128).

Clashes between organizational models

Chapter 2 opened with the story of the French general Bernadotte's culture shock after he became King of Sweden. Recently a French cosmetics company sent a Frenchman to Copenhagen as its regional sales manager for the four Nordic countries Denmark, Sweden, Norway, and Finland. Monsieur Dupont's culture shock started on his very first day in office. He called his secretary and gave her an order in the same way as he had always done in Paris. But instead of saying '*Oui, Monsieur*' as Parisian secretaries are supposed to do the Danish lady looked at him, smiled, and said 'Why do you want this to be done?'[1] A market model of the organization clashed with a pyramid model.

The models of organizations in people's minds also vary within countries. In whatever country, banks will function more like pyramids, post offices like machines, advertising agencies like markets, and orchestras like (autocratically led) families. We expect such differences, but when we cross national borders we run into differences in organizational models that were not expected. Potential victims of such pitfalls are:

- The individual tourist, migrant, or refugee trying to find his or her way in a foreign country's bureaucracy.
- The business firm or government agency trying to establish trade relationships abroad.
- The company involved in a merger, takeover, or joint venture with a partner from another country.

A considerable part of the failure of development assistance projects carried out by engineers from developed countries in the Third World is because of unrecognized organizational model differences. Take the story of a German engineering firm installing an irrigation system in an African country. Overcoming great technical difficulties, the engineers constructed an effective and easy-to-operate system. They provided all the necessary documentation for later use and repairs, translated into English and Swahili. Then they left. Four months later the system broke down and was never repaired. The local authority structure had not had an opportunity to adopt the project as its family property; it had no local 'master'.

Asian and African foreign students, migrants, and refugees often have great practical and emotional problems in understanding the impersonal, machine-like bureaucracies of Western countries. A Moroccan worker in the Netherlands was helped by a post office employee in filling out a customs declaration for sending a parcel home. Thankful, the Moroccan returned the next day with a present. The employee, visibly shocked, refused the present; the office rules would classify this as bribery. The Moroccan in turn felt insulted by the refusal of his friendly gesture.

Mergers, takeovers, and joint ventures across national borders are increasing. Decisions on mergers are usually made from a financial point of view only: mergers are part of a big money power game and seen as a defense against (real or imaginary) threats by competitors. Those making the decision rarely imagine the operating problems which arise inside the newly formed hybrid organizations. Mergers and takeovers within countries have a dubious success record, but cross-national ventures are even less likely to succeed (this will be discussed further in Chapters 8 and 9). Hidden differences in implicit organizational models are a main cause. In the new, integrated organization, the parts have to function in harmony, but how can this be if the key players have different mental models of what an organization should be?

Experience has shown that differences in power distance are more manageable than differences in uncertainty avoidance. In particular, organizations headquartered in smaller power distance cultures usually succeed in larger power distance countries. Local managers can adopt more authoritative management attitudes in the subsidiaries even if their international bosses behave in a more participative fashion.

Organizations headquartered in larger power distance cultures have more problems functioning in smaller power distance cultures. Even between headquarters in medium power distance USA and subsidiaries in countries with very low power distance, like Denmark and Sweden, problems often arise because US top managers feel uncomfortable with what they experience as a lack of respect for basic managerial prerogatives.

Countries with large power distance cultures have rarely produced large multinationals; multinational operations do not permit the centralization of authority without which managers at headquarters in these countries feel too uncomfortable.

Differences in uncertainty avoidance represent a serious problem in international ventures, whichever way they go. This is because if rules mean different things in different countries, it is difficult to keep the venture together. In weak uncertainty avoidance cultures, like the USA and even more in the UK and, for example, Sweden, managers and nonmanagers alike feel definitely uncomfortable with systems of rigid rules, especially if it is evident that many of these are never followed. In strong uncertainty avoidance cultures, like most of the Latin world, people feel equally uncomfortable without the structure of a system of rules, even if many of these are impractical and impracticable. At either pole of the uncertainty avoidance dimension people's feelings are fed by deep psychological needs, related to the control of aggression and to basic security in the face of the unknown (see Chapter 5).

The integration of national markets in the European Community increases the number of cross-national ventures among member countries. EC countries, from Denmark to Portugal, differ primarily along the upper-left to lower-right diagonal in Fig. 6.1: from small power distance, weak uncertainty avoidance to large power distance, strong uncertainty avoidance. But on this diagonal the differences among them are very considerable, and about as large as could be found anywhere in the world. Intra-EC cooperation is therefore rife with cultural problems; the EC can be considered the biggest laboratory in intercultural cooperation of today's world.

Keeping an international venture together demands flexibility in the use of different degrees of and bases for coordination in different countries. Most top managements, however, are not too fond of such cultural opportunism. If it is at all acceptable, then it is more so in headquarters cultures which themselves support weak uncertainty avoidance.

Cross-national mergers and takeovers have often turned out to be dramatic failures. Leyland–Innocenti, Chrysler UK, Imperial Typewriters, Vereinigte Flugzeugwerke–Fokker, Hoogovens–Hoesch, Citroen–Fiat are just a few of the more notorious ones. There is little doubt that the list will continue growing as long as management decisions about international ventures are based solely on financial considerations. Cultural aspects should at least carry equal weight. Even if cultural factors look favorable the cultural integration of the new cooperative structure should be managed; it does not happen by itself. Cultural integration takes time, energy, and lots of money unforeseen by the financial experts who designed the venture.

In Chapter 9 problems of and solutions to intercultural encounters in international business will be analyzed at greater length.

Management professors are human

Not only organizations are culture bound; theories about organizations are equally culture bound. The professors who wrote the theories are children of a culture: they grew up in families, went to schools, worked for employers. Their experiences represent the material on which their thinking and writing have been based. Scholars are as human and as culturally biased as other mortals.

For each of the four corners of Fig. 6.1 I selected a classical author who described organizations in terms of the model belonging to his corner of the diagram: the pyramid, the machine, the market, or the family. The four are approximate contemporaries; all were born in the mid-nineteenth century.

Henri Fayol (1841–1925) was a French engineer whose management career culminated in the position of *président-directeur-général* of a mining company. After his retirement he formulated his experiences in a pathbreaking text on organization: *Administration industrielle et générale*. On the issue of the exercise of authority Fayol wrote:

> 'We distinguish in a manager his *statutory* authority which is in the office, and his *personal* authority which consists of his intelligence, his knowledge, his experience, his moral value, his leadership, his service record, etc. For a good manager, personal authority is the indispensable complement to statutory authority.'[2]

In Fayol's conception the authority is both in the person *and* in the rules (the statute). We recognize the model of the organization as a pyramid of people with both personal power *and* formal rules as principles of coordination.

Max Weber (1864–1920) was a German academic with a university training in law and some years' experience as a civil servant. He became a professor of economics and a founder of German sociology. Weber quotes a seventeenth-century Puritan Protestant Christian textbook about: '. . . the sinfulness of the belief in authority, which is only permissible in the form of an impersonal authority.' (Weber, 1976, p. 224).

In his own design for an organization Weber describes the *bureaucracy*. The word was originally a joke, a classical Greek ending grafted onto a modern French stem. Nowadays it has a distinctly negative connotation, but to Weber it represented the ideal type for any large organization. About the authority in a bureaucracy Weber wrote:

> 'The authority to give the commands required for the discharge of (the assigned) duties should be exercised in a stable way. It is strictly delimited by rules concerning the coercive means ... which may be placed at the disposal of officials.'[3]

In Weber's conception the real authority is in the rules. The power of the 'officials' is strictly delimited by these rules. We recognize the model of the organization as a well-oiled machine which runs according to the rules.

Frederick Winslow Taylor (1856–1915) was an American engineer who, contrary to Fayol, had started his career in industry as a worker. He attained his academic qualifications through evening studies. From chief engineer in a steel company he became one of the first management consultants. Taylor was not really concerned with the issue of authority at all; his focus was on efficiency. He proposed to split the task of the first-line boss into eight specialisms, each exercised by a different person. Thus, each worker would have eight bosses, each with a different competence. This part of Taylor's ideas was never completely implemented, although we find elements of it in the modern 'matrix organization' in which an employee has two (or even three) bosses, usually one concerned with productivity and one with technical expertise.

Taylor's book *Shop Management* (1903) appeared in a French translation in 1913, and Fayol read it and devoted six full pages from his own 1916 book to Taylor's ideas. Fayol shows himself generally impressed but shocked by Taylor's 'denial of the principle of the Unity of Command' in the case of the eight-boss system. 'For my part,' Fayol writes, 'I do not believe that a department could operate in flagrant violation of the Unity of Command principle. Still, Taylor has been a successful manager of large organizations. How can we explain this contradiction?' (Fayol, 1970, p. 85). Fayol's rhetorical question had been answered by his compatriot Blaise Pascal two and a half centuries earlier: there are truths in one country which are falsehoods in another ('*Vérité en-deça des Pyrenées, erreur au-delà*').

In a 1981 article André Laurent, another of Fayol's compatriots, demonstrated that French managers in a survey reacted very strongly against a suggestion that one employee could report to two different bosses, while for example Swedish and US managers in the same survey showed fewer misgivings in this respect (Laurent, 1981). Matrix organization has never become as popular in France as it has in the USA. It is amusing to read Laurent's suggestion that in order to make matrix organizations acceptable in France they should be translated into hierarchical terms, i.e., one real boss plus one or more staff experts. Exactly the same solution was put forward by Fayol in his 1916 discussion of the Taylor system; in fact, Fayol wrote that he supposed this was how the Taylor system really worked in Taylor's companies.

Whereas Taylor dealt only implicitly with the exercise of authority in organizations, another American pioneer of organization theory, Mary Parker Follett (1868–1933), did address the issue squarely. She wrote:

> 'How can we avoid the two extremes: too great bossism in giving orders, and practically no orders given? . . . My solution is to depersonalize the giving of orders, to unite all concerned in a study of the situation, to discover the law of the situation and to obey that . . . One *person* should not give orders to another *person*, but both should agree to take their orders from the situation.'
> (Metcalf and Urwick, 1940, pp. 58–59).

In the concepts of Taylor and Follett the authority is neither in the person nor in the rules, but, as Follett puts it, in the situation. We recognize the model of the organization as a market, in which market conditions dictate what will happen.

Sun Yat-sen (1866–1925) was a scholar from the fourth corner of the power distance–uncertainty avoidance diagram, from China. He received a Western education in Hawaii and Hong Kong and became a political revolutionary. As China began industrialization much later than the West there is no indigenous theorist of industrial organization contemporary with Fayol, Weber, and Taylor. However, Sun was concerned with organization, albeit political. He wanted to replace the ailing government of the Manchu emperors by a modern Chinese state. He eventually became, for a short period, nominally the first President of the Chinese Republic. Sun's design for a Chinese form of government represents an integration of Western and traditional Chinese elements. From the West, he introduced the *Trias Politica*: the executive, legislative, and judicial branches. However, unlike in the West, all three are placed under the authority of the President. Two more branches are added, both derived from Chinese tradition and bringing the total up to five: the examination branch (determining access to the civil service) and the control branch, supposed to audit the government.

This remarkable mix of two systems is formally the basis of the present government structure of Taiwan, which has inherited Sun's ideas through the Kuomintang party. It stresses the authority of the President (large power distance): the legislative and judicial powers which in the West are meant to guarantee government by law are made dependent on the ruler and paralleled by the examination and control powers which are based on government of man (weak uncertainty avoidance). It is the family model with the ruler as the country's father and whatever structure there is, based on personal relationships.

Paradoxically in the other China which expelled the Kuomintang, the People's Republic, the Cultural Revolution experiment can also be interpreted as an attempt to maintain the authority of the ruler (in this case Chairman Mao) while rejecting the authority of the rules which were felt to suffocate the modernization of the minds. The Cultural Revolution is now publicly recognized as a disaster. What passed for modernization may in fact have been a revival of centuries-old unconscious fears.

Some countries with a Chinese inheritance, like Singapore and Hong Kong from the upper right-hand corner of the power distance–uncertainty avoidance diagram, have been doing very well in modernizing themselves. This cannot be explained from their implicit organizational models in Fig. 6.1. Chapter 7 will show evidence that it has something to do with the inheritance of Confucian values and explain how some of these have supported the modernization of East Asian countries.

In the previous paragraphs the models of organization in different cultures have been related to the theories of the founding fathers (including one founding mother) of organization theory. The different models can also be recognized in today's theories.

In the USA in the 1970s and 1980s it became fashionable to look at organizations from the point of view of 'transaction costs'. Economist Oliver Williamson (1975) opposed 'hierarchies' to 'markets'. The reasoning is that human social life consists of economic transactions between individuals. These individuals will form hierarchical organizations when the cost of the economic transactions (such as getting information, finding out whom to trust, etc.) is lower in a hierarchy than when all transactions would take place on a free market. What is interesting about this theory from a cultural point of view is that *the 'market' is the point of departure or base model*, and the organization is explained from market failure. A culture that produces such a theory is likely to prefer organizations that internally resemble markets to organizations that internally resemble more structured models, like pyramids. The ideal principle of control in organizations in the market philosophy is *competition* between individuals.

Williamson's compatriot and colleague William Ouchi (1980) has suggested *two* alternatives to markets: 'bureaucracies' and 'clans'; they come close to what this chapter calls the 'machine' and the 'family' model, respectively. If we take Williamson's and Ouchi's ideas together, we find all four organizational models described. The market, however, takes a special position as the theory's starting point, and this can be explained by the nationality of the authors.

In the work of both German and French organization theorists markets play a very modest role. German books tend to focus on formal systems—on the running of the machine. The ideal principle of control in organizations is a system of *formal rules* on which everybody can rely. French books usually stress the exercise of power and sometimes the defenses of the individual against being crushed by the pyramid (Kieser and Kubicek, 1983; Crozier and Friedberg, 1977; Pagès *et al.*, 1979). The principle of control is *hierarchical authority*; there is a system of rules, but contrary to the German case the personal authority of a superior prevails over the rules.

In China, in the days of Mao and the Cultural Revolution, neither markets nor rules nor hierarchy, but *indoctrination* was the attempted principle of control in organizations, in line with a national tradition that for centuries used comparative examinations as a test of adequate indoctrination. Political developments in 1989 showed this principle still to be popular with Chinese leaders.

Culture and organizational structure: elaborating on Mintzberg

Henry Mintzberg from Canada is one of today's most popular authors on organizational structure, at least in the English-speaking world. His achievement has been to summarize the academic state of the art into a small number of concepts, highly practical and easy to understand.

To Mintzberg, all good things in organizations come in fives.[4] Organizations in general contain up to five distinct parts:

1. The operating core (the people who do the work)
2. The strategic apex (the top management)
3. The middle line (the hierarchy in between)
4. The technostructure (people in staff roles supplying ideas)
5. The support staff (people in staff roles supplying services)

Organizations in general use one or more of five mechanisms for coordinating activities:

1. Mutual adjustment (of people through informal communication)
2. Direct supervision (by a hierarchical superior)
3. Standardization of work processes (specifying the contents of work)
4. Standardization of outputs (specifying the desired results)
5. Standardization of skills (specifying the training required to perform the work)

Most organizations show one of five typical configurations:

1. The simple structure. In this case, the key part is the strategic apex, and the coordinating mechanism is direct supervision.
2. The machine bureaucracy. Key part: the technostructure. Coordinating mechanism: standardization of work processes.
3. The professional bureaucracy. Key part: the operating core. Coordinating mechanism: standardization of skills.
4. The divisionalized form. Key part: the middle line. Coordinating mechanism: standardization of outputs.
5. The Adhocracy. Key part: the support staff (sometimes with the operating core). Coordinating mechanism: mutual adjustment.

Mintzberg, in his publications up till now, has not introduced the factor national culture in his typologies. He does recognize, however, that values play a role in the choice of coordinating mechanisms. For example, about formalization of behavior within organizations (a part of the standardization of work processes) he has written:

> 'Organizations formalize behavior to reduce its variability, ultimately to predict and control it . . . to coordinate activities . . . to ensure the machinelike consistency that leads to efficient production . . . to ensure fairness to clients . . . Organizations formalize behavior for other reasons as well, of more questionable validity. Formalization may, for example, reflect an arbitrary desire for order. . . . The highly formalized structure is above all the neat one; it warms the heart of people who like to see things orderly . . .' (Mintzberg, 1983, pp. 34–35).

Mintzberg's comment obviously represents his own values choice. The IBM research has demonstrated to what extent values about the desirability of centralization (reflected in power distance) and formalization (reflected in uncertainty avoidance) affect the implicit models of organizations in people's minds; and to what extent these models differ from one country to another. This suggests that it should be possible to link Mintzberg's typology of organizational configurations to national culture profiles based on the IBM data. The link means that, other factors being equal, people from a particular national background will prefer a particular configuration because it fits their implicit model, and that otherwise similar organizations in different countries will resemble different Mintzberg configuration types because of different cultural preferences.

The link between Mintzberg's five configurations and the quadrants of the power distance–uncertainty avoidance diagram is easy to make; it is presented in Fig. 6.2.

Mintzberg uses the term 'machine' in a different sense than Stevens and I do: in his 'machine bureaucracy' Mintzberg stresses the role of the technostructure, that is the higher educated specialists, but not the role of the highly trained workers who belong to his 'operating core'. Therefore Mintzberg's machine bureaucracy does not correspond with Stevens' 'machine' but with his 'pyramid'. In order to avoid confusion, I have in Fig. 6.2 renamed it 'full bureaucracy'. This is the term used for a very similar configuration in the Aston studies.[5]

The adhocracy corresponds with the 'village market' implicit organization model; the professional bureaucracy with the 'well-oiled machine' model; the full (machine) bureaucracy with the 'pyramid' model; the simple structure with the 'family' model, while the divisionalized form takes a middle position on both culture dimensions, containing elements of all four models. A typical country near the center of the diagram of Fig. 6.2 is the USA where the divisionalized form has been developed and enjoys great popularity.

Figure 6.2 explains a number of national characteristics known from the professional and anecdotal literature about organizations; these are especially clear in the 'preferred coordination mechanisms'. *Mutual adjustment* fits the market model of organizations and the stress on *ad hoc* negotiation in

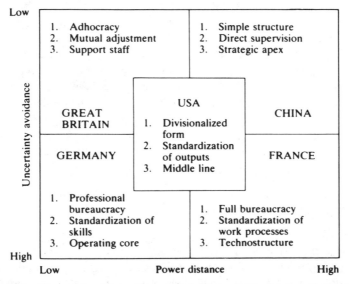

Fig. 6.2 Five preferred configurations of organizations according to Henry Mintzberg projected onto a power distance–uncertainty avoidance matrix with a typical country for each configuration

the Anglo countries. *Standardization of skills* explains the traditional emphasis in countries like Germany and Switzerland on the professional qualification of workers, and the high status in these countries of apprentice systems. *Standardization of work processes* fits the French concept of bureaucracy as it is pictured, for example, by Michel Crozier in his classic *The Bureaucratic Phenomenon* (1964). *Direct supervision* corresponds to what we know about Chinese organizations, also outside mainland China, which emphasize coordination through personal intervention of the owner and his relatives. *Standardization of outputs* is very much the preferred philosophy in the USA, even in cases where outputs are difficult to assess.[6]

Power distance, uncertainty avoidance, and motivation

This chapter has so far described the consequences of different combinations of power distance and uncertainty avoidance for organizations. The power distance–uncertainty avoidance matrix also relates to the motivation of individuals within organizations: why people act as they do. Arguments for the cultural relativity of motivation patterns were put forward earlier in Chapter 3, which dealt with Maslow's hierarchy of human needs, and in Chapter 5, which dealt with McClelland's theory of the achievement motive. This time another popular US theory about work motivation is up for discussion: Frederick Herzberg's 'motivation versus hygiene'. Herzberg *et al.* (1959) published a now classic study, which argues that the work situation contains elements with a positive motivation potential (the real motivators), and elements with a negative potential (the hygiene factors). The motivators are the work itself, achievement, recognition, responsibility, and advancement. These are often labeled the 'intrinsic' elements of the job. The hygiene factors, which have to be present in order to prevent *de*motivation but cannot motivate by themselves, are company policy and administration, supervision, salary, and working conditions: 'extrinsic' elements of the job. Herzberg assumes this distinction to be a universal characteristic of human motivation. It is the *job content* which makes people act, not the job context.

Herzberg's conclusion resembles the quote from his compatriot Mary Parker Follett earlier in this chapter, where she defends that people should seek the law of the situation: 'take their orders from the situation'. Culturally both fit an environment in which power distances are small and uncertainty avoidance is weak: neither dependence on more powerful superiors nor a need for rules are supposed to be functional or necessary for making people act.

Long before Herzberg, the issue of human motivation was raised by Sigmund Freud (1856–1939), one of the founding fathers of present-day psychology. According to Freud we are impelled to act by unconscious forces inside us which he calls our *id*. Our conscious conception of ourselves, our *ego* tries to control these forces. The ego in its turn is influenced by an inner pilot, again unconscious, our *superego*. The superego criticizes the thoughts and acts of the ego and causes feelings of guilt and anxiety when the ego is felt to be giving in to the id. The superego is developed in the young child, mainly by the influence of the parents.

Freud was an Austrian, and conceived his ideas in the Austrian intellectual environment of his day. Austria in the power distance–uncertainty avoidance matrix takes an extreme position in the lower left-hand corner: small power distance but strong uncertainty avoidance. The latter stands for a strong psychological need for rules; the former for psychological independence from a flesh-and-blood boss for enforcing these rules. The superego can be interpreted as an interiorized boss/father, who controls the individual through self-imposed guilt feelings. The superego concept thus reflects a distinct national culture pattern; it could hardly have been invented in, for example, the USA where uncertainty avoidance is weaker. Freud's ideas have been imported into the USA of course, but the international traffic of ideas is always a selective process. The superego has never become a very popular concept among US psychoanalysts, and it has played no role whatsoever in the motivation theories found in US management literature.

In Austria and other countries of the lower left-hand quadrant of the matrix, contrary to Herzberg's theory, rules as part of what Herzberg called 'company policy and administration' should not only be seen as 'hygiene'. Enforced by a superego (or in ordinary language a sense of duty) they can be real motivators in these countries.

In a similar way in the two right-hand quadrants of the matrix 'supervision' should not be seen as a hygienic factor. In these countries with large power distances, dependence on more powerful people is a basic need which can be a real motivator. In the lower right-hand quadrant, incorporating most Latin countries, the motivator could be labeled the *boss* in the sense of the formally appointed superior. At INSEAD business school in Fontainebleau (where Stevens did his analysis reported earlier in this chapter), leaderless discussion groups composed entirely of Frenchmen were known to often lose their time in internal fights for leadership at the expense of productivity, unlike groups of German or British students and also unlike internationally mixed groups.

In the upper right-hand corner, where we find Asian and African countries, the motivator should rather be labeled the *master*. He differs from the 'boss' in that his power is based on tradition and charisma more than on formal position.

All in all, this section has argued that Herzberg's theory, like the other US theories of motivation considered in previous chapters, is culturally constrained, and reflects the culture of (perhaps a part of?) the US environment in which its author grew up and did his research.

The culture of accounting systems

Not only managers and management professors but even accountants are human; moreover, they play a particular role in the culture of a society. Accounting and management control systems are manifestations of culture and reflect basic cultural assumptions. These have not been extensively studied, and this section is therefore based on impressions and conjectures.[7] In the English-speaking world there is an area of academic research called 'behavioral accounting' but in accordance with American individualism it usually focuses on the behaviors of individuals and small groups, and not so much on the cultural context in which accounting takes place.[8]

In Chapter 1 culture was shown to be manifested in the form of symbols, heroes, rituals, and values. Accounting is said to be the language of business: this means that accounting is the handling of *symbols* which have meaning to the initiated in business only. At the level of symbols one also finds money. Money has neither an intrinsic value, nor an intrinsic meaning, other than that which is attributed to it by convention. It also means different things to different people. For example, it means something else in the culture of accountants than in the culture of bankers. There is a national component to the meaning of money: in Chapter 4 the importance of money was associated with masculinity. In more masculine societies like the USA and Germany, accounting systems stress the achievement of purely financial targets more than in more feminine societies like Sweden or the Netherlands. In more individualist societies like the USA, the system's stress is more on short-term results than in more collectivist societies like Japan or even Germany, as in an individualist environment the responsible people may change employers at short notice.

Accountants are very unlikely to ever become *heroes* in organizations themselves but they have an important role in identifying and anointing heroes elsewhere in the organization, because they determine who are the good or the bad guys. Their major device for this purpose is called 'accountability': holding someone personally responsible for results. As measurable results are more important in masculine societies than in feminine ones, the former's accounting systems are more likely to present results in such a way that a responsible manager is shown either as a hero or as a villain.

From a cultural point of view accounting systems in organizations are best understood as uncertainty-reducing *rituals*, fulfilling a cultural need for certainty, simplicity, and truth in a confusing world, regardless of whether this truth has any objective base. Trevor Gambling from the UK, a professor and former accountant, has written that much of accounting information is after-the-fact justification of decisions that were taken for nonlogical reasons in the first place. The main function of accounting information, according to Gambling (1977, pp. 141–151), is maintaining morale in the face of uncertainty. The accountant 'enables a distinctly demoralized modern industrial society to live with itself, by reassuring that its models and data can pass for truth.'

This explains the lack of consensus across different countries on what represents proper accounting methods. For the USA these are collected in the accountant's holy book called the GAAP guide (Generally Accepted Accounting Principles). Being 'generally accepted' within a certain population is precisely what makes a ritual a ritual. It does not need any other justification. Once you have agreed on the ritual, a lot of problems become technical again, such as how to perform the ritual most effectively. Phenomenologically, accounting practice has a lot in common with religious practice (which also serves to avoid uncertainty). British journalist Graham Cleverley called accountants the 'priests' of business.[9] Sometimes we find explicit links between religious and accounting rules, as in Islam in the Koranic ban on calculating interest.

My own doctoral research dealt with the behavioral consequences of budgeting, and it unwittingly supported the ritual nature of budget accounting. This is remarkable, because the budget process is probably one of the most action-oriented parts of the accounting system. In those days I worked as a production manager in a Dutch textile mill, and I had been struck by the number of behavioral paradoxes when we introduced a budget system: observable behavior which was the opposite of what the system intended.

The main conclusion of the research was captured in the title of a dissertation: *The Game of Budget Control* (Hofstede, 1968). It was based on a field study in five Dutch business companies. It did not refer to rituals or culture but it found that for budget control to have a positive impact on results, it should be played as a game. Games in all human societies are a very specific form of ritual: they are activities carried out for their own sake. Basically the research showed that the proper ritual use of the system was a prime condition for its impact on results. The technical aspects of the system used—the things the professional literature worries most about—did not affect the results very much. The way the game was played gave the system its meaning in the minds of the actors, and this determined the impact. This was a cultural interpretation *avant la lettre*.

If accounting systems are uncertainty avoiding rituals one can expect that a society's score on uncertainty avoidance will strongly affect its accounting practices: more strongly uncertainty avoiding societies will have more precise rules on how to handle different cases; in less strongly uncertainty avoiding societies more will be left to the discretion of the organization or even of the accountant.

Behind the symbols, heroes, and rituals in accounting there are *values*. The less an activity is determined by technical necessity, the more it is ruled by values, and thus influenced by cultural differences. Accounting is a field in which the technical imperatives are weak: historically based conventions are more important to it than laws of nature. So, it is logical for accounting systems and the ways they are used to vary along national cultural lines.

In large power distance countries accounting systems will frequently be used to justify the decisions of the top power holder(s): they are seen as the power holder's tool to present the desired image, and figures will be twisted to this end.

In strong uncertainty avoidance countries, accounting systems will be not only more detailed, as argued above, but also, to a larger extent, theoretically based—pretending to derive from consistent general economic principles. In weak uncertainty avoidance countries, systems will be more pragmatic, *ad hoc*, and folkloristic. In the USA, which scores fairly low on this dimension, tendencies to accept accounting traditions as given have outweighed tendencies to base them on general postulates. In Germany, which scores higher on uncertainty avoidance, annual reports to shareholders are supposed to use the same valuation of the company's assets as is used for fiscal purposes; in the Dutch, British, and US systems, reports to the fisc are a completely different thing from reports to shareholders.

In individualist cultures the information in the accounting system will be taken more seriously and will be considered to be more indispensable than in collectivist ones. The latter, being 'high context' according to Edward Hall, possess many other and more subtle clues to find out about the well-being of organizations and the performance of people, so they rely less on the explicit information produced by the accountants. The accounting profession in such societies is therefore likely to carry lower status; the work of accountants is a ritual without practical impact on decisions.

Multinationals, when going abroad, have to impose universal accounting rules for consolidation purposes. If, as the research at IBM showed, even in this tightly coordinated corporation employees in different countries hold quite different personal values, it is likely that interpretations of accounting rules in the subsidiaries of multinationals will often deviate from what headquarters expect.

Differences between occupational value systems play a role in the communication between accountants and other organization members. US students majoring in accounting were found to attribute higher values to being 'clean' and 'responsible' and lower values to being 'imaginative' than other students, which suggests a self-selection on uncertainty-avoiding values (Baker, 1976). In a Dutch and an international sample, I found that accountants stress the form of information where people in operating roles will stress its content (Hofstede, 1978).

Accountants are also the people who determine the 'value' of the organization's assets. Ways of valuing assets reflect underlying nonrational value systems, such as the fact that machines are considered assets while people are not. Hardware is less uncertain than software.

This section has taken a cultural look at accounting systems because I had the opportunity to study such systems. This does not imply that accounting and accountants represent the only subsystem of organizations which merits being looked at from a cultural point of view. Personnel management systems, information systems, marketing systems, and financial management systems all have their cultural and ritual aspects too.

Notes

[1] Personal communication.

[2] (Fayol, 1970, p. 21) Translation by GH.

[3] (Weber, 1970, p. 196) Translated from *Wirtschaft und Gesellschaft*, 1921, Part III, Ch. 6, p. 650.

[4] (Mintzberg, 1983) This is a simplified version of Mintzberg (1979). In Mintzberg (1989), he has added a 'missionary configuration' with 'standardization of norms'. To me, this is an aspect of the other types rather than a type by itself. It deals with the 'strength' of an organization's culture which will be discussed in Chapter 8.

[5] See note 1 of this chapter and Hofstede (1980, p. 319; 1984, pp. 215–216).

[6] Examples are management by objectives for university professors, and PPBS (Program Planning Budgeting System) for the Federal Government. The latter was introduced in the early 1960s by Secretary of Defense Robert McNamara who came from the Ford Corporation; it is generally considered to have been a dramatic failure.

[7] This section uses parts of Hofstede (1987a, pp. 1–11). Hypotheses for research on the subject have been formulated by Sid J. Gray (1988).

[8] The association between accounting and culture was made in two humorous paperbacks: Cleverley, 1971; Page, 1972. Throughout history court jesters have been allowed to tell truths before the authorities could afford to do so.

[9] See note 8.

7

Virtue versus Truth

Dr Rajendra Pradhan is a Nepalese anthropologist who, in the period 1987–1988, did a 10-month field research project in the Dutch village of Schoonrewoerd. He thus reversed the familiar pattern which is for Western anthropologists to do field research in Eastern villages. Schoonrewoerd is a typical Dutch village in the rural heart of the province of South Holland, with 1500 inhabitants and two churches from different Calvinist Protestant denominations. Dr Pradhan became a regular churchgoer in both, and he established his contacts with the local population predominantly through the congregations. He was often invited to people's homes for coffee after church, and the topic, usually, was religion. He used to explain that his parents respected Hindu rituals, but that he stopped doing this, because it would take him too much time. His Dutch hosts always wanted to know what he *believed*—an exotic question to which he did not have a direct answer. 'Everybody over here talks about believing, believing, believing', he said, bewildered. 'Where I come from, what counts is the ritual, in which only the priest and the head of the family participate. The others watch and make their offerings. Over here so much is *mandatory*. Hindus will never ask "Do you believe in God?" Of course one should believe, but the important thing is what one *does*.'[1]

In an earlier and Europe-centered generation, Rudyard Kipling (1865–1936) wrote his famous poem which starts with 'Oh, East is East and West is West, and never the twain shall meet . . .' Today, of course, the twain do meet, not only in Pradhan's coffee visits but in world trade, technology, and politics. Both Kipling *and* Pradhan, however, suggest that there exist profound differences in thinking between East and West. In a world which can only survive through global cooperation, such differences should be explored and understood. Pradhan's project provides some enlightening insights into differences in handling religious matters between Hinduism and Calvinism. In an entirely different but complementary way, the results

159

of new value survey studies held in the 1980s have illuminated differences between Confucian thinking in the Chinese culture area and Western thinking in general.[2]

Cultural biases in the researchers' minds

The IBM studies, the results of which were described in earlier chapters, used a questionnaire composed by Western minds. The team that first composed it contained British, Dutch, French, Norwegian, and US members. If the arguments within the previous chapters about the cultural relativity of practices *and* theories are taken seriously, then this restrictive Western input into the research instrument should be a matter of concern. When the surveys were administered, not only Western but also non-Western respondents were confronted with Western questions. They dutifully answered them, but could the results really be supposed to express their values to the full? As a consequence of our own research findings, we (the researchers) have worried about this limitation of our instruments.

Almost simultaneously with the results of the IBM studies, the outcome of another cross-cultural values survey was published (Ng *et al.*, 1982, pp. 196–205). A group of academic researchers from nine Asian and Pacific countries administered a modified version of the Rokeach value survey (RVS) to 100 psychology students (50 men, 50 women) in each of 10 national or ethnic groups. The RVS is a well-known instrument developed by US psychologist Milton Rokeach on the basis of an inventory of values in US society around 1970. The IBM and RVS studies did not lead to directly comparable results because their data had been analyzed in quite different ways. One of the Asian researchers, Michael Bond from the Chinese University of Hong Kong, decided to re-analyze the RVS results following the same approach as was used for the IBM data. This re-analysis produced five dimensions in the RVS data. Four of these were each correlated with one of the four IBM values dimensions, across the six countries that were part of both the IBM and the RVS study. The fifth dimension could not be interpreted (Hofstede and Bond, 1984).

The discovery of correlated dimensions in completely different material represented strong support for the basic nature of the factors described in Chapters 2 through 5. With another questionnaire, other respondents (students instead of IBM employees), at another point in time (data collected around 1979 instead of 1970), and a restricted group of countries, four similar dimensions were found. One dilemma was not resolved, however. Both the IBM questionnaire and the RVS were products of Western minds. In both cases, respondents in non-Western countries were asked to answer Western questions. Some of these may have been irrelevant to them, but were answered anyway; other issues more relevant in the non-Western countries than in the West may not have been included.

The standard solution suggested in order to avoid cultural bias in research is *decentering*: a process which involves researchers from different cultures developing research questions out of different cultural environments. In this respect the IBM questionnaire was better than the RVS. The former was at least developed by a five-nationality team, and pre-tested in 10 countries. The latter is a purely American product, although the Asian–Pacific research team had adapted it somewhat by adding four values they felt to be relevant in their countries but missing on the Rokeach list.[3]

The problem about decentered research is the dynamics in the research team. All members are equal, but usually some are more equal than others. There is often a senior researcher, the one who took the initiative, and he (rarely she) is usually from a Western background. Researchers from countries in which prevail values such as respect for the senior guru and harmony within the team will often be almost too eager to follow the magic of the prestigious team leader. This means that the project team will maintain its Western bias even with a predominantly non-Western membership. When the chief researcher comes from a non-Western country he or she often studied in the West and sometimes overadopts Western value positions, becoming 'more Catholic than the Pope'.

Creating a non-Western bias: the Chinese value survey

Michael Bond, himself a Canadian but having lived and worked in the Far East since 1971, found a creative solution to the Western bias problem. He had a questionnaire designed with a deliberate non-Western bias, in this case a Chinese culture bias, which he used in the same way as Western questionnaires, so that the results could be compared. Bond asked a number of Chinese social scientists from Hong Kong and Taiwan to prepare in Chinese a list of at least 10 basic values for Chinese people. Through the elimination of overlap and, on the other side, adding some values which from his reading of Chinese philosophers and social scientists seemed to be similarly important, he arrived at a questionnaire of 40 items—the same number as in the previously used RVS. The new questionnaire was called the *Chinese value survey* (CVS). Its original Chinese version was translated into English, and through a series of checks by different bilingual persons a Chinese and an English version were prepared which were as close as possible.

Subsequently, the CVS was administered to 100 students (again 50 men, 50 women) in each of 22 countries around the world. After the initial publication of the results, data for (the People's Republic of) China were added, increasing the number of countries covered to 23. The students used the Chinese version, English version, or one of eight other language versions translated, where possible, directly from the Chinese. Respondents were taken from any class level, and from as wide a range of undergraduate majors as possible, within institutions of higher learning with relatively high admission standards according to the local rating. To a Western mind some of the items seemed strange, such as 'filial piety' (which was explained as 'honoring of ancestors and obedience to, respect for, and financial support of parents'). Of course, to the Chinese mind some of the items on the RVS or IBM questionnaire may have seemed equally unusual.

A statistical analysis of the CVS results from the 23 countries based, as in the case of the RVS and IBM survey, on the *relative* importance attached in a country to each value as opposed to the other values, again yielded four dimensions. Twenty out of the 23 countries had been covered in both the CVS and the IBM studies. For these 20 overlapping countries the scores on the CVS and IBM dimensions could be compared by correlation. The findings were striking. One CVS dimension was significantly correlated with power distance and collectivism, but somewhat more with power distance. Another CVS dimension was significantly correlated with individualism and also, but somewhat less, with power distance (with a negative sign). A third CVS dimension was significantly correlated with masculinity only. This again in spite of the completely different questions, different populations, different time periods, and different mix of countries.[4]

Few of the items in the CVS have direct equivalents in the IBM questionnaire. If we put the values that compose a CVS dimension next to those within the correlated IBM dimension we are in for some surprises. We should assume that the IBM dimensions represent a Western and the CVS dimensions an Eastern interpretation of common basic value complexes. Within each of these value complexes there is more than either the Western or the Eastern mind will detect by itself.

Large power distance (IBM) stands for a need for dependence on more powerful persons. The correlated CVS factor 'moral discipline' contains the following values:

- having few desires
- moderation, following the middle way
- keeping oneself disinterested and pure

The opposite pole, small power distance, stands for a need for *in*dependence. The corresponding opposite pole of the CVS factor shows the following values:

- adaptability
- prudence (carefulness)

It seems that the questions composed by Western minds have tapped, in particular, the power aspect of this dimension. The Eastern questions show that the inequalities in power go together with different virtues in one's personal life. The person in a large power distance culture should balance status with restraint; the person in a small power distance culture should move around with care.

Individualism (IBM) corresponds with one pole of a CVS dimension 'integration' which is associated with the biggest cluster of CVS values:

- tolerance of others
- harmony with others
- noncompetitiveness
- a close, intimate friend
- trustworthiness
- contentedness with one's position in life
- solidarity with others
- being conservative

The opposite pole, collectivism, is associated with opposite CVS values:

- filial piety (obedience to parents, respect for parents, honoring of ancestors, financial support of parents)
- chastity in women
- patriotism

These associations are more in line with what was already found in the IBM studies. In the individualist society, relationships with others are not obvious and prearranged, they are voluntary and have to be carefully fostered. In the collectivist society there is no need to make specific friendships: who one's friends are, is predetermined by one's group membership. This group membership is maintained by filial piety and chastity in women, and associated with patriotism. In later versions of the questionnaire originally developed for IBM a work goal 'serve your country' was added. This too was found to be strongly associated with collectivism.

Masculinity (IBM) corresponds with a CVS factor 'human-heartedness'. At the masculine pole we find:

- patience
- courtesy
- kindness (forgiveness, compassion)

At the opposite, feminine pole we find:

- patriotism (the same value was also associated with collectivism)
- a sense of righteousness

The IBM dimension at the masculine pole stresses the assertive, materialistic, performance-oriented side of this value complex. The CVS again shows that there are other virtues associated with masculinity. Courtesy reminds us of the chivalrous ideals of the Western medieval knights. Patience and kindness we would rather expect at the feminine pole, but the way of asking in the CVS is very different from the way of asking in the IBM questionnaire. The CVS asks for conscious endorsement of 'values as the desirable' or abstract virtues; the IBM work goals questions on which the masculine–feminine dimension is based asks for 'values as the desired' or personal objectives. The desirable and the desired do not always overlap; one may even compensate for the other. Chinese philosophers have always stressed that the masculine (*yang*) and the feminine (*yin*) elements in life are intertwined; the CVS-dimension 'human-heartedness' seems to support this postulate of Taoism. The feminine pole in the CVS stresses subordination to higher purpose: patriotism and righteousness.

The three dimensions common to the CVS and the IBM studies are those that refer to three types of expected social behavior: towards seniors or juniors, towards the group, and as a function of one's gender. These represent cultural choices so fundamental to any human society that they are found regardless of whether the questions asked were designed by Eastern or by Western minds. They are truly universal human issues in the sense that all societies share the same problems, but different societies have 'chosen' (historically rather than consciously) different answers to these problems.

Confucian dynamism as a fifth dimension
One dimension from the IBM studies is missing in the CVS results. None of the CVS factors is correlated with uncertainty avoidance. In Chapter 5 this dimension was associated among other things with man's search for Truth. It seems that for the Chinese minds which composed the CVS questions related to Truth were not relevant. Remember Rajendra Pradhan's embarrassment, related at the beginning of this chapter, at being asked what he *believed*. Both the Indian and the Chinese minds seem to take a position different from the Western one when it comes to the need for defining Truth.

The analysis of the CVS data revealed in the worldwide answers to the Chinese questions a fourth dimension unrelated to anything found with Western questions. Michael Bond called it 'Confucian dynamism', referring to the teachings of Confucius. In practical terms, it refers to a long-term versus a short-term orientation in life. It deals with values which the Western mind will clearly recognize, but which did not enter the inventory of key issues of the designers of Western questionnaires.

Confucius, whose ideas about inequality were already referred to in Chapter 2, was an intellectual of humble origins in China around 500 BC. He rather unsuccessfully sought to serve various of the local rulers in the divided China of his days. He did however gain a reputation for wit and wisdom, and in his later life was surrounded by a host of disciples who recorded what we know about his teachings. Confucius thus held a position rather similar to Socrates in ancient Greece, who was his virtual contemporary (Socrates lived 80 years later).

Confucius' teachings are lessons in practical ethics without any religious content. Confucianism is not a religion but a set of pragmatic rules for daily life derived from what Confucius saw as the lessons of Chinese history. The following are the key principles of Confucian teaching:

1. *The stability of society is based on unequal relationships between people* The *wu lun*, or five basic relationships already discussed in Chapter 2, are ruler–subject, father–son, older brother–younger brother, husband–wife, and senior friend–junior friend. These relationships are based on mutual and complementary obligations. The junior partner owes the senior respect and obedience. The senior owes the junior partner protection and consideration.

2. *The family is the prototype of all social organizations* A person is not primarily an individual; rather, he or she is a member of a family. Children should learn to restrain themselves, to overcome their individuality so as to maintain the harmony in the family (if only on the surface); one's thoughts remain free. Harmony is found in the maintenance of everybody's *face* in the sense of dignity, self-respect, and prestige. The importance of face in the collectivist family and society was described in Chapter 3. Losing one's dignity in the Chinese tradition is equivalent to losing one's eyes, nose, and mouth. Social relations should be conducted in such a way that everybody's face is maintained. Paying respect to someone is called 'giving face'.

3. *Virtuous behavior towards others consists of not treating others as one would not like to be treated oneself* (the Chinese Golden Rule is negatively phrased!) There is a basic human benevolence towards others, but it does not go as far as the Christian injunction to love one's enemies. Confucius is supposed to have said that if one should love one's enemies, what would remain for one's friends?

4. *Virtue with regard to one's tasks in life consists of trying to acquire skills and education, working hard, not spending more than necessary, being patient, and persevering* Conspicuous consumption is taboo, as is losing one's temper. Moderation is enjoined in all things.

The new dimension, Confucian dynamism, discriminating among the answers of students from 23 countries and first revealed by using the CVS, was composed of the following values: on the pole which could be labeled 'long-term orientation':

- persistence (perseverance)
- ordering relationships by status and observing this order
- thrift
- having a sense of shame

On the opposite pole 'short-term orientation':

- personal steadiness and stability
- protecting your 'face'
- respect for tradition
- reciprocation of greetings, favors, and gifts

Michael Bond chose the qualification 'Confucian' for this dimension because nearly all values, on both poles, seem to be taken straight from the teachings of Confucius. However, the values on the one pole are more oriented towards the future (especially perseverance and thrift); they are more dynamic. The values on the opposite pole are more oriented towards the past and present; they are more static.

Confucius and economic growth

'The second time Duke Ching called Confucius to an audience, he again asked him "What is the secret of good government?" Confucius replied, "Good government consists in being sparing with resources".'   (Kelen, 1983, p. 44)

In Table 7.1 the scores of 23 country student samples on the long-term orientation (LTO) dimension are listed. These scores were obtained in a

Table 7.1   Long-term orientation (LTO) index values for 23 countries

Score rank	Country or region	LTO score
1	China	118
2	Hong Kong	96
3	Taiwan	87
4	Japan	80
5	South Korea	75
6	Brazil	65
7	India	61
8	Thailand	56
9	Singapore	48
10	Netherlands	44
11	Bangladesh	40
12	Sweden	33
13	Poland	32
14	Germany FR	31
15	Australia	31
16	New Zealand	30
17	USA	29
18	Great Britain	25
19	Zimbabwe	25
20	Canada	23
21	Philippines	19
22	Nigeria	16
23	Pakistan	00

0–100 range in the same way as the scores for the IBM survey results in Chapters 2 through 5 (the score for China which exceeds 100 was added after the scale had been fixed). The figures represent *relative* positions of countries, not absolute.

The top five positions in Table 7.1 are taken by East Asian countries: China, Hong Kong, Taiwan, Japan, and South Korea. Singapore is in the ninth position. China, Confucius' homeland, is a case apart. The other five countries are known as the 'Five Dragons' because of their surprisingly fast economic growth over the past decades. Because of this, it should be no surprise that the 'Long Term Orientation' (LTO) Index across all 23 countries is strongly correlated with the economic growth data published by the World Bank for the period 1965–1987.[5]

The correlation between *certain* Confucian values and economic growth over the past decades is a surprising, even a sensational finding. The existence of a relationship between Confucius' teachings and recent economic growth had been suggested before but it had never been proven. One of its defendants was the American futurologist Herman Kahn (1922–1983) who formulated a 'Neo-Confucian hypothesis' (Kahn, 1979). In this he suggested that the recent economic success of the countries of East Asia could be attributed to common cultural roots going far back into history, and that this cultural inheritance under the world market conditions of the post Second World War period has constituted a competitive advantage for successful business activity. The data collected with the CVS prove Kahn right, and also specify *which* Confucian values are associated with economic growth.

A correlation does not yet prove a causal link. Causality could have gone either way, or there could have been a third factor acting as a common cause. Chapter 3 showed that national wealth was associated with individualism index scores, and, based on data from two points in time, causality was shown to have gone *from* wealth *to* individualism. The CVS study only provided data for one point in time. The direction of causality can merely be assumed. The nature of the values involved, however, makes it very likely that these values were the cause and economic growth was the effect, the link between the two being formed by East Asian entrepreneurship. The Chinese and Japanese were known to value thrift and perseverance before the present boom started; their belief in tradition, although still strong, has definitely been weakened by the historical events of the Second World War and the period thereafter.

East Asian entrepreneurship does not seem to be based only on the values of the entrepreneurs themselves. The way the CVS scores were found, by surveying student samples, suggests that the decisive values are held broadly within entire societies, among entrepreneurs and future entrepreneurs, among their employees and their families, and among other members of the society.

The values that together form the 'Confucian dynamism' dimension, long-term versus short-term orientation, will probably puzzle many Western readers. Their amazement is not surprising, because the dimension is composed precisely of elements that Western questionnaires had not registered. A Westerner would not normally find them important.

It is remarkable in itself that 'thrift' and 'perseverance' did not occur in, for example, the Rokeach value survey, which is supposed to have been based on a complete inventory of American values from the 1960s. Spending, not thrift, seems to be a value in the USA, both at individual and government level. The same holds for other Western societies. It applies least, it seems, to the Netherlands; the Dutch are often teased for their stinginess and have been called 'the Chinese of Europe'. Private savings as a share of gross national product in 1988 were reported as about 12 percent for Japan, 8 percent for the Federal Republic of Germany, 4 percent for the UK, and 3 percent for the USA. Herbert Stein, former Chairman of the Council of Economic Advisers of two Republican US presidents, said when asked why Americans do not save more:

> 'Economists have been unable to answer this question. Our savings quote . . . has always been lower than elsewhere . . . It is most likely a reflection of the American lifestyle, although this is no explanation.'[6]

The label 'Confucian' for the dimension could be seen as somewhat misleading. As we saw, *both* opposing poles of the dimension contain Confucian values. Some non-Confucian countries like Brazil and India score also fairly high on the index (Brazil has a sizeable Japanese minority, though). To the Western observer, the East Asian countries seem to be more oriented towards traditions and face than the West, but here the reader should be reminded that the index measures the *relative* value given to one side over the other. If the students in the East value tradition, they value thrift even more. Finally, the argument can be made that a number of very Confucian values are *not* related to the dimension, like 'filial piety' which appeared to be associated with collectivism.

In spite of this disclaimer, the values at the LTO pole are very Confucian *and* support entrepreneurial activity. *Persistence* (perseverance), tenacity in the pursuit of whatever goals, is an essential asset for a beginning entrepreneur. *Ordering relationships by status and observing this order* reflects the Confucian stress on unequal relationship pairs, the *wu lun*. A sense of a harmonious and stable hierarchy and complementarity of roles undoubtedly makes the entrepreneurial role easier to play. *Thrift* leads to savings and the availability of capital for reinvestment by oneself or one's relatives. The value of *having a sense of shame* supports interrelatedness through sensitivity to social contacts and a stress on keeping one's commitments.

At the short-term orientation pole, *personal steadiness and stability*, if overstressed, discourage the initiative, risk seeking, and changeability required of entrepreneurs in quickly changing markets. *Protecting one's face* if exaggerated would detract from pursuing the business at hand. Even if there is, in fact, a lot of face-saving going on in East Asia, the scores show that at the conscious level, the student respondents wanted to de-emphasize it. Too much *respect for tradition* impedes innovation. Part of the secret of the Five Dragons' economic success is the ease with which they have accepted Western technological innovations. In this respect they have been less traditional than many Western countries, and this explains the Dragons' relatively low scores on this value. Finally, *reciprocation of greetings, favors, and gifts* is a social ritual more concerned with good manners than with performance. Again, although definitely still very present in the East Asian countries, it seems to be consciously de-emphasized. In the Western countries which score relatively higher on the short-term and lower on the long-term orientation values, the equivalent of face, tradition, and reciprocation is a sensitivity to social trends in consumption, to 'keeping up with the Joneses', which is put above values like thrift and persistence.

Culture in the form of certain dominant values is a necessary but not a sufficient condition for economic growth. Two other conditions are the existence of a market and a political context that allows development. The need for a market explains why the growth of the Five Dragons started only after 1955 when, for the first time in history, the conditions for a truly global market were fulfilled. The need for a supportive political context was met in all five Dragon countries, but in very different ways, with the role of government varying from active support to *laissez faire*. Labor unions were weak and company oriented in all five countries, and a relatively egalitarian income distribution meant that support for revolutionary social changes was weak. The Confucian sense of moderation affected political life as well, in spite of occasional outbreaks of unrest and violence.

The influence of the political context is evident in the country that was the cradle of Confucianism, mainland China, suitably the top scorer on Confucian dynamism. The economic growth of China was hampered by the violence of the 1966–1976 Cultural Revolution; nevertheless China's average economic growth rate for the 23-year period that includes the Revolution is reported as 5.2 percent, higher than the 4.2 percent of Japan. Of course China started very low. Politics has played a major role in its economic development and will continue to do so. It is obviously immensely more difficult to turn around a nation of 1100 million people than one of 2.6 million like Singapore. The question is whether China's rulers can cope with the domestic political consequences of the country's economic opening towards the rest of the world. The dramatic suppression of student demonstrations at the Square of the Gate of Heavenly Peace in Beijing in June 1989 suggests that political control still prevails over economic modernization. If a solution to this dilemma is found, the mainland Chinese seem to have the mental software to make their country into a sixth and giant Dragon.

Western minds and Eastern minds

The economic success of the Five Dragons of East Asia was predicted by few economists. Even after it happened, many failed for a long time to recognize it. A forecast for the region in the prestigious *American Economic Review* (Chenery and Strout, 1966) did not even include Hong Kong and Singapore because they were considered insignificant; it underrated the performances of Taiwan and South Korea and overrated those of India and Sri Lanka. Fifteen years later Singapore with a population of 2.6 million exported more than India with 700 million.

After the Dragons' economic miracle had become undeniable, economists had no explanation for it. By economic criteria, Colombia for example, should have outperformed South Korea, while the reverse was true.[7] 'Culturists' like Herman Kahn used the Confucian heritage as an explanation, but this was considered speculation. It is remarkable that it took an East Asian instrument—the CVS—to find a true proof of the role of culture in the development of East Asia and an explanation of the economic success of the Five Dragons.

The importance of the cultural origin of the minds behind the questionnaire is a powerful illustration of how fundamental a phenomenon culture really is. It affects not only our daily practices: the way we live, are brought up, manage, are managed, and die; but also the theories we are able to develop to explain our practices. No part of our lives is exempt from culture's influence.

The comparison of the results of the (Western) IBM and RVS studies versus the (Eastern) CVS showed that three dimensions dealing with basic human relationships seem to be so universal that they somehow show up in whatever multicountry value study we do. These are the equivalents of the power distance, individualism–collectivism, and masculinity–femininity dimensions in the IBM study. A fourth dimension can be found, but its nature depends on the culture of the designers of the questionnaire. With the Western-made questionnaires (IBM and RVS) a dimension 'uncertainty avoidance' was found; with the CVS another dimension 'Confucian dynamism'.

Uncertainty avoidance was described in Chapter 5. It deals ultimately with a society's search for Truth. Uncertainty avoiding cultures foster a belief in an absolute Truth, and uncertainty accepting cultures take a more relativistic stance.

Confucian dynamism, or as this chapter renamed it, long-term versus short-term orientation, can be interpreted as dealing with a society's search for Virtue. It is no accident that this dimension relates to the teachings of Confucius. As mentioned earlier in this chapter, Confucius was a teacher of practical ethics without any religious content. He dealt with Virtue but he left the question of Truth open.

Eastern religions, Hinduism, Buddhism, Shintoism, and Taoism, are separated from Western religions, Judaism, Christianity, and Islam, by a deep philosophical dividing line. The three Western religions belong to the same thought family; historically, they grew from the same roots. As was argued in Chapter 5, all three are based on the existence of a Truth which is accessible to the true believers. All three have a Book. In the East, neither Confucianism, which is a nonreligious ethic, nor any major religion is based on the assumption that there is a Truth which a human community can embrace. They offer various ways in which a person can improve him/herself, however these do not consist in believing, but in ritual, meditation, or ways of living. Some of these may lead to a higher spiritual state, eventually to unification with God or Gods. Therefore Dr Pradhan was so puzzled by the question about what he believed. This is an irrelevant question in the East. What one *does* is important.[8] This is why a questionnaire invented by Western minds led to the identification of a fourth dimension dealing with Truth; a questionnaire invented by Eastern minds found a fourth dimension dealing with Virtue.

The Western concern with Truth is supported by an axiom in Western logic that a statement excludes its opposite: if A is true, B, which is the opposite of A, must be false. Eastern logic does not have such an axiom. If A is true, its opposite B may also be true, and together they produce a wisdom which is superior to either A or B. This is sometimes called the complementarity of *yang* and *yin*, using two Chinese characters which express the male and the female elements present in all aspects of reality. Human truth in this philosophical approach is always partial. People in East and South-East Asian countries can quite easily adopt elements from different religions, or adhere to more than one religion at the same time. In countries with such a philosophical background, a practical nonreligious ethical system like Confucianism can become a cornerstone of society. In the West, ethical rules tend to be derived from religion: Virtue from Truth.

During the Industrial Revolution which originated in the West 200 years ago the Western concern for Truth was at first an asset. It led to the discovery of the laws of nature which could then be exploited for the sake of human progress. It is surprising that Chinese scholars, despite their high level of civilization, never discovered Newton's laws: they were simply not looking for laws. The Chinese script also betrays this lack of interest in generalizing: it needs 5000 different characters, one for each syllable, while by splitting the syllables into separate letters Western languages need only about 30 signs. Western thinking is analytical, while Eastern thinking is synthetic.

By the middle of the twentieth century the Western concern for Truth gradually ceased to be an asset and turned instead into a liability. Science may benefit from analytical thinking, but management and government are based on the art of synthesis. With the results of Western, analytically derived technologies now being freely available, Eastern cultures could start putting these technologies into practice using their own superior synthetic abilities. What is true or who is right is less important than what works and how the efforts of individuals with different thinking patterns can be coordinated towards a common goal. Japanese management, especially with Japanese employees, is famous for this pragmatic synthesis. By showing the link between Confucian dynamism and recent economic growth, the CVS research project has demonstrated the strategic advantage of cultures that can practice Virtue without a concern for Truth.

From the Muslim countries covered by the CVS study Bangladesh scored 40 and Pakistan 0. Contrary to East Asia, many countries with a dominant Muslim tradition are still searching for ways of coping with modernity. Muslim countries which temporarily collected enormous riches from their oil resources have hardly adapted better to the modern world than those which remained poor. The oil benefits may have been a liability rather than an asset. None of the Five Dragons had any natural resources worth mentioning besides the mental software of their populations.

There was a period in history, from about the ninth to the fourteenth century AD, when the Muslim world was not only militarily but also scientifically advanced while Christian Europe was backward. With the Renaissance and the Reformation, Christian countries have entered the road to modernization, while the world of Islam has withdrawn into traditionalism. Contrary to what happens in East Asia, many opinion leaders in the Muslim world seem to interpret modern technology and Western ideas as a threat rather than as an opportunity. The concern for Truth which Muslim cultures share

Table 7.2   Key differences between short-term and long-term orientation societies

Short-term orientation	Long-term orientation
Respect for traditions	Adaptation of traditions to a modern context
Respect for social and status obligations regardless of cost	Respect for social and status obligations within limits
Social pressure to 'keep up with the Joneses' even if it means overspending	Thrift, being sparing with resources
Small savings quote, little money for investment	Large savings quote, funds available for investment
Quick results expected	Perseverance towards slow results
Concern with 'face'	Willingness to subordinate oneself for a purpose
Concern with possessing the Truth	Concern with respecting the demands of Virtue

with the Christians can be seen as a competitive disadvantage versus the Dragons which only search for Virtue.

Table 7.2 summarizes the key aspects of the short-term versus long-term orientation dimension described in this chapter. It is less extensive than the corresponding tables for the four IBM dimensions which are supported by the broad search for correlated phenomena from *Culture's Consequences* (Hofstede, 1980). However, the new dimension clearly covers issues extremely relevant for economic development and not found in relationship with the other dimensions.

A shift from a short-term towards a long-term orientation seems highly desirable, not only from a point of view of economic growth but also in view of the necessity of surviving with an increasing world population in a world with limited resources. Confucius' answer to Duke Ching: 'Good government consists in being sparing with resources' will become even more relevant in the future than it was 2500 years ago.

Notes
[1] Herman Vuijsje, '*Twee koffie, twee koekjes*,' in *NRC Handelsblad*, April 16, 1988. Quotes translated by GH.
[2] This chapter makes extensive use of an article by Hofstede and Bond (1988).
[3] Besides, they changed the scoring from ranking values relative to each other, to rating each value by itself.
[4] The details are described in an article authored by 'The Chinese Culture Connection' (1987), the collective name adopted by a team of 24 researchers orchestrated by Michael H. Bond. Across the 20 countries, a CVS factor labeled 'Moral discipline' correlates 0.55 power distance and −0.54 with individualism. A CVS factor labeled 'integration' correlates 0.65 with individualism, and −0.58 with power distance. A CVS factor labeled 'human-heartedness' correlates 0.67 with masculinity.
[5] The product moment correlation coefficient between LTO and percentage average annual growth rate 1965–1987 is 0.70, significant at the 0.001 level.

6 From an article by Dutch journalist Ben Knapen in *NRC Handelsblad*, February 9, 1989. Backtranslated by GH.

7 The per capita gross national product of Colombia was US$280 in 1965, $1240 in 1987. In South Korea the figures were $150 in 1965, $2690 in 1987 (*World Development Report*, 1989).

8 US mythologist Joseph Campbell (see Chapter 5, note 15) has compared Eastern and Western religious myths. He suggests that Judaism, Christianity, and Islam have dissociated matter and spirit, while Eastern religions and philosophers have kept them integrated. See Campbell (1988, pp. 71–75).

Part III

Organizational Cultures

8

From fad to management tool

Heaven's Gate BV is a 60-year-old production unit in the chemical industry of the Netherlands. Many of its employees are old-timers. Stories about the past abound. Workers tell about how heavy the jobs used to be when loading and unloading was done by hand. They tell about heat and physical risk. HGBV used to be seen as a rich employer. For several decades, the demand for its products exceeded the supply. Products were not sold, but distributed. Customers had to be nice and polite in order to be served. Money was made very easily.

HGBV's management style used to be paternalistic. The old general manager made his daily morning walk through the plant, shaking hands with everyone he met. This, people tell, is the root of a tradition which still exists and which they call the 'HGBV grip': when one arrives in the morning, one shakes hands with one's colleagues. This ritual greeting would be normal in France, but in the Netherlands it is unusual. Rich and paternalistic, HGBV has long been considered a benefactor, both to its employees in times of need and to the local community. Some of this has survived. Employees still feel HGBV to be a desirable employer, with good pay, benefits, and job security. A job with HGBV is still seen as a job for life. HGBV is a company one would like one's children to join. Outside, HGBV is a regular sponsor of local sports and humanitarian associations. 'No appeal to HGBV has ever been made in vain.'

The working atmosphere is good-natured, with a lot of freedom given to employees. The plant has been described as a club, a village, a family. Twenty-five year and forty-year anniversaries are given lots of attention; the plant's Christmas parties are famous. These celebrations represent rituals with a long history, which people still value. In HGBV's culture, or, as people express it, 'the HGBV way', unwritten rules for social behavior are very important. One does not live in order to work, one works in order to live. What one does, counts less than *how* one does it. One has to fit into the informal network, and this holds for all hierarchical levels. 'Fitting' means:

avoiding conflicts and direct confrontations; covering other people's mistakes; loyalty, friendliness, modesty, and good-natured cooperation. Nobody should be too conspicuous, either in a positive or in a negative sense.

HGBVers grumble, but never directly about other HGBVers. Also, grumbling is reserved for one's own circle: towards superiors or outsiders, one does not soil the nest. This concern for harmony and group solidarity fits well into the regional culture of the geographical area in which HGBV is located. Newcomers are quickly accepted, as long as they adapt. The quality of their work counts less than their social adaptation. Whoever disrupts the harmony is rejected, however good a worker she or he is. Disturbed relationships may take years to heal. 'We prefer to let a work problem continue for another month, even if it costs a lot of money, above resolving it in an unfriendly manner.' Company rules are never absolute. The most important rule, one interviewee said, is that rules are flexible. One may break a rule if one does it gently. It is not the rule-breaker who is at risk, but the one who makes an issue of it.

Leadership in HGBV, in order to be effective, should be in harmony with the social behavior patterns. Managers should be accessible, fair, and good listeners. The present general manager is such a leader. He does not give himself airs. He has an easy relationship with people of all levels and is felt to be 'one of us'. Careers in HGBV are made primarily on the basis of social skills. One should not behave too conspicuously; one need not be brilliant, but one does need good contacts; one should know one's way in the informal network, being invited rather than volunteering. One should belong to the tennis club. All in all, one should respect what someone called the strict rules for being a nice person.

This romantic picture, however, has recently been disturbed by outside influences. First, market conditions changed, and HGBV found itself in an unfamiliar competitive situation with other European suppliers. Costs had to be cut, and manpower reduced. In the HGBV tradition, this problem was resolved without collective layoffs, through early retirement. However, the old-timers who had to leave prematurely were shocked that the company did not need them any more.

Second, and even more seriously, HGBV has been attacked by environmentalists because of the pollution it causes, a point of view which has received growing support in political circles. It is not impossible that the licenses necessary for HGBV's operation will one day be withdrawn. HGBV's management has tried to counter this problem with an active lobby with the authorities, with a press campaign, and through organizing public visits to the company, but their success is by no means certain. Inside HGBV, this threat is belittled. People are unable to imagine that one day there may be no more HGBV. 'Our management has always found a solution. There will be a solution now'. In the meantime, attempts are made to increase HGBV's competitiveness through quality improvement and product diversification. These also imply the introduction of new people from the outside. These new trends, however, clash head-on with HGBV's traditional culture.[1]

The organizational culture craze

The short case study above is a description of an organization's culture. People working for Heaven's Gate BV have a specific way of acting and interacting which sets them apart from people working for other organizations, even within the same region. In earlier chapters, this book has mainly associated 'culture' with nationality. The attribution of a 'culture' to an organization is a relatively recent phenomenon. The term *organizational culture* first appeared casually in English-language literature in the 1960s as a synonym of 'climate'. The equivalent *corporate culture*, coined in the 1970s, gained popularity after a book carrying this title, by Terrence Deal and Allan Kennedy, appeared in the USA in 1982. It became common parlance through the success of a companion volume, from the same McKinsey/ Harvard Business School team, Thomas Peters and Robert Waterman's *In Search of Excellence* which appeared in the same year. Since then, an extensive literature has developed on the topic, which has also reached other language areas.

Peters and Waterman wrote:

> 'Without exception, the dominance and coherence of culture proved to be an essential quality of the excellent companies. Moreover, the stronger the culture and the more it was directed toward the marketplace, the less need was there for policy manuals, organization charts, or detailed procedures and rules. In these companies, people way down the line know what they are supposed to do in most situations because the handful of guiding values is crystal clear.'[2]

Talking about the 'culture' of a company or organization has become a fad, among managers, among consultants and, with somewhat different concerns, among academics. Fads pass, and this one, too, may be out of fashion one day, but not without having left its trace. Organizational/corporate culture has become as fashionable a topic as organizational structure, strategy, and control. There is no standard definition of the concept, but most people who write about it would probably agree that 'organizational culture' is:

- *holistic*   referring to a whole which is more than the sum of its parts
- *historically determined*   reflecting the history of the organization
- *related to the things anthropologists study*   like rituals and symbols

- *socially constructed*   created and preserved by the group of people who together form the organization
- *soft*   (although Peters and Waterman assure their readers that 'soft is hard')
- *difficult to change*   although authors disagree on *how* difficult

In Chapter 1 'culture' in general was defined as 'the collective programming of the mind which distinguishes the members of one group or category of people from another'. Consequently 'organizational culture' can be defined as *the collective programming of the mind which distinguishes the members of one organization from another*.

Organizations with 'strong' cultures, in the sense of the quote from Peters and Waterman, arouse positive feelings in some people, negative in others. The attitude towards strong organizational cultures is partly affected by national culture elements. The culture of the IBM Corporation, one of Peters and Waterman's most excellent companies, was depicted with horror by Max Pagès, a leading French social psychologist, in a 1979 study of IBM France; he called it *'la nouvelle église'*: the new church. French society as compared to US society is characterized by a greater dependence of the average citizen on hierarchy and on rules (see Chapters 2, 5, and 6). French academics are also children of their society and therefore more likely than American academics to stress intellectual rules, that is, rational elements in organizations. At the same time French culture according to Chapter 3 is individualistic so there is a need to defend the individual against the rational system.[3] Even in the USA some people have reacted to Peters and Waterman's book by the slogan 'I'd rather be dead than excellent.'

Another type of reaction is found in the Nordic countries, Denmark, Sweden and, to some extent, Norway and Finland. In their case society is *less* built on hierarchy and rules than in the USA. The idea of 'organizational cultures' in these countries is greeted with approval because it tends to stress the irrational and the paradoxical. This does not at all prevent a basically positive attitude towards organizations (see Westerlund and Sjöstrand, 1975; March and Olsen, 1976; Broms and Gahmberg, 1983; Brunsson, 1985).

There is also a distinction among writers on organizational cultures between those who see culture as something an organization *has*, and those who see it as something an organization *is* (Smircich, 1983). The former leads to an analytic approach and a concern with change. It predominates among managers and management consultants. The latter supports a synthetic approach and a concern with understanding and is almost exclusively found among pure academics.[4]

Differences between organizational and national cultures

Using the word 'culture' for both nations and organizations suggests that the two kinds of culture are identical phenomena. This is incorrect: a nation is not an organization, and the two types of 'culture' are of a different nature.

The difference between national and organizational cultures is due to the different roles played in each by the manifestations of culture described in Chapter 1 (in the 'onion diagram', Fig. 1.2: symbols, heroes, rituals, and values, of which the first three were subsumed under the name 'practices').

Among national cultures—comparing otherwise similar people—the IBM studies found considerable differences in values, in the sense described in Chapter 1 of broad, nonspecific feelings of good and evil, etc. This notwithstanding similarities in practices among IBM employees in similar jobs but in different national subsidiaries. When people write about national cultures in the modern world becoming more similar, the evidence cited is usually taken from the level of practices: people dress the same, buy the same products, and use the same fashionable words (symbols); they see the same television shows and movies (heroes); they perform the same sports and leisure activities (rituals). These rather superficial manifestations of culture are sometimes mistaken for all there is; the deeper, underlying level of values, which moreover determine the meaning for people of their practices, is overlooked. Studies at the values level continue to show impressive differences among nations; not only the IBM studies from around 1970 described in earlier chapters, but also, to take a more recent example, the European value systems study from 1981 which used representative samples of entire populations (see Chapter 2, note 9).

Most of this chapter will be based on the results of a research project carried out between 1985 and 1987 under the auspices of IRIC (Institute for Research on Intercultural Cooperation), now at the University of Limburg at Maastricht, the Netherlands. It made intensive use of the experience collected during the cross-national IBM studies. Paradoxically, the cross-national research at IBM did not reveal any direct information about IBM's corporate culture: all units studied shared the same corporate culture, and there were no outside points of comparison. The cross-national study, however, was useful from a methodological point of view. It served as a model of how a cross-organizational study could be designed. Instead of one corporation in many countries, this time we should study many different organizations in one and the same country: a similar approach but replacing national by organizational differences.

IRIC's research project on organizational cultures found the roles of values versus practices to be exactly reversed with respect to the national level. Comparing otherwise similar people in different organizations showed

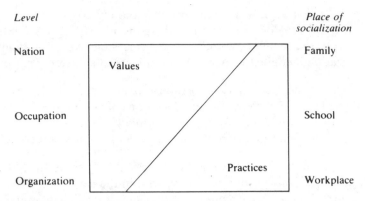

Fig. 8.1 The nature of cultural differences: the national, occupational, and organizational levels

considerable differences in practices but much smaller differences in values. This is shown in Fig. 8.1.

Figure 8.1 illustrates that at the national level cultural differences reside mostly in values, less in practices (as long as we compare otherwise similar people). At the organizational level, cultural differences reside mostly in practices, less in values. An occupational culture level has been placed halfway between nation and organization, suggesting that entering an occupational field means the acquisition of both values and practices.

The differences in the values–practices balance pictured in Fig. 8.1 can be explained by the different places of 'socialization' (learning) for values and for practices; these have been listed at the right-hand side of the diagram. Values are acquired in one's early youth, mainly in the family and in the neighborhood, and later at school. By the time a child is 10 years old, most of its basic values have been programmed into its mind. Organizational practices, on the other hand, are learned through socialization at the workplace, which most people enter as adults, that is, with the bulk of their values firmly in place. For occupational values the place of socialization is the school or university, and the time is in between childhood and adult-hood.

Figure 8.1, which is based on the experience of two large empirical studies, one (the IBM study) cross-national and the other cross-organizational, suggests that national cultures and organizational cultures are phenomena of a different order. Using the same term 'cultures' for both can be misleading. The conclusions from the diagram are at variance with the popular literature on 'corporate cultures' which insists, following Peters and Waterman, that shared values represent the core of a corporate culture. On the basis of the research described below *shared perceptions of daily practices* should be considered to be the core of an organization's culture. In IRIC's organization cultures study the employees' values differed more according to criteria like the nationality, age, and education of the employees than according to their membership of the organization *per se*.[5]

An explanation for the difference between Peters and Waterman (and many other US authors) and our findings about the nature of organizational cultures could be that the US management literature rarely distinguishes between the values of founders and significant leaders, and the values of the bulk of the organization's members. Descriptions of organizational cultures are often only based on statements by corporate heroes. Our research has assessed to what extent leaders' messages have come across to members. The values of founders and key leaders undoubtedly shape organizational cultures, but the way these cultures affect ordinary members is through shared practices. Founders–leaders' values become members' practices.

If members' values depend primarily on criteria other than membership in the organization, the way these values enter the organization is through the hiring process: a company hires people of a certain nationality, age, education, sex.[6] Their subsequent socialization in the organization is a matter of learning the practices: symbols, heroes, and rituals. Personnel departments which preselect the people to be hired play a very important role in maintaining an organization's values (for better or for worse), a role of which many personnel managers are not quite conscious.

A qualitative–quantitative study of organizational cultures: the IRIC project

Studies of organizational cultures can be divided into those based on soft, qualitative information versus those seeking hard, quantitative data. One article by an Italian and a British author associates soft with feminine and hard with masculine, and assumes the latter is more appealing in a man's world (Gherardi and Turner, 1987). This may, however, depend on national models of masculinity and femininity (see Chapter 4). Peters and Waterman's slogan 'soft is hard' has justifiably drawn attention to soft information in a masculine society. Qualitative data usually means case studies; many organizational culture studies are about one single case. With all their appeal such studies inevitably raise questions as to reliability (would another observer have perceived the same phenomena?) and generalization (how does this case help us to understand other cases?).

Hard, quantitative studies of organizational cultures are few and far between and not necessarily very convincing. Culture assessment based on hard or semi-hard data (directly or indirectly quantifiable) has the advantage of reliability (independence of the person of the researcher), and stability of the instrument over time, thus allowing 'longitudinal' research. More easily than soft-data-based research it helps to overcome resistance to bad news among the people concerned ('on how many interviews do you base this opinion?'). Managers who operate in a hard-data, bottom-line culture can incorporate it more readily in their consciousness. However, this risks missing the essence of culture as a whole: it can easily become mechanistic, giving rise to the idea that organizational culture can be manipulated. For all these reasons the IRIC study was designed to include both a qualitative and a quantitative element, so as to get the best of both worlds: it used in-depth interviews as well as a paper-and-pencil survey.

Achieving access to a sufficient number of organizations proved quite a problem. Whereas the cross-national IBM study could use existing data, collected via the infrastructure and on the budget of the corporation, IRIC's cross-organizational project had to raise its own funds and find its own participant firms. Selling a joint research project to a number of different organizations is not easy—certainly not if they have to pay for it themselves. In the beginning everybody wants to know who else will be in it, but this is precisely what the researchers do not know yet ('if you come, we have a party'). Eventually a sufficient number of organizations was reached by including *two* national environments in the study: Denmark and IRIC's home base, the Netherlands. On the IBM national culture dimensions these two countries have fairly similar scores: they belong to the same Nordic–Dutch cluster.

Within these national contexts IRIC sought access to a wide range of different work organizations. By showing how different organizational cultures can be, one acquires a better insight into how different is different, and how similar is similar. Units of study were both entire organizations and parts of organizations, which their management assumed to be culturally reasonably homogeneous (the research outcome later allowed this assumption to be tested). Altogether the IRIC project covered 20 units from 10 different organizations, 5 in Denmark, 5 in the Netherlands. These units were engaged in the activities shown in Table 8.1. Unit sizes varied from 60 to 2500 persons. The number of 20 units was small enough to allow studying each unit in depth, qualitatively, as a separate case study. At the same time, it was large enough to permit statistical analysis of comparative quantitative data across all cases.

The first, qualitative phase of the research consisted of in-depth person-to-person interviews of 2–3 hours duration each with nine informants per unit (thus, a total of 180 interviews). These interviews served both to acquire a qualitative feel for the whole (the *Gestalt*) of the unit's culture, and to collect issues to be included in the questionnaire for the ensuing survey. Informants were hand-picked in a discussion with the person who served as the researchers' contact in the unit, on the basis that they would have something

Table 8.1 Activities of work organizations involved in IRIC project

Private manufacturing companies (electronics, chemicals, consumer goods)	
total divisions or production units	6
head office or marketing units	3
research and development units	2
Private service companies (banking, transport, trade) units	5
Public institutions (telecommunication, police) units	4
Total number of units studied	20

interesting and informative to say about the culture. The group of informants included in all cases the unit top manager and his (never her) secretary; it also comprised a selection of people in different jobs from all levels, both old-timers and newcomers, women and men. Sometimes the gatekeeper or doorman was found to be an excellent source of information; an employee representative (equivalent to a shop steward) was always included.

The interview team consisted of 18 members (Danish or Dutch), most of them with a social science training, but deliberately naive about the type of activity going on in the unit studied. Each unit's interviews were divided between two interviewers, one woman and one man, as the gender of the interviewer might affect the observations obtained. All interviewers received the same project training beforehand, and all used the same broad checklist of open-ended questions.

The interview checklist contained questions like:

- *About organizational symbols* What are special terms here which only insiders understand?
- *About organizational heroes* What kind of people are most likely to advance quickly in their career here? Whom do you consider as particularly meaningful persons for this organization?
- *About organizational rituals* In what periodic meetings do you participate? How do people behave during these meetings? Which events are celebrated in this organization?
- *About organizational values* What things do people very much like to see happening here? What is the biggest mistake one can make? Which work problems can keep you awake at night?

Interviewers were free to probe for more and other information if they felt it was there. Interviews were taped and the interviewers wrote a report for each interview using a prescribed sequence, quoting as far as possible the respondents' actual words.

The second, quantitative phase of the project consisted of a paper-and-pencil survey with precoded questions, administered contrary to the first phase to a strictly *random* sample from the unit. This sample was composed of about 25 managers (or as many as the unit counted), 25 college-level nonmanagers (professionals) and 25 non-college-level nonmanagers. The questions in the survey included those used in the cross-national IBM study plus a number of later additions; most, however, were developed on the basis of the interviews of the first phase. Questions were formulated about all issues which the interviewers suspected would differ substantially between units. These included, in particular, many of the perceptions of daily practices, which had been missing in the cross-national studies.

The results of both the interviews and the surveys were discussed with the units' management and sometimes fed back to larger groups of employees if the management agreed with it.

Results of the in-depth interviews: the SAS case

The 20 units studied produced as many case studies, insightful descriptions of each unit's culture composed by the interviewers after the interviews and with the survey results as a check on their interpretations. The case of Heaven's Gate BV at the beginning of this chapter was taken from the survey results. One more case will now be described: the Scandinavian Airlines System (SAS) Copenhagen Passenger Terminal.

SAS in the early 1980s went through a spectacular turnaround process. Under the leadership of their new President Jan Carlzon the company switched from a product-and-technology orientation to a market-and-service orientation. Before, planning and sales had been based on realizing a maximum number of flight hours with the most modern equipment available. Pilots, technicians, and disciplinarian managers were the company's heroes. Deteriorating results forced the reorganization.

Carlzon was convinced that in the highly competitive air transport market success depended on a superior way of catering to the needs of the present and potential customers. These needs should be best known by the employees with daily face-to-face customer contact. In the old situation these people had never been asked for their opinions: they were a disciplined set of uniformed soldiers, trained to follow the rules. Now they were considered 'the firing line', and the organization was restructured to support them rather than order them around. Superiors were turned into advisors; the firing line received considerable discretion in dealing with customer problems on the spot. They only needed to report their decisions to superiors after the fact, which meant a built-in acceptance of employees' judgment with all risks involved (Carlzon, 1987).

One of the units participating in the IRIC study was the SAS passenger terminal at Copenhagen airport. The interviews were conducted three years after the turnaround operation. The employees and managers were uniformed, disciplined, formal, and punctual. They seemed to be the kind of people who *like* to work in a disciplined structure. People worked shift hours with periods of tremendous work pressure alternating with periods of relative inactivity. They showed considerable acceptance of their new role. When talking about the company's history they tended to start from the time of the turnaround; only some managers referred to the earlier years.

The interviewees were very proud of the company: their identity seemed to a large extent derived from it. Social relationships outside the work situation were frequently with other SAS people. Carlzon was often mentioned as a company hero. In spite of their being disciplined, relationships between colleagues seemed to be good-natured, and there was a lot of mutual help. Colleagues who met with a crisis in their private lives were supported by others and by the company. Managers of various levels were visible and accessible, although clearly managers had more trouble accepting the new role than nonmanagers. New employees entered via a formal introduction and training program with simulated encounters with problem clients. This served also as a screening device, showing whether the newcomer had the values and the skills necessary for this profession. Those who successfully completed the training felt quickly at home in the department. Towards clients the employees demonstrated a problem-solving attitude: they showed considerable excitement about original ways in which to resolve customers' problems: ways in which some rules could be stretched in order to achieve the desired result. Promotion was from the ranks and was felt to go to the most competent and supportive colleagues.

It is not unlikely that this department benefited from a certain 'Hawthorne effect'[7] because of the key role it had played in a successful turnaround. At the time of the interviews the euphoria of the successful turnaround was probably at its highest. Observers inside the company commented that people's values had not really changed, but that the turnaround had transformed a discipline of obedience towards superiors into a discipline of service towards customers.

Results of the survey: six dimensions of organizational cultures
The IBM studies had led to the identification of four dimensions of *national* cultures (power distance, individualism–collectivism, masculinity–femininity, and uncertainty avoidance). These were dimensions of *values*, because the national IBM subsidiaries primarily differed on the cultural

values of their employees. The 20 units studied in the IRIC cross-organizational study, however, differed only slightly with respect to the cultural values of their members, but they varied considerably in their practices, as illustrated by Fig. 8.1.

Most questions in the paper-and-pencil survey measured *people's perceptions of the practices in their work unit*. These were presented in a 'Where I work . . .' format, for example:

Where I work:

| Meeting times are | | Meeting times are |
| kept very punctually | 1 2 3 4 5 | only kept approximately |

| Quantity prevails | | Quality prevails |
| over quality | 1 2 3 4 5 | over quantity |

Each item thus consisted of two opposite statements: which statement was put in the right and which in the left column was decided on a random basis, so that their position could not suggest their desirability.

All 61 'Where I work . . .' questions were designed on the basis of the information collected in the open interviews, and were subjected to a statistical analysis very similar to the one used in the IBM studies (see Chapter 2). They produced six entirely new dimensions: of practices, not of values. What was used was a factor analysis of a matrix of 61 questions × 20 units; for each unit, a mean score was computed on each question across all respondents, who were one-third managers, one-third professionals and one-third nonprofessionals. This analysis produced six clear factors reflecting dimensions of (perceived) practices distinguishing the 20 organizational units from each other. These six dimensions were mutually independent, i.e., they occurred in all possible combinations.

Choosing labels for empirically found dimensions is a subjective process: it represents the step from data to theory. The labels chosen have been changed several times. Their present formulation has been discussed at length with people in the units. As much as possible, the labels had to avoid suggesting a 'good' and a 'bad' pole for a dimension. Whether the score of a unit on a dimension should be interpreted as good or bad depends entirely on where those responsible for managing the unit want it to go. The terms finally arrived at are the following:

1. Process oriented vs. results oriented
2. Employee oriented vs. job oriented
3. Parochial vs. professional
4. Open system vs. closed system
5. Loose control vs. tight control
6. Normative vs. pragmatic

The order of the six cross-organizational dimensions (their number) reflects the order in which they appeared in the analysis, but it has no theoretical meaning; number 1 is not more important than number 6. A lower number only shows that the questionnaire contained more questions dealing with dimension 1 than with dimension 2, etc.; but this can very well be seen as a reflection of the interests of the researchers who designed the questionnaire.

For each of the six dimensions three key 'Where I work . . .' questions were chosen to calculate an index value of each unit on each dimension, very much in the same way as in the IBM studies index values were computed for each country on each cross-national dimension. The unit scores of the three questions chosen were strongly correlated with each other.[8] Their content was such that together they would convey the essence of the dimension, as the researchers saw it, to the managers and the employees of the units in the feedback sessions.

Dimension 1 opposes a concern with means (*process oriented*) to a concern with goals (*results oriented*). The three key items show that in the process-oriented cultures people perceive themselves as avoiding risks and making only a limited effort in their jobs, while each day is pretty much the same. In the results-oriented cultures people perceive themselves as comfortable in unfamiliar situations and put in a maximal effort, while each day is felt to bring new challenges. On a scale from 0 to 100 in which 0 represents the most process-oriented and 100 the most results-oriented unit among the 20, HGBV, the chemical plant described earlier, scored 02 (very process oriented, little concern for results) while the SAS passenger terminal scored 100: it was the most results-oriented unit of all. For this dimension it is difficult not to attach a 'good' label to the results-oriented pole and a 'bad' label to the other side. Nevertheless, there are operations for which a single-minded focus on the process is essential. Our most process-oriented unit (score 00) was a production unit in a pharmaceutical firm. Drug manufacturing is an example of a risk-avoiding, routine-based environment in which it is doubtful whether one would want its culture to be results oriented. Similar concerns exist in many other organizations. So even a results orientation is not always 'good' and its opposite not always 'bad'.

One of the main claims from Peters and Waterman's book *In Search of Excellence* is that 'strong' cultures are more effective than 'weak' ones. A problem in verifying this proposition is that in the existing organizational/corporate culture literature one will search in vain for a practical (operational) measure of culture strength. As the issue seemed important, in the IRIC project we developed our own method for measuring the strength of a culture. A 'strong' culture was interpreted as a homogeneous culture, i.e., one in which all survey respondents gave about the same answers on the key questions, regardless of their content. A weak culture was a heterogeneous one: this occurred when answers among different people in the same unit varied widely. The survey data showed that across the 20 units studied, culture strength (homogeneity) was significantly correlated with results orientation.[9] To the extent that 'results oriented' stands for 'effective', Peters and Waterman's proposition about the effectiveness of strong cultures has therefore been confirmed in our data.

Dimension 2 opposes a concern for people (*employee oriented*) to a concern for completing the job (*job oriented*). The key items selected show that in the employee-oriented cultures people feel their personal problems are taken into account, that the organization takes a responsibility for employee welfare, and that important decisions tend to be made by groups or committees. In the job-oriented units people experience a strong pressure to complete the job, they perceive the organization as only interested in the work employees do, not in their personal and family welfare; and they report that important decisions tend to be made by individuals. On a scale from 0 to 100 HGBV scored 100 and the SAS passenger terminal 95—both of them extremely employee oriented. Scores on this dimension reflected the philosophy of the unit or company's founder(s), but also the possible scars left by past events: units that had recently been in economic trouble, especially if this had been accompanied by collective layoffs, tended to score job oriented, even if according to our informants the past had been different. Opinions about the desirability of a strong employee orientation differed among the leaders of the units in the study. In the feedback discussions some top managers wanted their unit to become more employee oriented but others desired a move in the opposite direction.

The employee-oriented–job-oriented dimension corresponds to the two axes of a well-known US leadership model: Blake and Mouton's *Managerial Grid* (1964). Blake and Mouton developed an extensive system of leadership training on the basis of their model. In this training, employee orientation and job orientation are treated as two independent dimensions: a person can be high on both, on one, or on neither. This seems to conflict with our placing the two orientations at opposite poles of a single dimension. However, Blake and Mouton's grid applies to individuals, while the IRIC study compared organizational units. What the IRIC study shows is that while individuals may well be both job *and* employee oriented at the same time, organizational cultures tend to favor one or the other.

Dimension 3 opposes units whose employees derive their identity largely from the organization (*parochial*) to units in which people identify with their type of job (*professional*). The key questions show that members of parochial cultures feel the organization's norms cover their behavior at home as well as on the job; they feel that in hiring employees, the company takes their social and family background into account as much as their job competence; and they do not look far into the future (they probably assume the organization will do this for them). On the other side, members of professional cultures consider their private lives their own business, they feel the organization hires on the basis of job competence only, and they do think far ahead. Sociology has long known this distinction as 'local' versus 'cosmopolitan', the contrast between an internal and an external frame of reference (Merton, 1968). The parochial type of culture is often associated with Japanese companies. Predictably in our survey, unit scores on this dimension are correlated with the unit members' level of education: parochial units tend to have employees with less formal education. SAS passenger terminal employees scored quite parochial (24); HGBV employees scored about halfway (48).

Dimension 4 opposes *open systems* to *closed systems*. The key items show that in the open system units members consider both the organization and its people open to newcomers and outsiders; almost anyone would fit into the organization, and new employees need only a few days to feel at home. In the closed system units, the organization and its people are felt to be closed and secretive, even among insiders; only very special people fit into the organization, and new employees need more than a year to feel at home (in the most closed unit, one member of the managing board confessed that he still felt an outsider after 22 years). On this dimension, HGBV again scored halfway (51) and SAS extremely open (9). What this dimension describes is the communication climate. It was the only one of the six 'practices' dimensions associated with nationality: it seems that an open organizational communication climate is a characteristic of Denmark more than of the Netherlands. However, one Danish organization scored very closed.

Dimension 5 refers to the amount of internal structuring in the organization. According to the key questions, people in *loose control* units feel that no one thinks of cost, meeting times are only kept approximately, and jokes about the company and the job are frequent. People in *tight control* units describe their work environment as cost-conscious, meeting times are kept punctually, and jokes about the company and/or the job are rare. It appears from the data that a tight formal control system is associated, at least statistically, with strict unwritten codes in terms of dress and dignified behavior. On a scale of 0 = loose and 100 = tight, SAS, with its uniformed personnel, scored extremely tight (96), and HGBV scored once more halfway (52); but halfway is quite loose for a production unit, as comparison with other production units shows.

Dimension 6, finally, deals with the popular notion of 'customer orientation'. *Pragmatic* units are market driven; *normative* units perceive their task towards the outside world as the implementation of inviolable rules. The key items show that in the normative units the major emphasis is on correctly following organizational procedures, which are more important than results; in matters of business ethics and honesty, the unit's standards are felt to be high. In the pragmatic units, there is a major emphasis on meeting the customer's needs, results are more important than correct procedures, and in matters of business ethics, a pragmatic rather than a dogmatic attitude prevails. The SAS passenger terminal was the top scoring unit on the pragmatic side (100), which shows that Jan Carlzon's message had come across. HGBV scored 68, also on the pragmatic side. In the past as it was described in the HGBV case study, the company may have been quite normative towards its customers, but it seems to have adapted to its new competitive situation.

Business cultures and the scope for competitive advantages in cultural matters

Inspection of the scoring profiles of the 20 units on the 6 dimensions shows that dimensions 1, 3, 5, and 6 (process vs. results, parochial vs. professional, loose vs. tight, and normative vs. pragmatic) relate to the type of work the organization does, and to the type of market in which it operates. In fact, these four dimensions partly reflect the *business or industry culture*, a frequently neglected component of the organizational culture. In Fig. 8.1 it should be located somewhere in between the occupational and the organizational level, because a given industry employs specific occupations and it also maintains specific organizational practices, for logical or traditional reasons. On dimension 1 most manufacturing and large office units scored process oriented; research/development and service units scored more results oriented. On dimension 3 units with a traditional technology scored parochial; high-tech units scored professional. On dimension 5 units delivering precision or risky products or services (such as pharmaceuticals or money transactions) scored tight, those with innovative or unpredictable activities scored loose. To our surprise the two city police corps we studied scored on the loose side (16 and 41): the work of a policeman, however, is highly unpredictable, and police personnel have considerable discretion in the way they want to carry out their task. On dimension 6 service units and those operating in competitive markets scored pragmatic while units involved in the implementation of laws and those operating under a monopoly scored normative.

While the task and market environment thus affect the dimension scores, the IRIC study has also produced its share of surprises: production units with an unexpectedly strong results orientation even on the shop floor, or a unit like HGBV with a loose control system in relation to its task. These surprises represent the distinctive elements in a unit's culture as compared to similar units, and the competitive advantages or disadvantages of a particular organizational culture. The other two dimensions, 2 and 4 (employee vs.

job and open vs. closed) seem to be less constrained by task and market but rather based on historical factors like the philosophy of the founder(s) and recent crises. In the case of dimension 4, open vs. closed system, the national cultural environment was already shown to play an important role.

Figure 8.1 indicates that although organizational cultures are *mainly* composed of practices, they do have a modest values component. The cross-organizational IRIC survey included the values questions from the cross-national IBM studies. The organizations differed somewhat on three clusters of values. The first resembles the cross-national dimension of uncertainty avoidance, although the differences show up on other survey questions than those used for computing the country UAI scores. A cross-organizational uncertainty avoidance measure is correlated with dimension 4 (open vs. closed), with weak uncertainty avoidance obviously on the side of an open communication climate. The relationship is reinforced by the fact that the Danish units, with one exception, scored much more open than the Dutch ones. Denmark and the Netherlands, though similar on most national culture scores, differ most on their national uncertainty avoidance scores, Denmark scoring much lower.

A second cluster of cross-organizational values bears some resemblance to power distance. It is correlated with dimension 1 (process vs. results oriented): larger power distances are associated with process orientation and smaller ones with results orientation.

Clusters of cross-organizational value differences associated with individualism and masculinity were not found in the IRIC study. It is possible that this was because the study was restricted to business organizations and public institutions. If, for example, health and welfare organizations had been included the study might have shown a wider range of values with regard to helping other people, which would have produced a feminine–masculine dimension. But this is just conjecture awaiting further research.

Questions which in the cross-national study composed the individualism and masculinity dimensions formed a different configuration in the cross-organizational study which we labeled *work centrality* (strong or weak): the importance of work in one's total life pattern. It was correlated with dimension 3: parochial vs. professional. Obviously work centrality is stronger in professional organizational cultures. In parochial cultures, people do not take their work problems home with them.

From the six organizational culture dimensions the numbers 1, 3 and 4 were thus to some extent associated with values. For the other three dimensions: 2, 5, and 6, no link with values was found at all. These dimensions just describe practices to which people have been socialized without their basic values being involved.

Organizational culture and other organizational characteristics

In the IBM studies national culture's antecedents and consequences were proven by correlating the country scores with all kinds of external data. These included economic indicators like the country's per capita gross national product, political measures like an index of press freedom, and demographic data like the population growth rate. Comparisons were also made with the results of other surveys covering the same countries but using different questions and different respondents. The IRIC cross-organizational study has included a similar 'validation' of the dimensions against external data. This time, of course, the data used consisted of information about the organizational units obtained in other ways and from other sources.

Besides the interviews and the survey the IRIC study included the collection of quantifiable data about the units as wholes. Examples of such information (labeled *structural data*) are total employee strength, budget composition, economic results, and the ages of key managers. All structural data were personally collected by the author of this book. Finding out what meaningful structural data *could* be obtained was a heuristic process which went along with the actual collection of the data. This process was too complicated to be shared across researchers. The informants for the structural data were the top manager, the chief personnel officer, and the chief budget officer. They were presented with written questionnaires which were followed up by personal interviews.

Out of a large number of quantifiable characteristics tried, about 40 provided usable data. For these 40 characteristics, the scores for each of the 20 units were correlated with the unit scores on the 6 practice dimensions.[10] In the following paragraphs, for each of the 6 practice dimensions the most important relationships found are described.

There was a strong correlation between the scores on practice dimension 1, process orientation versus results orientation, and the balance of labor versus material cost in the operating budget (the money necessary for daily functioning). Any operation can be characterized as labor-intensive, material-intensive, or capital-intensive, depending on which of the three categories of cost takes the largest share of its operating budget. Labor-intensive units (holding number of employees constant) scored more results oriented, while material-intensive units (again holding number of employees constant) scored more process oriented. If an operation is labor intensive, the effort of people, by definition, plays an important role in its results. This appears more likely to breed a results-oriented culture. The yield of material-intensive units tends to depend on technical processes, which seems to stimulate a process-oriented culture. It is therefore not surprising that one finds research/development and service units on the results-oriented side; manufacturing and office units, in these days of automation, are more often found on the process-oriented side

The second highest correlation of results orientation was with lower absenteeism. This is a nice validation of the fact that, as one of the key questions formulated it, 'people put in a maximal effort'. Next, there were three significant correlations between results orientation and the structure of the organizations. Flatter organizations (larger span of control for the unit top manager) scored more results oriented. This confirms Peters and Waterman's seventh maxim 'simple form, lean staff'. Three simplified scales were used based on the Aston studies of organizational structure referred to in Chapter 6 (Pugh and Hickson, 1976), in order to measure centralization, specialization and formalization. Both specialization and formalization were negatively correlated with results orientation: more specialized and more formalized units tend to be more process oriented. Centralization was not correlated with this dimension. Results orientation was also correlated with having a top management team with a lower education level, which has been promoted from the ranks: doers rather than figureheads. Finally, in results-oriented units, union membership among employees tended to be lower.

The strongest correlations with dimension 2 (employee vs. job oriented) were with the way the unit is controlled by the organization to which it belongs. Where the top manager of the unit stated that *his* superiors evaluated him on profits and other financial performance measures, the members scored the unit culture as job oriented. Where the top manager of the unit felt his superiors evaluated him on performance vs. a budget, the opposite was the case: members scored the unit culture to be employee oriented. It seems that operating against external standards (profits in a market) breeds a less benevolent culture than operating against internal standards (a budget). Where the top manager stated he allowed controversial news to be published in the employee journal, members felt the unit to be more employee oriented, which validated the top manager's veracity.

The remaining correlations of employee orientation were with the average seniority (years with the company) and age of employees (more senior employees score a more job-oriented culture), with the education level of the top management team (less-educated teams correspond with a more job-oriented culture) and with the total invested capital (surprisingly not with the invested capital per employee). Large organizations with heavy investment tended to be more employee than job oriented.

On dimension 3 (parochial vs. professional), units with a traditional technology tended to score parochial; high-tech units professional. The strongest correlations of this dimension were with various measures of size: not surprisingly, the larger organizations fostered the more professional cultures. Also not surprisingly, professional cultures had less labor union membership. Their managers had a higher average education level and age. Their organization structures showed more specialization. An interesting correlation was with the time budget of the unit top manager: the way the unit top manager claimed to spend his time. In units with a professional culture we found the top managers claiming to spend a relatively large share of their time in meetings and person-to-person discussions. Finally, the privately owned units in our sample tended to score more professional than the public ones.

Dimension 4 (open vs. closed system) was responsible for the single strongest correlation with external data, i.e., between the percentage of women among the employees and the openness of the communication climate.[11] The percentage of women among *managers* and the presence of at least one woman in the top management team were also correlated with openness. However, this correlation is affected by the bi-national composition of the research population. Among developed European countries, Denmark has one of the highest participation rates of women in the work force, and the Netherlands one of the lowest (although steeply increasing). Also, as mentioned earlier, Danish units as a group (with one exception) scored more open than Dutch units. This does not necessarily exclude a causal relationship between the participation of women in the work force and a more open communication climate: it could very well be the explanation *why* the Danish units were so much more open. All in all, the relationship between female participation in the labor force and openness of the organization's communication climate is an interesting finding which merits further research.

Also connected with the open vs. closed dimension are an association of formalization with a more closed culture (a nice validation of both measures), of admitting controversial issues in the employee journal with an open culture (obviously), and of higher average seniority with a more open culture.

The strongest correlation of dimension 5 (loose vs. tight control) was with an item in the self-reported time budget of the unit top manager: where the top manager claimed to spend a relatively large part of his time reading and writing reports and memos from inside the organization, we found tighter control. This makes perfect sense. We also found that material-intensive units have more tightly controlled cultures. As the results of such units often depend on small margins of material yields, this makes sense too.

Tight control was also correlated with the percentage of female managers and of female employees, in this order. This is most likely a consequence of the simple, repetitive, and clerical activities for which, in the organizations we studied, the larger number of women tended to be hired. Tighter control was found in units with a lower education level among male and female employees and also among its top managers. This reminds us of the finding in Chapter 2 that lower educated occupations maintain larger power distances. In units in which the number of employees had recently increased, control was felt to be looser; where the number of employees had been reduced, control was perceived as tighter. Employee layoffs are obviously associated with budget squeezes. Finally, absenteeism among employees was lower where control was perceived to be less tight. Absenteeism is evidently one way of escape from the pressure of a tight control system.

For dimension 6 (normative vs. pragmatic) only one meaningful correlation with external data was found. Privately owned units in the sample were more pragmatic, public units (such as the police corps) more normative.

Missing from the list of external data correlated with culture are measures of the organizations' performance. This does not mean that culture is not related to performance; only that we did not find comparable yardsticks for the performance of so varied a set of organizational units.

The relationships described in this section show objective conditions of organizations which are associated with particular culture profiles. They point to the things one has to change to modify an organization's culture: for example, certain aspects of its structure, or the priorities of the top manager. The last section of this chapter will be devoted to what this means for the management of organizational cultures.

Sense and nonsense about organizational cultures

The IRIC research project has thus produced a six-dimensional model of organizational cultures, defined as perceived common practices: symbols, heroes, and rituals. The research data came from twenty organizational units in two Northwest European countries, and one should therefore be careful not to claim that the same model applies to any organization anywhere. Certain important types of organizations, like those concerned with health and welfare, government, and the military, were not included. We do not know whether new practice dimensions may still be found in other countries. Nevertheless we believe that the fact that organizational cultures can be meaningfully described by a number of practice dimensions is probably universally true. Also it is likely that such dimensions will generally resemble, and partly overlap with, the six described in this chapter.[12]

This does not mean that the dimension scores together *are* the culture. Organizational cultures are wholes (*Gestalts*) and their flavor can only be fully appreciated by insiders. Outsiders need empathy to understand them. However, most managers of organizations live in a world of hardware and bottom-line figures and have difficulty with a fuzzy concept like a *Gestalt*. For them, a framework providing some grasp on the complexities of an organization's culture is an asset. It allows a comparison of the cultures of different organizations or parts of organizations in meaningful terms.

Practical uses of such a comparison for the management and members of an organization are:

1. Identifying the subcultures in one's own organization. In the course of the IRIC project we found that some of the units studied contained quite varied subcultures.[13] As Fig. 8.2 illustrates, organizations may be culturally divided according to hierarchical levels: top management, middle and lower level managers, professional employees, office employees, and shop floor employees. Other potential sources of internal cultural divisions are functional area (such as, sales vs. production vs. research), product/ market division, country of operation, and for organizations having gone through mergers, former merger partners. We have met cases in which 20 years after a merger the cultural traces of the merged parts could still be found. Not all of these

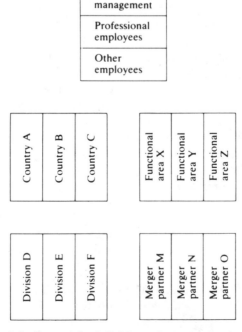

Fig. 8.2 Potential subdivisions of an organization's culture

potential divisions will be equally strong but it is important for the managers and members of a complex organization to know its cultural map—which, as we found, is often not the case.

2. Testing whether the culture fits the strategies set out for the future. Cultural constraints determine which strategies are feasible for an organization and which are not. For example, if a culture is strongly normative, a strategy for competing on customer service does not have much chance of success.

3. In the case of mergers and acquisitions, identifying the potential areas of culture conflict between the partners. This can either be an input to the decision whether or not to merge, or, if the decision has been made, an input to a plan for managing the post-merger integration so as to minimize friction losses and preserve unique cultural capital.

4. Measuring the development of organizational cultures over time, by repeating a survey after one of more years. This will show whether attempted culture changes have, indeed, materialized, as well as the cultural effects of external changes which occurred after the previous survey.

The six dimensions describe the culture of an organization but they are not prescriptive: no position on one of the six dimensions is intrinsically good or bad. In Peters and Waterman's book *In Search of Excellence* eight conditions for excellence are presented as norms. The book suggests there is 'one best way' towards excellence. The results of the IRIC study refute this. What is good or bad depends in each case on where one wants the organization to go, and a cultural feature that is an asset for one purpose is unavoidably a liability for another. Labeling positions on the dimension scales as more or less desirable is a matter of strategic choice, and this should vary from one organization to another. In particular the popular stress on customer orientation (becoming more pragmatic on dimension 6) is highly relevant for organizations engaged in services and the manufacturing of custom-made quality products, but may be unnecessary or even harmful for, for example, the manufacturing of standard products in a competitive price market.

This chapter referred earlier to the controversy about whether an organization *is* or *has* a culture. On the basis of the IRIC research project, we propose that practices are features an organization *has*. Because of the important role of practices in organizational cultures, the latter can be considered *somewhat* manageable. Changing collective values of adult people in an intended direction is extremely difficult, if not impossible. Values do change, but not according to someone's master plan. Collective practices, however, depend on organizational characteristics like structures and systems, and can be influenced in more or less predictable ways by changing these. Nevertheless, as argued above, organizational cultures are also, in a way, integrated wholes or *Gestalts*, and a *Gestalt* can be considered something the organization *is*. Changes in practices represent the margin of freedom in influencing these wholes. Because they are wholes, an integrating and inspiring type of leadership is needed to give these structural and systems changes a meaning for the people involved. The outcome should be a new and coherent cultural pattern, as was illustrated by the SAS case.

Managing (with) organizational culture

Practically, what can one do about one's organization's culture? Firstly, this depends on one's position in, or with regard to, the organization. A classic study by Eberhard Witte from Germany concluded that successful innovations in organizations required the joint action of two parties: a *Machtpromotor* and a *Fachpromotor*; in English, a power holder and an expert (Witte, 1973, 1977). Witte's model was developed on German data and may well be entirely valid only for countries like Germany with small power distance (accessibility of power holders) and strong uncertainty avoidance (belief in experts). Nevertheless, even for different national cultures it makes sense to distinguish the two roles. Both are crucial for culture innovations. The support of a power holder is indispensable; preferably a person with some charisma, not a pure administrator. However, expertise in making the right diagnosis and choosing the right therapy is also indispensable. Witte's research suggests that in Germany at least the *Machtpromotor* and the *Fachpromotor* should be two different persons; trying to combine the roles compromises one of them.

The *Fachpromotor* should provide a proper diagnosis of the present state of the organization's culture and subcultures. It is dangerous to assume one knows one's organization's present cultural map and how it should be changed. Organizations can look very different from the top than from the middle or bottom where the actual work is done. In the IRIC research project, when feeding back the interview and survey results to the units' management we always asked them to guess where their organization stood on the various dimensions, before showing how their people had answered our questions. Some managers were uncannily insightful and correct in their guesses, but others were way off. Wishful thinking and unfounded fears often affected their answers. So a proper diagnosis is essential.

With sound diagnostic information, the *Machtpromotor* should then make cultural considerations part of the organization's *strategy*. What are the strengths and weaknesses of the present cultural map? Can the strengths be better exploited and the weaknesses circumvented? Can the organization continue to live with its present culture? If management wants it to change, is this feasible? Do the benefits outweigh the costs (which are always higher than expected)? Are the material resources and human skills available which will be needed for changing the culture? And if it has been decided that the culture should change, what steps will be taken to implement it? Does the *Machtpromotor* realize his or her own crucial and lasting role in this process? Will he or she be given enough time by superiors, directors, or banks to take the process to its completion (and it always takes longer than one thinks)? Can a sufficient amount of support for the necessary changes be mobilized within the organization? Who will be the supporters? Who will be the resisters? Can these be circumvented or put in positions where they can do no harm?

Although culture is a 'soft' characteristic, changing it calls for 'hard' measures. *Structural changes* may mean closing departments, opening other departments, merging or splitting activities, or moving people and/or groups geographically. The general rule is that when people are moved as individuals, they will adapt to the culture of their new environment; when people are moved as groups, they will bring their group culture along. People in groups have developed, as part of their culture, ways of interacting which are quite stable and difficult to change. Changing them means that all interpersonal relationships have to be renegotiated. However, if new tasks or a new environment force such a renegotiation there is a good chance that undesirable aspects of the old culture will be cleaned up.

Process changes mean new procedures; eliminating controls or establishing new controls; automation or disautomation; short-circuiting communications or introducing new communication links. An example is a company in the bulk chemicals market which wanted to move into speciality chemicals. For the latter it had to eliminate a lot of the controls established for bulk chemicals production (like detailed yield figures) and instead establish quite different controls, like delivery time checks and customer satisfaction surveys. In the field of controls the main issue is whether activities are controlled on the basis of their output or through their inputs. The former, of course, if possible, is more effective. Especially in the public sector many activities whose outputs can be clearly defined are nevertheless only controlled by their inputs, for traditional budget reasons (see Hofstede, 1981).

Personnel changes mean new hiring and promoting policies. The gatekeeper role of the personnel department should be recognized. Personnel managers unconsciously maintain hero models for the organization which in a new culture may have to be revised. Could the hero be a heroine? Can a man with an earring be promoted? Training programs, often the first thing managers think of when wanting to change cultures, are only functional after the need for retraining has been established by structural, process, and personnel changes (as in the SAS case). Training programs without the support of hard changes usually remain at the level of lip service and are a waste of money. In

Table 8.2 Key Steps and considerations regarding organizational culture

MANAGING (WITH) ORGANIZATIONAL CULTURE

Is a task of top management which cannot be delegated

Demands both power and expertise

Should start with a cultural map of the organization
    Demands a culture diagnosis

Demands strategic choices:
    Is present culture matched with strategy?
    If not, can strategy be adapted?
    If not, what change of culture is needed?
    Is this change feasible—do we have the people?
    What will be the costs in terms of management attention and money?
    Do the expected benefits outweigh these costs?
    What is a realistic time span for the changes?
    If in doubt, better change strategy anyway
    Different subcultures may demand different approaches

Create a network of change agents in the organization
    Some key people at all levels
    If key people start, others will follow
    Can resisters be circumvented?

Design necessary structural changes
    Opening or closing departments
    Merging or splitting departments or tasks
    Moving groups or individuals?
    Are tasks matched with talents?

Design necessary process changes
    Eliminating or establishing controls
    Automation or disautomation
    Establishing or cutting communication links
    Replace control of inputs by control of outputs?

Revise personnel policies
    Reconsider criteria for hiring
    Reconsider criteria for promotion
    Is personnel management up to its new task?
    Design timely job rotation
    Be suspicious of plans to train others; need for training has to be felt by trainees
    themselves

Continue monitoring development of organizational culture
    Sustained attention, persistence
    Periodically repeat culture diagnosis

general, one should always be suspicious about suggestions to train *someone else*. Training is only effective if the trainee wants to be trained.

In attempted culture changes, new symbols often receive a lot of attention. They are easily visible: a new name, logo, uniforms, slogans, and portraits on the wall; all that belongs to the fashionable area of 'corporate identity'.

But symbols are only the most superficial level of culture. New symbols without the support of more fundamental changes at the deeper levels of heroes, rituals, and the values of key leaders just mean a lot of hoopla, the effects of which wear out quickly. Culture change in an organization needs persistence and sustained attention by the *Machtpromotor*. If the process is started by a culture diagnosis, it is evidently useful to repeat this diagnosis after sufficient time has passed for the planned changes to have become noticeable. In this way, a process of monitoring is started, in which changes actually found are compared with intended changes and further corrections can be applied. If organizational culture is *somewhat* manageable, this is the way to go about it.

In Table 8.2 the main steps in managing (with) culture have been summarized as a practical checklist for the reader. They may help in turning this fad into a management tool.

Notes

1   This case is derived from Hofstede *et al.* (1990). The remainder of this chapter also draws heavily upon this paper.
2   (Peters and Waterman, 1982, pp. 75–76). The Dutch organization sociologist Lammers has shown that Peters and Waterman's 'excellent' type has been described by European and US sociologists for more than half a century. See Lammers (1988).
3   This is also noticeable in French organization sociology, such as in the work of Michel Crozier. An example is Crozier and Friedberg (1977).
4   The concern with understanding is dominant among people who study organizational symbolism: see Pondy *et al.* (1983) and Berg (1986).
5   What we called 'practices' can also be labeled 'conventions', 'customs', 'habits', 'mores', 'traditions', 'usages'. They were recognized as part of culture by Edward B. Tylor in the last century: 'Culture is that complex whole which includes knowledge, beliefs, art, morals, law, customs and any other capabilities and habits acquired by man as a member of society' (Tylor, 1924).
6   In a study across six certified public accountant firms operating in the Netherlands, Sjo Soeters and Hein Schreuder found evidence of self-selection of new employees according to the national values dominant in the firm (US or Dutch), but not of socialization to the firm's values after entering. See Soeters and Schreuder (1986).
7   A Hawthorne effect means that employees selected for an experiment are so motivated by their being selected that this alone guarantees the experiment's success. It is named after the Hawthorne plant of Western Electric Corporation in the USA, where Professor Elton Mayo in the 1920s and 1930s conducted a series of classic experiments in work organization.
8   In a factor analysis of only these $6 \times 3 = 18$ questions for the 20 units, they accounted for 86 percent of the variance in mean scores between units.
9   Culture strength was statistically operationalized as the mean standard deviation, across the individuals within a unit, of scores on the 18 key practices questions (3 per dimension): a low standard deviation meaning a strong culture. Actual mean standard deviations varied from 0.87 to 1.08, and the Spearman rank order correlation between these mean standard deviations and the 20 units' scores on 'results orientation' was -0.71.

10 The product moment correlation matrix contained 15 correlations significant at the 0.01 level and beyond, and 28 at the 0.05 level. Crossing 40 characteristics with 6 dimensions we could expect 2 or 3 correlations at the 0.01 level by chance, and 12 at the 0.05 level. Chance therefore can only account for a minor part of the relationships found.

11 A product moment correlation coefficient of 0.78, significant at the 0.001 level.

12 We are not the only ones suggesting this kind of model. In Switzerland, management consultant Cuno Pümpin has described a model with seven dimensions of which five are similar to ours (results orientation, employee orientation, company orientation, cost orientation, and customer orientation); his publications do not explain how these dimensions were found (Pümpin, 1984; Pümpin, *et al.*, 1985). In India, Professor Pradip Khandwalla in a study of managers across 75 organizations, using five-point survey questions similar to our 'Where I work . . .' questions, found a first factor closely resembling our process vs. results orientation (Khandwalla, 1985).

13 In a later study conducted by IRIC for a large service company, culture data were collected from the full population of about 2500 employees, divided into 130 departments. A statistical technique called 'hierarchical cluster analysis' revealed four clear subcultures; one of these presented almost the opposite profile from the culture to which top management belonged.

Part IV

Implications

9

Intercultural encounters

The English Elchi (ambassador) had reached Tehran a few days before we arrived there, and his reception was as brilliant as it was possible for a dog of an unbeliever to expect from our blessed Prophet's own lieutenant . . . . The princes and noblemen were enjoined to send the ambassador presents, and a general command issued that he and his suite were the Shah's guests, and that, on the pain of the royal anger, nothing but what was agreeable should be said to them.

All these attentions, one might suppose, would be more than sufficient to make infidels contented with their lot; but, on the contrary, when the subject of etiquette came to be discussed, interminable difficulties seemed to arise. The Elchi was the most intractable of mortals. First, on the subject of sitting. On the day of his audience of the Shah, he would not sit on the ground, but insisted upon having a chair; then the chair was to be placed so far, and no farther, from the throne. In the second place, of shoes, he insisted upon keeping on his shoes, and not walking barefooted upon the pavement; and he would not even put on our red cloth stockings. Thirdly, with respect to hats: he announced his intention of pulling his off to make his bow to the king, although we assured him that it was an act of great indecorum to uncover the head. And then, on the article of dress, a most violent dispute arose: at first, it was intimated that proper dresses should be sent to him and his suite, which would cover their persons (now too indecently exposed) so effectually that they might be fit to be seen by the king; but this proposal he rejected with derision. He said, that he would appear before the Shah of Persia in the same dress he wore when before his own sovereign.

James Morier, *The Adventures of Hajji Baba of Ispahan.*

James J. Morier (1780–1849) was a European and *The Adventures of Hajji Baba of Ispahan* is a work of fiction. Morier however knew what he wrote about. He was born and raised in Ottoman Turkey as a son of the British consul at Constantinople. Later, he spent altogether seven years as a British diplomat in Persia, the present Iran. When *Hajji Baba* had been translated into Persian, the readers refused to believe that it had been written by a foreigner. 'Morier was by temperament an ideal traveller, revelling in the surprising interests of strange lands and peoples, and gifted with a humorous sympathy that enabled him to appreciate the motives actuating persons entirely dissimilar to himself,' to quote the editor of the 1923 version of his book.[1] Morier obviously read and spoke Turkish and Persian. For all practical purposes he had become bicultural.

Intended versus unintended intercultural conflict

Human history is composed of wars between cultural groups. Joseph Campbell (1904–1987), an American author on comparative mythology, finds the primitive myths of nonliterate peoples without exception affirming and glorifying war. In the Old Testament, a Holy Book of both Judaism and Christianity and a source document for the Muslim Koran, there are many quotes like:

> 'But in the cities of these people that the Lord your God gives you for an inheritance, you shall save alive nothing that breathes, but you shall utterly destroy them, the Hittites and the Amorites, the Canaanites and the Perizzites, the Hivites and the Jebusites, as the Lord your God has commanded'.
>
> (Deuteronomy 20:16–18).

This is a religiously sanctified call for genocide.[2] The fifth commandment 'thou shalt not kill' from the same Old Testament obviously only applies to members of the ingroup. Territorial expansion of one's own tribe by killing off others is not only permitted but supposed to be ordered by God. Not only in the land of the Old Testament, but also in many other parts of the world, territorial conflicts involving the killing or expelling of other groups continue to this day. The Arabic name of the modern Palestinians who dispute with the Israelis the rights on the land of Israel is 'Philistines', the same name by which their ancestors are described in the Old Testament.

Territorial expansion is not the only *casus belli* (reason for war). Human groups have found many other excuses for collectively attacking others. An external enemy has always been one of the most effective ways to maintain internal cohesion. In Chapter 5 it was shown that a basic belief in many cultures is 'What is different, is dangerous.' Racism assumes the innate superiority of one group over another and uses this to justify using violence for the purpose of maintaining this superiority. Totalitarian ideologies like apartheid impose definitions of which groups are better and which are inferior; definitions which may be changed from one day to another. Culture pessimists wonder whether human societies can exist without enemies.

Whereas cultural processes have a lot to do with issues of war and peace, war and peace will not be a main issue in this chapter. They represent 'intended conflict' between human groups and this is an issue too big for this book. The purpose of the present chapter is to look at the *unintended conflicts* which often arise during intercultural encounters and which happen although nobody wants them and all suffer from them. They have at times contributed to the outbreak of wars. However, it would be naive to assume that all wars could be avoided by developing intercultural communication skills.

Owing to modern travel and communication technology, intercultural encounters have multiplied in the modern world at a prodigious rate. Embarrassments, such as those between Morier's English Elchi and the courtiers of the Shah, today occur between ordinary tourists and locals, between schoolteachers and the parents of their immigrant students, and between business people trying to set up international ventures. More subtle misunderstandings than those pictured by Morier but with similar roots still play an important role in negotiations between modern diplomats and political leaders. Intercultural communication skills can contribute to the success of negotiations on whose results depend the solutions for crucial global problems. Avoiding such unintended cultural conflicts will be the theme of this chapter.

Culture shock and acculturation

There exist a number of standard psychological and social processes which tend to accompany intercultural encounters. The simplest form of intercultural encounter is between one foreign individual and a new cultural environment.

The foreigner usually experiences some form of *culture shock*. As illustrated over and over again in earlier chapters, our mental software contains basic values. These have been acquired early in our lives, and they have become so natural as to be unconscious. Based upon them are our conscious and more superficial manifestations of culture: rituals, heroes, and symbols (see Fig. 1.2). The inexperienced foreigner can make an effort to learn some of the symbols and rituals of the new environment (words to use, how to greet, when to bring presents) but it is unlikely that he or she can recognize, let alone feel, the underlying values. In a way, the visitor in a foreign culture returns to the mental state of an infant, in which he or she has to learn the simplest things over again. This usually leads to feelings of distress, of helplessness, and of hostility towards the new environment. Often one's physical functioning is affected. Expatriates and migrants have more need for medical help shortly after their displacement than before or later.

People on temporary assignment to a foreign cultural environment often report an *acculturation curve* like Fig. 9.1.[3] In this diagram, feelings (positive or negative) are plotted on the vertical axis; time on the horizontal one. Phase 1 is a (usually short) period of *euphoria*: the honeymoon, the excitement of travelling and of seeing new lands. Phase 2 is the period of *culture shock* when real life starts in the new environment, as described above. Phase 3, *acculturation*, sets in when the visitor has slowly learned to function under the new conditions, has adopted some of the local values,

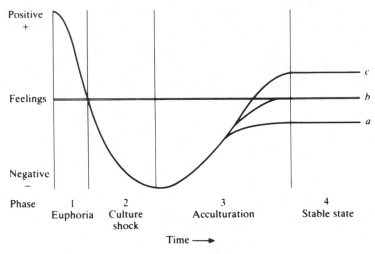

Fig. 9.1 The acculturation curve

finds increased self-confidence and becomes integrated into a new social network. Phase 4 is the *stable state* of mind eventually reached. It may remain negative compared to home (4a), for example if the visitor continues feeling alien and discriminated against. It may be just as good as before (4b), in which case the visitor can be considered to be biculturally adapted, or it may even be better (4c). In the last case the visitor has 'gone native'—she or he has become more Roman than the Romans.

The length of the time scale in Fig. 9.1 is arbitrary; it seems to adapt to the length of the expatriation period. People on short assignments of up to three months have reported euphoria, culture shock, and acculturation phases within this period; people on long assignments of several years have reported culture shock phases of a year or more before acculturation set in.

Culture shocks and the corresponding physical symptoms may be so severe that assignments have to be terminated prematurely. Most international business companies have experiences of this kind with some of their expatriates.[4] There have been cases of expatriate employees' suicides. Culture shock problems of accompanying spouses, more often than those of the expatriated employees themselves, seem to be the reason for early return. The expatriate, after all, has the work environment which offers a cultural continuity with home. There is the story of an American wife, assigned with her husband to Nice, France, a tourist's heaven, who locked herself up inside their apartment and never dared to go out.

Among refugees and migrants there is a percentage that fall seriously physically or mentally ill, commit suicide, or remain so homesick that they have to return, especially within the first year.

Expatriates and migrants who successfully complete their acculturation process and then return home will experience a 'reverse culture shock' in readjusting to their old cultural environment. Migrants who have returned home sometimes find they do not fit any more and emigrate again, this time for good. Expatriates who successively move to new foreign environments report that the culture shock process starts all over again. Obviously, culture shocks are environment specific. For every new cultural environment there is a new shock.

Ethnocentrism and xenophilia

There are also standard types of reactions within host environments exposed to foreign visitors. The people in the host culture receiving a foreign culture visitor usually go through another psychological reaction cycle. The first phase is *curiosity*—somewhat like the euphoria on the side of the visitor. If the visitor stays and tries to function in the host culture, a second phase sets in: *ethnocentrism*. The hosts will evaluate the visitor by the standards of their culture, and this evaluation tends to be unfavorable. The visitor will show bad manners, like the English Elchi; he or she will appear rude, naive, and/ or stupid. Ethnocentrism is to a people what egocentrism is to an individual: considering one's own little world to be the centre of the universe. If foreign visitors arrive only rarely, the hosts will probably stick to their ethnocentrism. If regularly exposed to foreign visitors, the hosts may move into a third phase: *polycentrism*, the recognition that different kinds of people should be measured by different standards, and the ability to understand the foreigner according to the foreigner's standards. This is a mild form of bi- or multiculturality.[5]

As we saw in Chapter 5, uncertainty avoiding cultures will resist polycentrism more than uncertainty accepting cultures. However, individuals within a culture vary around the cultural average, so in intolerant cultures one may meet tolerant hosts and vice versa. The tendency to apply different standards to different kinds of people may also turn into *xenophilia*, that is, the belief that in the foreigner's culture, everything is better. Some foreigners will be pleased to confirm this belief. There is a tendency among expatriates to idealize what one remembers from home. Neither ethnocentrism nor xenophilia is a healthy basis for intercultural cooperation, of course.

Group encounters: auto- and heterostereotypes

Intercultural encounters among groups rather than with single foreign visitors provoke group feelings. Contrary to popular belief, intercultural contact among groups does *not* automatically breed mutual understanding. It usually confirms each group in its own identity. Members of the other group are not perceived as individuals but in a stereotyped fashion: all Chinese look alike; all Scots people are stingy. As compared to the *heterostereotypes* about members of the other group, *autostereotypes* are fostered about members of one's own group. Such stereotypes will even affect the perception of actual events: if a member of one's own group attacks a member of the other group, one may be convinced ('I saw it with my own eyes') that it was the other way round.

As we saw in Chapter 3, the majority of people in the world live in collectivist societies, in which people remain throughout their lives members of tight ingroups which provide them with protection in exchange for loyalty. In such a society, groups with different cultural backgrounds are outgroups to an even greater extent than outgroups from their own culture. Integration across cultural dividing lines in collectivist societies is even more difficult to obtain than in individualist societies. This is *the* major problem of many decolonized nations, like those in Africa where national borders were inherited from the colonial period which in no way respected ethnic and cultural dividing lines.

Establishing true integration among members of culturally different groups requires environments in which these people can meet and mix as equals. Sports clubs, universities, work organizations, and armies can assume this role. Some ethnic group cultures produce people with specific skills, like sailors or traders, and such skills can become the basis for their integration in a larger society.

Language and humor

In most intercultural encounters the parties also speak different mother languages. Throughout history this problem has been resolved by the use of trade languages like Malay, Swahili or, more and more, derivations from English. Trade languages are 'pidgin' forms of original languages, and the trade language of the modern world can be considered a form of business pidgin English. Language differences contribute to mistaken cultural perceptions. In an international training program within IBM, trainers used to rate participants' future career potential. A longitudinal follow-up study of actual careers showed that the trainers had consistently overestimated participants whose native language was English (the course language) and underestimated those whose languages were French or Italian, with native German speakers taking a middle position (Hofstede, 1975).

Communication in trade languages or pidgin limits communications to those issues for which these simplified languages have words. To establish a more fundamental intercultural understanding, the foreign partner must acquire the host culture language. Having to express oneself in another language means learning to adopt someone else's reference frame. It is doubtful whether one can be bicultural without also being bilingual. Although the words of a language are 'symbols' in terms of the onion diagram (see Fig. 1.2),

Table 9.1   Ability to converse in foreign languages in 12 EC countries

Country	Percentage speaking the following number of foreign languages				Mean number
	None	One	Two	Three	
Luxemburg	1	10	47	42	2.3
Netherlands	28	29	32	12	1.3
Denmark	40	30	25	6	1.0
Belgium Dutch	46	22	20	11	1.0
Belgium French	56	23	16	6	0.6
Germany FR	60	33	6	1	0.5
Greece	66	27	5	2	0.4
France	67	26	6	1	0.4
Spain	68	26	5	1	0.4
Portugal	76	14	8	2	0.4
Great Britain	74	20	5	1	0.3
Italy	76	19	5	1	0.3
Ireland (Republic of)	80	17	3	0	0.2

Source: *Eurobarometer* No. 28, December 1987, pp. 76–78, EEC.

which means that they belong to the surface level of a culture, they are also the vehicles of culture transfer. Moreover, words are obstinate vehicles: our thinking is affected by the categories for which words are available in our language.[6] Many words have migrated from their language of origin into others because they express something unique: management, computer, apartheid, machismo, perestroika, geisha, sauna, Weltanschauung, mafia, savoir-vivre.

The skill of expressing oneself in more than one language is very unevenly distributed across countries. For example, among the 12 countries of the European Community a public opinion survey in 1987 produced figures about the ability to participate in a conversation in a foreign language (see Table 9.1). The champions are the small, wealthy, Germanic-language countries: Luxemburg (where virtually everybody speaks other languages besides the local *Letzebürgisch*), the Netherlands, Denmark, and the Dutch (Flemish)-speaking part of Belgium. Switzerland is missing on the list because it is not an EC member but it certainly also scores high. The same holds for the Nordic countries Finland, Norway, and Sweden. These countries possess a strategic advantage in intercultural contacts in that they nearly always have people available who speak several foreign languages; and whoever speaks more than one language will more easily learn additional languages. At the low end in the EC table we find Italy and the English-speaking countries Great Britain and the Republic of Ireland. If the USA had participated, it would almost certainly have scored even lower.

Paradoxically, having English, the world trade language, as one's mother tongue is a liability, not an asset, for truly communicating with other cultures. Native English speakers do not always realize this. One farmer from Kansas, USA, is supposed to have said 'If English was good enough for Jesus Christ, it is good enough for me.'[7] I once met an Englishman working near the Welsh border who said he had turned down an offer of a beautiful home across the border, in Wales, because in there his young son would have had to learn Welsh as a second language at school. In my view he missed a unique contribution to his son's education as a world citizen.

Language and culture are not so closely linked that sharing a language implies sharing a culture; nor should a difference in language always impose a difference in cultural values. In Belgium, where Dutch and French are the two dominant national languages (there is a small German-speaking area too) the scores of the Dutch- and French-speaking regions on the four dimensions of the IBM studies were very similar, and both regions scored very much like France and very different from the Netherlands. This reflects Belgian history: the middle and upper classes used to speak French, whatever the language of their ancestors, and adopted the French culture; the lower classes spoke Dutch whatever the language of their ancestors, but when upclassed they conformed to the culture of the middle classes. The IBM studies include a similar comparison between the German- and French-speaking regions of Switzerland. In this case the picture is very different: the German-speaking part scored similar to Germany and the French-speaking part scored similar to France. Switzerland's historical development was very different from Belgium's: in Switzerland the language distribution followed the cantons (independent provinces), rather than the social class structure. This also helps to understand why language is a hot political issue in Belgium, but not in Switzerland (Hofstede, 1980, pp. 335–339; 1984, pp. 228–231).

Without knowing the language one misses a lot of the subtleties of a culture and is forced to remain a relative outsider. One of these subtleties is humor. What is considered funny is highly culture-specific. Many Europeans consider that Germans have no sense of humor, but this simply means they have a different sense of humor. In intercultural encounters the experienced traveller knows that jokes and irony are taboo until one is absolutely sure of the other culture's conception of what represents humor.

Raden Mas Hadjiwibowo, the Indonesian businessman whose description of Javanese family visits was quoted in Chapter 3, has written an insightful analysis of the difference between the Indonesian and the Dutch sense of humor. One of his case studies runs as follows:

'It was an ordinary morning with a routine informal office meeting. They all sat around the meeting table, and found themselves short of one chair. Markus, one of the Indonesian managers, looked in the connecting office next door for a spare chair.

The next-door office belonged to a Dutch manager, Frans. He was out, but he would not mind lending a chair; all furniture belonged to the firm anyway. Markus was just moving one of Frans' chairs through the connecting door when Frans came in from the other side.

Frans was in a cheerful mood. He walked over to his desk to pick up some papers, and prepared for leaving the room again. In the process he threw Markus a friendly grin and as an afterthought he called over his shoulder: "You're on a nice stealing spree, Markus?". Then he left, awaiting no answer.

When Frans returned to his office after lunch, Markus was waiting for him. Frans noticed Markus had put on a tie, which was unusual. "Markus, my good friend, what can I do for you?" Frans asked. Markus watched him gloomily, sat straight in his chair and said firmly and solemnly: "Frans, I hereby declare that I am not a thief."

Dumbfounded, Frans asked what the hell he was talking about. It took them another forty-five minutes to resolve the misunderstanding.'[8]

In the Dutch culture in which the maintenance of face and status is not a big issue, the 'friendly insult' is a common way of joking among friends. 'You scoundrel' or 'you fool', if pronounced with the right intonation, expresses warm sympathy. In Indonesia where status is sacred, an insult is always taken at its face value. Frans should have known this.

Intercultural encounters in tourism

Tourism represents the most superficial form of intercultural encounter. With mass tourism the traveller may spend two weeks in Morocco, Bali, or Cancun without finding out anything about the local culture at all. Host country personnel working in tourism will learn something more about the culture of the tourists, but their picture of the way the tourists live at home will be highly distorted. What one picks up from the other group is on the level of symbols (see Fig. 1.2): words, fashion articles, music, etc.

The economic effects of mass tourism on the host countries may or may not be favorable. Traditional sources of income are often destroyed and the revenues of tourism go to governments and foreign investors, so that the local population may suffer more than it benefits. The environmental effects can be disastrous. Tourism is, from many points of view, a mixed blessing.

Tourism can nevertheless be the starting point for more fundamental intercultural encounters. It breaks the isolation of cultural groups, and creates an awareness that people exist who have other ways. The seed planted in some minds may ripen later. Some tourists start learning the language and history of the country they have visited and where they want to return. Hosts start learning the tourists' languages to promote their business. Personal friendships develop between the most unlikely people in the most unlikely ways. From an intercultural encounter point of view, the possibilities of tourism probably outweigh the disadvantages.

Intercultural encounters in schools

An American teacher at the foreign language institute in Beijing exclaimed in class 'You lovely girls, I love you.' Her students, according to a Chinese observer, were terrified. An Italian professor teaching in the United States complained bitterly about the fact that students were asked formally to evaluate his course. He did not think that students should be the judges of the quality of a professor. An Indian lecturer at an African university saw a student arrive six weeks late for matriculation, but he had to admit him because he was from the same village as the dean. Intercultural encounters in schools can lead to much perplexity.

Most intercultural encounters in schools are of one of two types: between local teachers and foreign, migrant, or refugee students, or between expatriate teachers, hired as foreign experts, or sent as missionaries, and local students. Different value patterns in the cultures from which the teacher and the student have come are one source of problems. In Chapters 2 through 5 consequences for the school situation of differences in values related to power distance, individualism, masculinity, and uncertainty avoidance have already been described. They usually affect the relationships between teacher and students, among students, and between teacher and parents.

As language is the vehicle of teaching, what was mentioned earlier about the role of language in intercultural encounters applies in its entirety to the teaching situation. The chances for successful cultural adaptation are better if the teacher is to teach in the students' language than if the student has to learn in the teacher's language, because the teacher has more power over the learning situation than any single student. The course language affects the learning process.

At INSEAD international business school in France I taught the same executive course in French to one group and in English to another; both groups were composed of people from several nationalities. Discussing a case study in French led to highly stimulating intellectual discussions but few practical conclusions. When the same case was discussed in English, it would not be long before someone asked 'So what?' and the class tried to become pragmatic. Both groups used the same readings, partly from French authors translated into English, partly vice versa. Both groups liked the readings originally written in the class language and condemned the translated ones as 'unnecessarily verbose, with a rather meagre message which could have been expressed on one or two pages.' The comments of the French-language class on the readings translated from English therefore were identical to the comments of the English-language class on the readings translated from

French. What is felt to be a 'message' in one language does not necessarily survive the translation process. Information is more than words: it is words which fit into a cultural framework.

Beyond differences in language, students and teachers in intercultural encounters run into differences in cognitive abilities. 'Our African engineers do not think like engineers, they tend to tackle symptoms, rather than view the equipment as a system' is a quote from a British training manager, unconscious of his own ethnocentrism. Fundamental studies by development psychologists have shown that the things we have learned are determined by the demands of the environment in which we grew up. A person will become good at doing the things that are important to him or her and that he or she has occasion to do often. Being from a generation which predates the introduction of pocket calculators in schools, I can do many calculations by heart, for which my children need a machine. Learning abilities, including the development of memory, are rooted in the total pattern of a society. In China, the nature of the script (between 3000 and 15 000 complex characters of up to 23 strokes) develops children's ability at pattern recognition, but it also imposes a need for rote learning.

Intercultural problems arise also because expatriate teachers bring irrelevant materials with them. A Zaïrese friend, studying in Brussels, recalled how at primary school in Lubumbashi her teacher, a Belgian nun, made the children recite in her history lesson '*Nos ancêtres, les Gaulois*': our ancestors, the Gauls. A British lecturer repeated his organizational behavior course word for word during a visiting teaching assignment to China. Much of what students from poor countries learn at universities in rich countries is hardly relevant in their home country situation. What is the interest for a future manager in an Indian company of mathematical modeling of the US stock market? The know-how supposed to make a person succeed in an industrial country is not necessarily the same as that which will help the development of a country presently poor.

Finally, intercultural problems can be based on institutional differences in the societies from which the teachers and students have come; differences which generate different expectations as to the educational process and the role of various parties in it. From what types of family are students and teachers recruited? Are educational systems élitist or anti-élitist? A visiting US professor in a Latin American country may think he contributes to the economic development of the country, while in actual fact he only contributes to the continuation of élite privileges. What role do employers play in the educational system? In Switzerland and Germany, traineeships in industry or business are a respected alternative to a university education, allowing people to reach the highest positions, but this is not the case in most other countries. What role do the state and/or religious bodies play? In some countries (France, Russia) the government prescribes the curriculum in great detail, in others the teachers are free to define their own. In countries where both private and public schools exist, the private sector may be for the élites (USA) or for the dropouts (the Netherlands, Switzerland). Where does the money for the schools come from? How well are teachers paid and what is their social status? In China, teachers are traditionally highly respected, but presently very poorly paid. In the UK the status of teachers has traditionally been low; in Germany, high.

Intercultural encounters in development cooperation

'Alain was from Antwerp. He was travelling with his Chinese counterpart Li. They were going to Hefei, but they did not know that Hefei was the new center of student protest . . . They were telephone engineers in a Belgian–Chinese joint venture to upgrade the telephone system . . .

He was the complete Foreign Expert. He did not speak Chinese. He had no interest in politics. Chinese art to him was the enamelled ashtrays and bamboo back-scratchers they sold at the friendship stores. Apart from Qingdao and Hefei and Shanghai, he had not travelled anywhere . . . Their field was telephones— wiring, systems, satellites, exchanges, link-ups, computers. They had this very narrow but deep area of expertise, and it was all they cared about. They could talk animatedly about computer telephone systems, but about nothing else. Mention the rain in Guangdong or the snow in Harbin and they looked blank. Don't mention books.'[9]

The relationship between rich and poor countries has changed completely since the Second World War. Until the war, most poor countries were colonies of rich countries. In the 30 years after the war nearly all former colonies became independent. At first they were called 'underdeveloped areas', a term which betrays a carryover of colonial condescension. After 1950, programs of development aid were gradually started, financed by the rich countries and with the poor ones as receivers. The colonial jargon faded out: the receiving countries were renamed 'developing countries' (even if they did not develop) or 'Third World', and development 'aid' became 'assistance' and after that 'development cooperation'.

In Chapter 4 it was shown that the percentage of their gross national products which governments of rich countries have allocated to development cooperation varies considerably (Norway spending in 1988 nearly five times as much as Austria), and that this percentage is strongly correlated with the rich countries' femininity scores. Development assistance money is allocated according to the (psychological) needs of the donor countries more than according to the material needs of the receivers.

The effectiveness of much of the development assistance has been dismal. With some notable exceptions in East Asia (see Chapter 7), in spite of aid, rich countries have become richer and poor countries poorer. Development assistance has not been able to prevent the debt crisis which has stricken many Latin American and African countries since the late 1970s.

Developing a country has for decades been considered primarily an economic and technical problem; it has been in the hands of technocrats at the giving, and often also at the receiving, end. Citizens of the receiving countries obtained technical or business degrees from universities in the donor countries, but they were not necessarily successful in applying their knowledge back home. It has slowly become evident that the quality of development cooperation depends on the effectiveness of the intercultural encounter of members of two very different societies. Nobody can develop a country but its own inhabitants; so foreign experts are only effective to the extent that they can transfer their know-how in the local context, and to the extent that the proposed aid fits in with felt needs and priorities in the receiving countries. This demands intercultural understanding, communication, and training skills.

There is always a cultural gap between donor and receiving countries on the dimension of individualism–collectivism. Donor countries, by definition rich, are also culturally more individualist and receiving countries more collectivist. This implies that receivers will want the aid to benefit certain ingroups over others (a particularist way of thinking) while donors will want to serve certain *categories*, like the urban poor or the small farmers, regardless of ingroup affiliation (a universalist way of thinking). Leaders in the receiving countries may, for example, want to repay their own village or tribe for its sacrifices in providing them with an education and enabling them to get into their present power position.

Usually there is also a gap on the dimension of power distance. Most donor countries score considerably lower on this dimension than the receivers, and the donors' representatives try to promote equality and democratic processes at the receiving end. Donors tend to be disturbed by the fact that they cannot avoid powerful local leaders who want to use at least part of the aid to maintain or increase existing inequalities. These leaders rarely have any commitment to the kind of democracy the donors have in mind.

There may or may not be gaps on masculinity–femininity and on uncertainty avoidance, but in these cases they can be in either direction: the donor country could score higher or lower than the receiver. Such differences demand insight into the specifics of both cultures, donor agents understanding the receiving culture *and their own*, and receiving agents understanding the donor country culture and their own.

Intercultural encounters in the context of development cooperation have an institutional and an interpersonal side. On the institutional level many receiving countries, as well as many donor countries, lack the organizational framework to make the cooperation a success. Usually the primitive institutional structures in the receiving countries are blamed. On the donor side, however, the situation is not always much better. Many development agencies have grown out of the foreign service, the main objective of which is the promotion of the donor country's interests abroad. Diplomats lack both the skills and the organizational culture to act as successful entrepreneurs for development consulting activities. Development aid money often has political strings attached to it: it has to be spent in a way which satisfies the values of the donor country citizens and politicians, regardless of whether these values are shared by citizens and politicians at the receiving end. Projects funded by *international* agencies like the World Bank do not have this constraint, but they have to satisfy the agency's objectives which often also conflict with the receivers'.

The institutional problem at the receiving end is most serious for countries whose traditional institutional frameworks were destroyed during the periods of colonization and decolonization, especially in sub-Saharan Africa. Where institutional traditions no longer exist, personal interests may prevail unchecked. Some politicians are out to enrich themselves without being controlled by traditional norms. Institutions cannot be created from scratch: they are living arrangements, rooted in values and history, which have to grow. The economic success of the countries of East Asia can also be explained from the fact that these countries all possessed centuries-old institutional frameworks which were adapted to modern times. A research project by a Nigerian MPA (Master of Public Administration) candidate within the Post and Telecommunication Services of Kenya showed how effective managers used traditional authority models in their modern organization: a vertical structure derived from the extended family, and a horizontal structure derived from the council of family heads in the traditional village.[10]

In many cases, donor countries may set the wrong priorities based on their perception of the receivers' needs which differs from the real needs. In 1988 the development cooperation agencies of the four Nordic countries Denmark, Finland, Norway, and Sweden commissioned an 'Evaluation of the Effectiveness of Technical Assistance Personnel'. The receiving countries involved were Kenya, Tanzania, and Zambia in East Africa, major receivers of aid from the Nordic countries. The report criticized the priorities set by the donor agencies. The three receiving countries in 1987 hosted some 900 Nordic Technical Assistance Persons (TAPs) at an annual cost of one million Swedish Crowns apiece (a total annual cost of approximately US $150 million). From these, 65 percent were implementers (carrying out projects themselves), 17 percent controllers on behalf of the aid agencies, 11 percent trainers of local personnel, and 7 percent assistants in local institution building. According to the researchers these ratios do not correspond to the real and exposed needs of the receiving countries at all. The manpower development in African countries has made rapid progress since independence, so in many areas there is a sufficient supply of qualified locals. The work done by the foreign implementers could often be done by locals with the foreigners acting as trainers and consultants; this would also produce a better multiplying effect of the know-how in the receiving country. It would sharply reduce the number of TAPs needed and change the profile of skills required from them.[11]

A landmark study on the interpersonal communication qualities demanded from experts in development cooperation, sponsored by the Canadian International Development Agency, was published in 1979. The researchers questioned 250 Canadian expatriates in six host countries as well as 90 host country counterparts (Hawes and Kealey, 1979). They identified *overseas effectiveness* as consisting of three components:

1. Intercultural interaction and training, related to involvement with the local culture and people, and with transfer of skills.
2. Professional effectiveness, related to the performance of daily tasks, duties, and responsibilities on the job.
3. Personal/family adjustment and satisfaction, related to the capacity for basic satisfaction while living abroad, as an individual and as a family unit.

From these three, the expatriates were found to be generally competent on components 2 and 3, but lacking on component 1. Local counterparts stressed the transfer of job skills through intercultural interaction and training as the most crucial dimensions of expatriate success.

In summary, intercultural encounters in the context of development cooperation will be productive if there is a two-way flow of know-how: technical know-how from the donor to the receiver, and cultural know-how about the context in which the technical know-how should be applied, from the receiver to the donor. A technical expert meets a cultural expert, and their mutual expertise is the basis for their mutual respect.

Both parties in development cooperation have to recognize and accept that they each bring their own cultural values. This will, for example, affect the setting of priorities and time schedules. Donors often find politicians at the receiving end unduly interested in prestige projects, but in many cases prestige is a greater cultural value in the receiving than in the donor country. Receivers, on the other hand, will benefit from an insight into the differing values of different donor countries, so they can involve a donor in projects to which this donor can feel committed. Parties should compromise, but never to the extent that projects are started where failure is predictable. Improving the quality of intercultural interactions in development cooperation still has a long way to go. It deserves the allocation of funds which now are too quickly reserved for technical resources.

Intercultural encounters between host countries and migrants

The number of people in today's world who have left their native country and moved to a completely different environment is larger than ever before in human history. The 'great peoples' migration' of the early centuries AD involved far smaller numbers of people than the present migration waves. The reasons are wars and other political upheavals as well as poverty in one place versus presumed riches in another. The effect in all cases is that people and entire families are parachuted into cultural environments vastly different from the ones in which they were mentally programmed, often without any preparation.

This section has been written with particular reference to the situation of Mediterranean and South Asian migrant workers and refugees in Western Europe. Much of it, however, will equally apply to legal or illegal migrants in North America, Australia, and New Zealand. In most of these cases people move from a collectivist to a more individualist society. Where they migrate as a family, they try to maintain collectivist values inside the family, and the migrant family tries to protect itself against adulteration by the individualist environment. This is easier if a migrant *community* can be established in the country of migration, which serves as a source of mutual support. Unfortunately the individualist values of host country politicians usually make them dislike migrant ghettos, and migrants are dispersed among the rest of the population, assuming this will speed up their adaptation. The opposite is often the case: migrants who have the support of a migrant community feel safer and offer less resistance to the new environment than migrants who feel isolated.

Next to gaps on the dimension of individualism–collectivism, migrants usually experience differences in power distance. Host societies tend to be more egalitarian than the places the migrants have come from. As in the case of development cooperation, differences on masculinity–femininity and on uncertainty avoidance between migrants and hosts may go either way, and the adaptation problems in these cases are specific to the pair of cultures involved.

Migrant families in their new environment experience standard dilemmas. At work, in shops and public offices, and usually also at school, migrants interact with locals and are re-programmed to local values. At home they try to maintain the values and relationship patterns from their country of origin. They are marginal people between two worlds and they alternate daily between one and the other.

The effect of this marginality is different for the different family members. The *father* tries to maintain his traditional authority in the home. At work his status is often low: migrants take the jobs nobody else wants. The family knows this and he loses face towards his relatives. If he is unemployed this makes him lose face even more. He frequently has problems with the local language which makes him feel a fool. Sometimes he is illiterate even in his own language. He has to call for the help of his children or of social workers in filling out forms and dealing with the authorities. He is often discriminated against by employers, policemen, and neighbors.

The *mother* in some migrant cultures is virtually a prisoner in the home, locked up when the father has gone to work. In these cases she has no contact with the host society, does not learn the language, and remains completely dependent on her husband and children. In other cases the mother too has a job. She may be the main breadwinner of the family, a severe blow to the father's self-respect. She meets other men and her husband may suspect her of unfaithfulness. The marriage sometimes breaks up.

The *sons* go to local schools, although not necessarily the best ones. While they actually need extra attention to make the switch from one society to another, they often receive even less attention than most local children. They become the real marginals, spending part of their time in the hostile freedom of the street and part in the warm tyranny of the family. Some succeed nevertheless, and benefit from the better educational opportunities and enter skilled and professional occupations. Some drop out of school and run away from parental authority at home; together with other migrant boys they may find collectivist protection in street gangs. In any case, they risk becoming the new underclass in the host society.

The *daughters* also go to school where they are exposed to an equality among the sexes unknown in the traditional society from which they have come. Fathers and brothers are supposed to defend the girls' purity and they often see school influences as threatening it. Migrant girls are not allowed to participate in school trips which would mean that they would spend a night away from home. They are not allowed to have dates. Often they are taken out of school as quickly as possible and hurried into the safety of an arranged marriage with a compatriot. Many Muslim cultures are endogamous, i.e., they allow marriage between first cousins (see Todd, 1983), and girls are conveniently married to relatives back home.

These are grim pictures but there is another side to it. Whoever has seen the migrants during their vacations in their home countries knows that over there, they are the cosmopolitans who spread Western values and tastes. Migrants on vacation, and even more so those who have returned for good, do experience a reverse culture shock. They have absorbed more from the country in which they spent part of their lives than they realized themselves, and if they meet a citizen of that country they welcome him or her warmly as a compatriot. The children often do not fit into the country of origin at all any more, and not infrequently they return to the host country with or without their parents' permission.

The host society is often ill prepared to deal with the migrants and help them to make most of their stay. I have already referred to the unfortunate tendency among some politicians to want to spread migrants geographically, rather than allowing them the social support of a community of compatriots. Those agents of the host society who interact frequently with migrants need to acquire special skills and experience. These are teachers, policemen, social workers, doctors, nurses, personnel officers, and counter-clerks in government offices. Some of them recognize the challenge of the intercultural encounters and develop creative ways of dealing with them. A schoolteacher in the Netherlands found out that his authority weighed heavily with Turkish fathers and that most fathers were honored and delighted to be invited for an interview. He could often convince the father that his daughter deserved to finish her school education, could safely participate in school excursions, and even continue towards a higher education. Many of his colleagues, he felt, took the negative reactions of Turkish fathers towards their daughters' careers for granted and did not realize how much influence they could exercise as teachers.[12]

There is, I believe, a need for simple training programs for locals interacting with migrants in which the locals learn to look at the situation from the migrants' point of view and are stimulated to find ways of approach which are effective towards both cultures. Some people go further: a group of policemen in the Netherlands took courses in the Turkish language and organized a vacation trip to Turkey (the Turks are the largest ethnic minority in the Netherlands, being about 1.5 percent of the population).

The opposite reaction is for locals, and in particular people interacting with migrants, to turn to ethnocentric and racist philosophies. Policemen, journalists, some teachers, and parts of the public do adhere to racist points of view, compounding the felony of the migrants' inadaptation. 'What is different is dangerous': these are primitive manifestations of personal uncertainty avoidance. Among migrants there is also a tendency towards ethnocentrism. They have a better excuse, because more than the locals they live in a hostile environment. Religious fundamentalism thrives among migrants who at home were hardly religious at all. But even in the host society, religious fundamentalism is often found among marginal groups in society, and the migrants are the new marginals.

Intercultural encounters in international negotiations

In the USA several books have appeared on the art of negotiation; it is a popular theme for training courses. Negotiations have even been simulated in computer programs, which use a mathematical theory of games to calculate the optimal choice in a negotiation situation. These approaches are largely irrelevant for international negotiations such as take place between diplomats and/or politicians and/or business representatives. The American approaches are based upon both parties holding American values and objectives accepted in American society. In international negotiations no assumptions about common values and objectives can be made. Every player in the game plays according to his or her own rules.

Experienced diplomats from whatever country have usually acquired a professional *savoir-faire* which enables them to negotiate successfully with other diplomats on issues on which they are empowered to decide themselves. The problem, however, is that in issues of real importance diplomats are usually directed by politicians who have the power but not the diplomatic *savoir-faire*. Politicians often make statements intended for domestic use, which the diplomats are supposed to explain to foreign negotiation partners. The amount of discretion left to diplomats is in itself a cultural characteristic which varies from one society and political system to another. Modern communication possibilities contribute to limiting the discretion of diplomats; Morier's English Elchi did have a lot of discretionary power by the simple fact that communicating with England took at least three months in those days.

Yet there is no doubt that the quality of intercultural encounters in international negotiations can contribute to avoiding unintended conflict, *if* the parties are of the proper hierarchical level for the decisions at stake. This is why summit conferences are so important—here are the people who *do* have the power to negotiate. Unfortunately they have usually risen to their present position because they hold strong convictions in harmony with the national values of their country, and for this same reason they have difficulty recognizing that others function according to different mental programs. A trusted foreign minister or ambassador who has both the ear of the top leader *and* diplomatic sensitivity is a great asset to a country.

In business negotiations, too, it is culturally very important to send persons with appropriate power and status, even if the actual negotiations are done by someone lower down. The model of the joint operation of a *Machtpromotor* and a *Fachpromotor* described in Chapter 8 as a condition for successful cultural innovations can also be applied to the business negotiation case.

Intercultural encounters in international business organizations

Since the 1960s, for the first time in history, the world has become one market. Although the protection of home markets survives it has become a relative rather than an absolute impediment to businesses operating on a world scale. Inside international business organizations very intensive intercultural encounters take place. The IBM studies from which Chapters 2 to 6 have been drawn are a proof of the cultural variety inside one and the same multinational; and this variety has to be bridged through intercultural interaction.

One way in which international businesses coordinate their activities is through the expatriation of managers. Nonmanagerial personnel are also sometimes expatriated, but usually for the performance of specific technical tasks with a limited need for interaction with locals. Managers, however, are sent abroad for the explicit purpose of interacting with other nationals.

The psychological processes affecting expatriates were described earlier in this chapter. Expatriates' effectiveness in carrying out their task depends on more than serving their full term abroad, of course. It is often difficult for the headquarters' superiors of an expatriate manager to assess his or her effectiveness. Not only should short-term tasks be carried out, but long-term interests should be served as well, including the training of local successors, the breeding of loyalty for and pride in the corporation among local colleagues and employees, and the establishment of good relationships with local stakeholders: customers, suppliers, unions, and government officials. Culturally clumsy expatriates can cause damage which is only noticed after their repatriation and which will easily be a multiple of the direct cost of their expatriation. This direct cost is not negligible: including provision for their families, expatriates easily cost between US $100 000 and 200 000 annually on top of their salary.

More and more, businesses expand by foreign mergers and takeovers. These imply a dramatic importance of intercultural interactions, in which not only national but also organizational cultures are involved. Five methods of international expansion can be distinguished: (1) the greenfield start; (2) the foreign takeover; (3) the international merger; (4) the foreign joint venture; (5) the partial cooperation with a foreign partner. Their cultural implications differ considerably.

The *greenfield start* means that the corporation sets up a foreign subsidiary from scratch, usually sending over one expatriate or a small team, who hire locals and gradually build up a local business. Greenfield starts are by their very nature slow, but their cultural risk is limited. The founders of the subsidiary are able to select carefully from the population of the host country employees who will fit the culture of the corporation. The culture of the subsidiary will become a combination of national elements (mainly values, see Chapter 8) and corporate elements (mainly practices, see again Chapter 8). Greenfield starts have a high success rate. IBM has almost exclusively grown through greenfield starts; the same is true for many of the older multinationals. International certified public accountant firms used to set up subsidiaries the greenfield way until the wave of mergers occurred in their business in the late 1980s.

The *foreign takeover* is the exact opposite of the greenfield start: a local company is purchased wholesale by a foreign buyer. The existing company, its own organizational culture and, of course, elements of the host country national culture are brought in at one fell swoop. Foreign takeovers are a fast way of expanding, but their cultural risk is enormous. To use an analogy from family life (such analogies are very popular for describing the relationships between parts of corporations), foreign takeovers are to greenfield starts as the bringing up of a foster child, adopted in puberty, is to the bringing up of one's own child. In order to overcome the problems of integrating the new member, one solution is to keep it at arm's length: that is, not to integrate it but to treat it as a portfolio investment. But usually this is not why the foreign company has been purchased. When integration is imperative, the cultural clashes are often resolved by brute power: key people are replaced by the corporation's own men. In other cases, key people have not waited for this to happen and have left on their own account. Foreign takeovers often lead to the destruction of human capital which is eventually the destruction of financial capital as well. The same applies to takeovers in the home country, but abroad the cultural risk is much larger. The problem is that decisions about takeovers tend to be made by financial experts who believe they have resolved the problem when they have established the proper price. From a culture management point of view, this is when the problem starts. It is highly desirable to let foreign (and domestic) takeovers be preceded by an analysis of the culture of the corporation and the takeover candidate. If the decision is still to go ahead, such a match analysis can be used as the basis for a culture management plan.

The *international merger* resembles the foreign takeover, except that now the partners are of roughly equal size or importance. The cultural risk is the same as in the case of the foreign takeover, but the possibility of resolving cultural problems by a one-sided show of power no longer exists. International mergers therefore have an abysmally low success rate, probably not more than 25 percent (see Grunberg, 1981). Again the financial experts tend to dominate the merger negotiations; when the share ratio and the composition of the new board have been decided, some top managers believe the merging process has been achieved. This, of course, is just where it starts. Even more than in the case of the foreign takeover, an analysis of the corporate and national cultures of the potential partners should be part of the decision process. If the merger is concluded, this analysis can again be the basis of a culture integration plan which needs the active and permanent support of a *Machtpromotor* (see Chapter 8), probably the chief executive.

The cases where international mergers have been successful (Shell and Unilever, both British–Dutch, are the oldest examples) show a few common characteristics: *two* head offices are maintained so as to avoid the impression that the corporation is run from only one of the two countries; there has been strong and charismatic leadership during the integration phase; there has been an external threat which kept the partners together for survival; and governments have kept out of the business.

The *foreign joint venture* means creating a new business by pooling resources from two or more founding parties. A foreign joint venture can be started greenfield, or the local partner may transfer part of its people collectively to the venture. In the latter case, it transfers part of its culture as well. Foreign joint ventures represent a lower risk than foreign takeovers and mergers, provided clear agreements are made about which partner supplies which resources, including which part of management. Joint ventures in which one partner provides the entire management have a higher success rate than those in which management is shared between the partners. Sometimes foreign joint ventures will develop quite new and creative cultural characteristics, showing a synergy of elements from the founding partners. Foreign joint ventures are a limited-risk way of entering an unknown country and market. Some foreign joint ventures survive for a restricted time only, after which one of the partners buys the other out; but when this happens they have served their purpose of supplying know-how.

The *partial cooperation with a foreign partner* represents the most prudent way of going international. Without setting up a new venture, the partners agree to collaborate on specific products and/or markets for mutual benefit. As the risks are limited to the project at hand, this is a safe way of learning to know each other; neither party feels threatened. The acquaintance could develop into a merger, but in this case the partners know much more about each other's culture than with a 'cold' merger.

Large numbers of cooperative projects of this kind have been started in Europe in an attempt to compete against Japanese and US competition. No European country by itself is large enough or rich enough to take up global competition. On the other hand, the negative experiences with all-out international mergers have made companies careful. Partial cooperation contracts are seen as a solution. Many cooperative projects are bundled in 'Eureka', an EC-sponsored program to bring research partners from different European countries (even including non-EC members) together: in 1989 it covered about 300 different projects with a total budget of US $8000 million. The coordination of such projects through an international program is no guarantee against cultural clashes: many of the European cooperation projects flounder or fail due to the prevalence of national or company interests but also due to naïveté about the problems of intercultural encounters. Europe is learning about intercultural cooperation the hard way, but what it has learned will become a competitive advantage over the other economic superpowers.

One of the most visible international projects which is a combination of a cooperation agreement and a joint venture is the Airbus Consortium in Toulouse, France. They have become the world's second largest aircraft manufacturer. Parts of the planes are manufactured by the participating companies in the UK, Germany, and Spain and flown over to Toulouse where the planes are assembled by a thoroughly multinational manpower.

Coordinating multinationals: structure should follow culture[13]

Most multinational corporations cover a range of different businesses and/ or product/market divisions, in a range of countries. They have to bridge both national and business cultures. The profound nature of national culture differences, rooted in values, has already been shown. Business culture differences consist of occupational and organizational components. They reside more in people's practices than in their values.

The purpose of any organizational structure is the coordination of activities. These activities are carried out in 'business units', each involved in one type of business in one country. The design of a corporate structure is based on three choices for each business unit, whether explicit or implicit:

1. Which of the unit's inputs and outputs should be coordinated from elsewhere in the corporation?
2. Where should the coordination take place?
3. How tight or loose should the coordination be?

Multinational, multibusiness corporations face the choice between coordination along type-of-business lines or along geographical lines. The key question is whether business know-how or cultural know-how is more crucial for the success of the operation. The classic solution is a 'matrix' structure. This means that every manager of a business unit has two bosses, one who coordinates the particular type of business across all countries, and one who coordinates all business units in the particular country. For a time in the 1970s, matrix structures were very popular but in practice they are an imperfect answer to the coordination problem. They are costly, often meaning a doubling of the management ranks, and their functioning may raise more problems than it resolves. A single structural principle is unlikely to fit for an entire corporation. In some cases the business structure should dominate, in others geographical coordination should have priority. This means a patchwork structure which may lack beauty, but it does follow the needs of markets and business unit cultures.

Variety within the environment in which a company operates should be matched with appropriate internal variety. Too often, top managers look for uniform principles in structuring their entire corporation. These may satisfy their need for simple solutions, but they are bound to violate the needs of some parts of the organization. The diversity in structural solutions advocated is not only one of place, but also one of time: optimal solutions are very likely to change over time, so that the periodic reshufflings which any large organization will experience, should be seen as useful.

Since even multinationals are held together by people, the best structure at a given moment depends primarily on the availability of suitable people. It makes no sense to design structures which demand skills from people who are impossible to find. Two roles are particularly crucial:

1. *The country business unit manager*   The top person in a business unit in a country. He or she should be able to function in two cultures: the culture of the business unit, and the corporate culture which is usually heavily affected by the nationality of origin of the corporation.
2. *Corporate diplomats*   Home country or other nationals impregnated with the corporate culture, multilingual, from various occupational backgrounds, and experienced in living and functioning in various foreign cultures. They are essential to make multinational structures work, as liaison persons in the various head offices or as temporary managers for new ventures.

The availability of such people represents a major challenge for multinational personnel management. Timely recruitment of future managerial talent from different nationalities, career moves through planned transfers in view of acculturation in the corporate ways, and cultural awareness training for business experts who will have to operate in foreign countries are steps to ensure that the right people will be available when they are needed.

Learning intercultural communication
The acquisition of intercultural communication abilities passes through three phases: awareness, knowledge, and skills. *Awareness* is where it all starts: the recognition that I carry a particular mental software because of the way I was brought up, and that others brought up in a different environment carry a different mental software for equally good reasons. Without awareness, one may travel around the world feeling superior and remaining deaf and blind to all clues about the relativity of one's own mental programming. With awareness, one may become a bit like James Morier as he was described at the beginning of this chapter: '. . . gifted with a humorous sympathy that enabled him to appreciate the motives actuating persons entirely dissimilar to himself.'

Knowledge should follow. If we have to interact with particular other cultures, we have to learn about these cultures. We should learn about their symbols, their heroes, and their rituals; while we may never share their values, we may at least obtain an intellectual grasp of where their values differ from ours.

Skills are based on awareness and knowledge, plus practice. We have to recognize and apply the symbols of the other culture, recognize their heroes, practice their rituals, and experience the satisfaction of getting along in the new environment, being able to resolve first the simpler, and later on some of the more complicated, problems of life among the others.

Intercultural communication can be taught. Some students are more gifted in learning it than others. People with unduly inflated egos, a low personal tolerance for uncertainty, a history of emotional instability, or known racist or extreme left- or right-wing political sympathies should be considered bad risks for training which, after all, assumes people's ability to distance themselves from their own cherished beliefs. Such persons are probably unfit for expatriation anyway; if a family is to be expatriated it is wise to make sure that the spouse and children, too, have the necessary emotional stability.

There are two types of intercultural communication course. The more traditional ones focus on *specific knowledge* of the other culture; they are sometimes called 'expatriate briefings'. They inform the future expatriates, and preferably their spouses too, and sometimes their children, about the new country, its geography, some history, customs, hygiene, 'do's and don'ts', what to bring; in short: how to live. They do not provide much introspection into the expatriates' own culture. They are extremely useful, but the strongly motivated expatriate-to-be can also obtain this information from books and videos. In fact the institutes offering this type of training usually maintain good book and video libraries for urgent individual preparation.

An even better preparation for a specific assignment is, of course, learning the local *language*. There are plenty of crash courses but unless the learner is exceptionally gifted, learning a new language at business level will take several months full-time; a bit less if the course takes place in the foreign country so that the learner is fully immersed. Most employers do not plan far enough ahead to allow their expatriates such an amount of time for language learning, to their own detriment. If the expatriate has this chance, it is very important to involve the spouse as well. Women, on average, are faster learners of languages than men. They are also better at picking up nonverbal cultural clues.

The other type of intercultural communication course focuses on *awareness* of and *general knowledge* about cultural differences. Awareness training focuses on one's own mental software and where it may differ from others. It is not specific to any given country of expatriation; the knowledge and skills taught apply in any foreign cultural environment. They deal not so much with the question of how to live in the other culture, but more with how to work: how to get a job done. Besides the (future) expatriate the course may be attended by the spouse too, because an understanding spouse is a major asset during the culture shock period.[14] It should, however, definitely be attended by the expatriate's boss at head office and by staff specialists who communicate with the expatriates. Experience has taught that a major problem of expatriates is to obtain the understanding and support of the persons who are not expatriated themselves, but who act as their contacts in the home country organization. The home front should acquire the same cultural sensitivity demanded of the expatriate.

The awareness and general cultural knowledge course I helped to design[15] takes three days. It uses an intercultural business game, exercises, lectures, case studies, and group discussions. It has been attended by experienced expatriates, and they, even more than the novices, found the course useful: it enabled them to re-interpret their experiences. The main message is that you and I have a culture and that people who were brought up elsewhere have cultures which in more-or-less predictable ways differ from ours. This message can be transferred and digested in three days. After that, the learner will have to acquire the additional knowledge and skills for him- or herself. Some will attend an expatriate briefing course for the country of expatriation as well. Others acquire their knowledge by reading. Skills will have to be further developed in the country of destination. The effect of the training is that the expatriate learns that more knowledge and skills are needed and where to look for them. She or he will use sympathetic locals and more experienced expatriates in acquiring more information and practice. She or he will pick up more clues and ask more questions.

A different target group for intercultural training consists of those persons inside a culture who in their daily work deal with foreigners: with migrants, refugees, tourists, or foreign students. Such 'interface persons' are school-teachers, police personnel, doctors, nurses, social workers, immigration officials, lawyers, judges, and personnel officers of organizations employing minorities. An adapted type of awareness training is suitable for these groups; unfortunately, their motivation to be trained and the willingness of their employers to invest time and money in training are less common for this group than in the case of the expatriates. In the case of the interface persons, it is likely that the ones who most need it, because of prejudices and a lack of sensitivity, are those least likely to seek training, and vice versa.

A now classic but very useful instrument for *self-training*, suitable for interface persons, is the *culture assimilator* (CA). The CA is a programmed learning tool consisting of about 100 short case descriptions, each illustrating an intercultural encounter in which someone behaves in a particular way. After the case, four explanations are given of this behavior. One of these is the explanation shared by the majority of those inside the foreign culture. The three others are naive explanations by outsiders. The student chooses one answer and looks on the next page for the corresponding comment. The comment explains why the answer chosen is correct (corresponding to the insiders' view) or incorrect (naive).

CAs were developed since the late 1960s in the USA by Fred Fiedler, Terence Mitchell, and Harry Triandis (1971). The CAs of this period were culture specific both towards the majority and towards the minority culture. They therefore were costly to make and had relatively limited distribution. Nevertheless, an evaluation of their long-term effects showed that they did create awareness among students and led to greater sensitivity in dealing with persons from the other group (Albert, 1983). Under the leadership of Dr Richard Brislin of the East–West Center, University of Hawaii, a team in the 1980s composed a general culture assimilator incorporating the main common themes that were found to occur in the earlier specific ones. It has however retained a strong US flavor and the differences it covers are almost exclusively those between the USA and Third World cultures: most deal with the power distance and individualism–collectivism dimensions (Brislin *et al.*, 1986).

Cultural sensitivity is subtle, and bias is always looming around the corner. When in 1976 children of Vietnamese refugees went to regular schools in small towns in the USA, the Office of Education issued an instruction for teachers *On Teaching the Vietnamese*. Part of it runs:

> 'Student participation was discouraged in Vietnamese schools by liberal doses of corporal punishment, and students were conditioned to sit rigidly and to speak only when spoken to. This background . . . makes speaking freely in class hard for a Vietnamese. Therefore, don't mistake shyness for apathy.'[16]

To most West European and North American readers, this instruction looks okay at first. However, it becomes more problematic when we look for all the clues about US culture which the quote supplies, which are as many sources of bias. In fact, the US Office of Education ascribes to the Vietnamese all the motivations of young Americans—like a supposed desire to participate—and explains their submission by corporal punishment, rather than, for example, respect. At a doctoral seminar I taught in Sweden, one of the participants[17] opened the eyes of the others by reversing the statement—supposing American students would have to attend Vietnamese schools:

'Students' proper respect for teachers was discouraged by a loose order and students were conditioned to behave disorderly and to chat all the time. This background makes proper and respectful behavior in class hard for an American student. Therefore, don't mistake rudeness for lack of reverence.'

Notes

1 (Morier, 1923) edited with Introduction and Notes by C. W. Stewart. The quote from the text is from pp. 434–435; the quote from the Editor from p. vi.
2 This paragraph has been inspired by Joseph Campbell, 'Mythologies of War and Peace', in Campbell (1988, pp. 174–206).
3 For a review of studies with regard to the acculturation curve see Furnham and Bochner (1986, pp. 130–136).
4 Professor Rosalie Tung from the USA has compared the expatriation policies of US, European and Japanese multinationals and shown that US corporations tend to have higher expatriate failure rates than the others. See Tung (1982).
5 Professor Howard V. Perlmutter of the Wharton School, Philadelphia, USA, has developed the sequence ethnocentric, polycentric, geocentric as three phases in the development of a multinational business corporation. In the case of a host population, it is unlikely that they will ever become 'geocentric'—abolishing all nation-specific standards.
6 In cultural anthropology the phenomenon that our thinking is influenced by our language is known as the Sapir–Whorf theorem, after Edward Sapir and Benjamin Lee Whorf who formulated it.
7 Attributed to Henry Louis Mencken (1880–1956), US critic and satirist.
8 From a speech by R. M. Hadjiwibowo to Semafor Senior Management College, the Netherlands, September 1983. Translation from the Dutch by GH with suggestions by the author.
9 Paul Theroux, *Riding the Iron Rooster: By Train through China*. Reproduced by permission from Hamish Hamilton, London, 1988, pp. 390–391.
10 From an MPA thesis by Cukwugozie Ndinkora for the Institute of Social Sciences, the Hague, the Netherlands, 1972.
11 (Forss *et al.*, 1988) This study continued a pilot study by IRIC in the Netherlands. IRIC's design had been to combine development agencies *and* multinationals in the same study about factors leading to the effectiveness of expatriates. See Andersson and Hofstede (1984). After the proposed public/private cooperation fell through, the Nordic development agencies decided to go ahead on their own.
12 Dutch journalist Maria Hendriks in *De Volkskrant*, July 9, 1984.
13 This section uses parts of an article by Hofstede (1989).
14 Professor Nancy Adler from Canada has focused on the role of the executive spouse and produced a video series *A Portable Life* including interviews with spouses. See also Adler (1986).
15 Now offered by ITIM International, Celebesstraat 96, NL–2585 TP The Hague, The Netherlands. Telephone 31–70–350.5054. Fax 31–70–355.2003.
16 This example is taken from a paper by Alfred J. Kraemer, presented at the 1978 Congress of Applied Psychology at Munich, Germany.
17 Åke Phillips.

10

Surviving in a multicultural world

... the English, of any people in the universe, have the least of a national character; unless this very singularity may pass for such.

David Hume, Essay XXI, 1742

The Germans live in Germany, the Romans live in Rome,
the Turkeys live in Turkey; but the English live at home.

from a nursery rhyme by J.H. Goring, 1909[1]

The message of this book

In terms of the quotes above, the message of the book has been that everybody is like Hume's or Goring's English. Everybody looks at the world from behind the windows of a cultural home and everybody prefers to act as if people from other countries have something special about them (a national character) but home is normal. Unfortunately, there is no normal position in cultural matters. This is an uncomfortable message, as uncomfortable as Galileo Galilei's claim in the seventeenth century that the Earth is not the center of the Universe.

Culture in Chapter 1 has been described through the metaphor of 'mental software'—a usually unconscious conditioning which leaves individuals considerable freedom to think, feel, and act but within the constraints of what his or her social environment offers in terms of possible thoughts, feelings, and actions. These constraints are present in all spheres of life, and in order to understand them, human life should be seen as an integrated whole.

Cultural programming starts in the environment in which a young child grows up, usually a family of some kind. It continues at school, and what happens in schools can only be understood if one knows what happens before and after school. It continues at work. Workers' behavior is an extension of behavior acquired at school and in the family. Managers' behavior is an extension of the managers' school and family experiences, as well as a mirror image of the behavior of the managed. Politics and the relationships between citizens and authorities are extensions of relationships in the family, at school, and at work, and in their turn they affect these other spheres of life. Religious beliefs, secular ideologies, and scientific theories are extensions of mental software demonstrated in the family, the school, at work, and in government relations, and they reinforce the dominant patterns of thinking, feeling, and acting in the other spheres.

Cultural programs differ from one group or category of people to another in ways which are rarely acknowledged and often misunderstood. The cultural category to which most of the book has been devoted is the nation state; some attention has been given to differences according to social class, gender, generation, and work organization. Every nation has a considerable moral investment in its own dominant mental software, which amply explains the common hesitation to make cultural differences discussable. The origins of the differences from one nation to another, and sometimes between ethnic, religious, or linguistic subgroups within nations, are hidden in history. In some cases causal explanations are possible; in many other cases one should assume that a small difference arose many centuries ago, and that in being transferred from generation to generation this small difference grew into the large difference it is today.

The main cultural differences among nations lie in values. Systematic differences exist (and are described in the Chapters 2 to 5 and in 7) with regard to values about power and inequality, with regard to the relationship between the individual and the group, with regard to the social roles expected from men or women, with respect to ways of dealing with the uncertainties in life, and with respect to whether one is mainly preoccupied with the future or with the past and present.

Chapters 6 and 8 have been devoted to the consequences of national culture differences for the functioning of organizations, and to the supposed phenomenon of 'organizational cultures': differences in mental software between those employed by different corporations or other bodies. The national culture impact on organizations is profound and affects both businesses and governments. The organizational culture component is much less profound than is often claimed, to the extent that the use of the same term 'culture' for both nations and organizations is slightly misleading. Organizational cultures are mainly expressed not in members' values but in more superficial manifestations like common symbols, heroes, and rituals.

The various chapters analyzing and describing cultural differences allow the reader to locate his or her own cultural value framework versus those in other countries and groups. Chapter 9, *Intercultural Encounters*, represents the culmination of the message: if we think, feel, and act so differently, how can we manage one world together? An increased consciousness of the constraints of our mental programs versus those of others is essential for our common survival. The message of the book is that such a consciousness can be developed and that while we should not expect to become all alike, we can at least aspire to become more cosmopolitan in our thinking.

The moral issue

Some people wonder whether the advocated consciousness of the limits of one's own value system does not lead to moral laxity. Chapter 1 contains a call for 'cultural relativism': the recognition that, as a famous French anthropologist expressed it, 'one culture has no absolute criteria for judging the activities of another culture as "low" or "noble".' But this is no call for dropping values altogether. As a matter of fact, the entire book shows that no human being can escape from using value standards all the time. Successful intercultural encounters presuppose that the partners believe in their own values. If not, they have become alienated persons, lacking a sense of identity. A sense of identity provides the feeling of security from which one can encounter other cultures with an open mind. The principle of surviving in a multicultural world is that one does not need to think, feel, and act in the same way in order to agree on practical issues and to cooperate. The IBM research to which the Chapters 2 to 6 have been devoted has illustrated this. The value differences among employees in different countries working for this multinational have been shown to be quite considerable. Nevertheless, IBMers the world over have cooperated in reasonable harmony towards practical goals. There is nothing unique about IBMers in this respect; other people can and do cooperate across national borders too. The fact that organizational cultures are relatively superficial and value-free phenomena, as was demonstrated in the IRIC research reported in Chapter 8, is precisely the reason why international organizations can exist and be composed of different nationals each with their own different national values.

People from cultures very dissimilar on the national culture dimensions of power distance, individualism, masculinity, uncertainty avoidance, and long-term orientation as described in the various chapters of this book can cooperate fruitfully. Yet, people from some cultures will cooperate more easily with foreigners than others. The most problematic are nations and groups within nations which score very high on uncertainty avoidance, and thus feel that 'What is different, is dangerous.' Also problematic is the cooperation with nations and groups scoring very high on power distance, because such cooperation depends on the whims of powerful individuals. In a world kept together by intercultural cooperation, such cultural groups will certainly not be forerunners. They may have to be left alone for some time until they discover they have no other choice but to join.

Cultural convergency and divergency

Research about the development of cultural values has shown repeatedly that there is very little evidence of international convergency over time, except an increase of individualism for countries that have become richer. Value differences between nations described by authors centuries ago are still present today, in spite of continued close contacts. For the next few hundred years countries will remain culturally very diverse.

Not only will cultural diversity among countries remain with us: it even looks as though differences within countries are increasing. Ethnic groups arrive at a new consciousness of their identity and ask for a political recognition of this fact. Of course these ethnic differences have always been there. What has changed is the intensity of contact between groups, which has confirmed group members in their own identities. Also, the spread of information on how people live elsewhere in the world, by international media, has affected minorities who compare their situation to the life of others whom they suppose to be better off. World news media also spread information of suffering and strife much wider than ever before. Pogroms, uprisings, and violent repression are no new inventions. In the past, relatively few people beyond those directly involved would know about them; now they are visible on TV screens around the world.

Educating for intercultural understanding: suggestions for parents

In this and the three following sections some of the conclusions from this book will be translated into practical advice. Such advice is unavoidably subjective, for which I beg the reader's tolerance.

The basic skill for surviving in a multicultural world, as this book has argued, is understanding first one's own cultural values (and that is why one needs a cultural identity of one's own), and next the cultural values of the others with whom one has to cooperate. As parents, we have more influence on creating multicultural understanding in future world citizens than in any other role. Values are mainly acquired during the first 10 years of a child's life. They are absorbed by observation and imitation of adults and older children rather than by indoctrination. The way parents live their own culture provides the child with its cultural identity. The way parents talk about and behave towards persons and groups from other cultures determines the degree to which the child's mind will be opened or closed for cross-cultural understanding.

Growing up in a bicultural environment can be an asset to a child: for example, having parents from different nationalities, or living abroad during childhood, or going to a foreign school. Whether such biculturality really is an asset or instead becomes a liability depends on the parents' ability to cope with the bicultural situation themselves. Having foreign friends, hearing different languages spoken, travelling with parents who awake the children's interests in things foreign are definite assets. Learning at least one other language—whatever the language—is a unique ingredient of education for multicultural understanding. This presupposes, of course, that the teaching of the other language is effective: a lot of language classes in schools are a waste of time. The stress should be on full immersion, whereby using the foreign language becomes indispensable for practical purposes. Becoming really bi- or multilingual is one of the advantages of children belonging to a minority or to a small nation. It is more difficult for those belonging to a big nation.

Coping with cultural differences: suggestions for managers

The previous chapters have offered many examples of the way in which cultural values affect the practices and theories of organizations. Culturally a manager is the follower of his or her followers: she or he has to meet the subordinates on these subordinates' cultural ground. There is free choice in managerial behavior but the cultural constraints are much tighter than most of the management literature admits.

The work situation is basically a suitable laboratory for intercultural cooperation, as the problems are practical and results are visible to everybody. Yet managers, workers, and worker representatives are rarely in the front ranks for promoting intercultural understanding. Narrow economic interest viewpoints tend to prevail on all sides. An exception is perhaps the increasing use of expatriate manager training. When managers are sent abroad, their organizations offer more and more opportunities for some cross-cultural training or briefing. Managers chronically underestimate cultural factors in the case of mergers and acquisitions, as was argued in Chapter 9.

In world business there is a growing tendency for tariff and technological advantages to wear off, which automatically shifts competition towards cultural advantages or disadvantages. Most people recognize the importance of cultural factors in the competitive success of Japan and other East Asian countries. In Chapter 7 it was shown which cultural values seem to make the difference in the competition between East and West.

On the four cultural dimensions found in the IBM studies and described in the Chapters 2 through 5, any position of a country offers potential

Table 10.1 Culture and international competition: competitive advantages of different cultural profiles

Power distance small: acceptance of responsibility	Power distance large: discipline
Collectivism: employee commitment	Individualism: management mobility
Femininity: personal service custom-made products agriculture biochemistry	Masculinity: mass production efficiency heavy industry bulk chemistry
Uncertainty avoidance weak: basic innovations	Uncertainty avoidance strong: precision

competitive advantages as well as disadvantages. Table 10.1 summarizes suggested advantages of particular national cultural positions. The table serves to show that no country can be good at everything. Chapter 8 arrived at a similar conclusion with regard to organizational cultures. This is a strong argument for making cultural considerations part of strategic planning, and locating activities in countries, in regions, and in organizational units which possess the cultural characteristics necessary for competing in these activities.

Spreading multicultural understanding: suggestions for the media

Media people—journalists, reporters, and radio and TV producers—play a uniquely important role in creating multicultural understanding—or misunderstanding. The battle for survival in a multicultural world may be to a large extent fought in the media. Media people are human: they have cultural values of their own. With regard to other cultures their position is ambiguous. On the one hand, they cater to a public and their success depends on the extent to which they write or speak what the public wants to read or hear. On the other hand they are in a position to direct people's attention: to create an image of reality which to many people becomes reality itself. All except the most sophisticated citizens carry the beliefs about other cultures reflected in their favorite television shows, radio programs, and newspapers.

The consciousness that people in other parts of one's society, and people in other societies, think, feel, and act on the basis of other but not necessarily evil value assumptions, may or may not be recognized by media people and reflected in their productions. Simple information for the public can avoid big misunderstandings. There undoubtedly exist reporters who only want simple black-and-white messages, or even have a vested interest in showing who are the good guys and who the bad ones. For those with higher ambitions there still is a big untapped potential for spreading understanding about differences in cultural values and practices. For example, using the television eye to compare similar aspects of daily behavior in different countries can be extremely powerful and is still too seldom done.[2]

A problem particular to small countries like my own, the Netherlands, is that both television and newspapers buy materials from larger countries without stressing the different cultural contexts in which these materials were produced. An example are newspaper articles reporting on survey research about trends in society. The material used is most frequently from the USA, and the evident assumption of the editor responsible is that the conclusions are valid for the Netherlands as well. If one realizes the large distance between the two societies on the masculinity–femininity dimension (see Chapter 4), which affects many societal phenomena, Dutch readers should at least be cautioned when interpreting US data. The funny thing is that no journalist would dream of producing Japanese or German statistics with the tacit assumption that these apply in the Netherlands, whereas in some cases they may very well be relevant.

Global challenges call for intercultural cooperation

Mankind today is threatened by a number of disasters which have all been man-made: they are disasters of culture rather than the disasters of nature to which our ancestors were regularly exposed. Their common cause is that man has become both too fertile and too clever for the limited size of our globe. The only way towards survival is to become even cleverer so that the negative consequences of our cleverness can be compensated for. This demands concerted action on issues for which, unfortunately, different cultural values make people disagree rather than agree. In these circumstances, intercultural cooperation has become a prime condition for the survival of mankind.

A number of value-laden world problems have been indicated in this book. There are the economic problems: international economic cooperation versus competition; the distribution of wealth and poverty across and within countries. There are the technology-induced problems. In the past, whenever new technology had been invented it could also be applied. This is no longer the case and decisions have to be taken as to whether some of the things man can make should be made, and if so, subject to which precautions. Such decisions should be agreed upon on a world scale, and if countries, groups, or individuals do not respect the decisions or the precautions they should be forced to do so. Examples are certain uses of nuclear energy for both peaceful and aggressive purposes; certain chemical processes and products; certain uses of computers; certain applications of genetic manipulation. An example of the latter is that doctors may become able to influence whether a baby will be born a boy or a girl. In certain cultures the desirability of having boys over girls is very strong. In view of both ethical and demographic considerations, should this technology be allowed to spread? If so, where and under what conditions, and if not so, can one stop it?

The combined effect of world population growth, economic development, and technological developments affects the world ecosystem in ways which are only partly known. Acid rain in many parts of the world is already now destroying forests. The problem of the reduction of the ozone layer is known but its seriousness is not. Long-term climate changes due to the 'greenhouse effect' of increased emission of CO_2 and other gases are already noticeable; they have a built-in delay of decades, so that even if we were to stop emitting now, the greenhouse effect will increase for a long time. Coping with these problems needs worldwide research and political decision-making in areas in which both perceived national interests and cultural values are in conflict. Decisions about sacrifices made today for benefits to be reaped by the next generation have to be made by politicians whose main concern is with being re-elected next year or surviving a power struggle tomorrow. In addition, the sacrifices may lie in parts of the world other than the main benefactors. The greenhouse effect can be reduced if the tropical countries preserve their rain forests. These countries are mainly poor, and their governments want the revenue from selling their hardwoods. Could a world fund be created which compensates them for leaving intact what remains of their rain forests?

The trends described are threats to mankind as a whole. They represent the common enemy of the future. A common enemy has always been the most effective way of making leaders and groups with conflicting values and interests cooperate. Maybe these threats will force us to achieve a global intercultural cooperation which has never existed. Chapter 9 has referred to the predominance of intended intercultural conflict, of wars and genocide, in human history. A new level of intercultural cooperation is the only alternative to common doom.

Speculations on political developments

Worldwide intercultural cooperation does not mean worldwide democracy. Authoritarian governments will, at least for the next few centuries, continue to prevail in most of the world. 'Authoritarian' is not the same as 'totalitarian'. The latter is based on political fundamentalism (strong uncertainty avoidance) and tries to control all aspects of people's lives. The former is based on large power distance and means a concentration of power in a few hands.

Western-style democratic government presupposes not only a not too large power distance but also, and even more, fairly strong individualism which guarantees freedom of expression and of the formation of political parties.

As Chapters 2 and 3 of this book have shown, both individualism and small power distance are correlated with a country's wealth. Figure 3.2 illustrated that there are few democracies with a 1990 per capita gross national product below US $5000. Western-style democratic government is a luxury which only rich countries can afford: illiterate and underfed populations make poor democrats. On the other hand, rich countries need not in all cases become democratic, as Singapore, Hong Kong, and the oil sheikdoms show. Wealth is a necessary but not a sufficient condition for democracy.

The concern of the US government with establishing democracies in Central America is not very realistic in view of the 1990 per capita GNPs of these countries which range from $590 in Honduras to $1900 in Panama. The only way to establish democracies in these countries would be to stimulate their economic development and help them across the poverty limit, but as was argued in Chapter 9, economic development cannot be imported into a country; only its own citizens can develop a country.

The chances for viable democracies (instead of 'people's democracies') in Eastern European and other formerly state-controlled economies are not all that bad, now that the system has changed. The situation differs from one country to the next. What kind of governments will come about can to some extent be predicted on the basis of pre-existing levels of economic development. During the 1980s the economies of these countries deteriorated dramatically, which eventually led to the revolutions or reforms of 1989. The last more or less 'normal' year and the last year that the World Bank published GNP data for most communist countries was 1980. In that year the 'democracy limit' was about US $4000. Although the figures should undoubtedly be taken with a degree of skepticism, they suggest that Eastern Germany ($7180) and Czechoslovakia ($5820) were well over this democracy limit. The Soviet Union ($4550), Poland ($3900), Hungary ($4180), and Bulgaria ($4150) were close to the limit. Yugoslavia ($2620), Romania ($2340) and Albania ($840 in 1979) were below; outside Europe, Mongolia ($780 in 1979), Cuba ($1410 in 1979), North Korea ($1130 in 1979), and China ($290). From these, the Soviet Union and Yugoslavia were federations of economically more and less developed republics that have proven unstable.

On the basis of the 1980 per capita GNPs the chances for a 'Western' type democracy were best for East Germany (which in the meantime is in the process of resolving the issue through reunification with its Western neighbor) and for Czechoslovakia. The latter comprised of richer Czechia and poorer Slovakia, which split in 1992 at the initiative of Slovakia. It is doubtful whether the population of Slovakia supported the separation, but the political leaders did. Czechia has clearly become a democracy; the case for Slovakia is unclear. Democracy looks feasible for Poland, Hungary, and

Bulgaria, and for the wealthier republics from the former Soviet Union (in particular the Baltic States Estonia, Latvia and Lithuania) and from the former Yugoslavia (in any case, Slovenia and maybe Croatia), but less so for Romania, the poorer parts of the former Yugoslavia and of the former Soviet Union, and unlikely for Albania, Cuba, and China. From this point of view, the Chinese leaders who in June 1989 rejected Western-style democratic reforms were correct; however, this does not prohibit other reforms, of course, or condone the way in which the requests for reforms were crushed.

If the establishment of Western-style democracies depends on a country's level of economic development as I argued, whoever wants to make the whole world democratic should face the economic and ecological consequences of this goal. At present, the rich countries' standard of living also implies a standard of environmental pollution and depletion of resources which makes it utterly impossible to extend this standard of living to the entire world population. Therefore, achieving the goal of democracy for everybody requires an entirely new way of handling our ecosystem: sustaining the rich countries' quality of life but drastically reducing its ecological cost. The concept of 'economic growth' may in this respect already be obsolete; another measure for the survival power of economic/ecological systems will have to be found.

Political fundamentalisms of the Marxist or fascist kind seem to have lost popularity in most places, but religious fundamentalisms hold sway in many parts of the world. In this book they are considered manifestations of uncertainty avoidance (see Chapter 5), and a fluctuating phenomenon—as world history has amply shown. They are a basic expression of human anxiety and as such they will never disappear, nor, fortunately, ever triumph for long or in large parts of the world. They hurt themselves against the variety in values which will always exist in the world; and because of their absolute claims they carry the seeds of their own schisms and bankruptcy.

Much will depend on the acquisition of intercultural cooperation skills as part of the mental software of politicians. Glen Fisher, a retired US Foreign Service Officer, has written a perceptive book called *Mindsets* on the role of culture in international relations. About the relationship between economics, culture, and politics, he writes:

'An interdisciplinary approach to international economic processes hardly exists. Most important, routine applications of conventional economic analysis cannot tolerate 'irrational' behavior. But, from a cross-national and cross-cultural perspective, there is a real question as to what is rational and what irrational; both are very relative terms and very much culture bound; one person's irrationality might turn out to be another's orderly and predictable behavior.' And later on: 'Despite the frequent assertion that sentimentality and the pursuit of economic interests don't mix, economic systems are in fact ethical systems. Whether by law and regulation or by custom, some economic activities are sanctioned while others are not. And what is sanctioned differs from culture to culture.'

(Fisher, 1988, pp. 144, 153)

Both what is 'rational' and what is 'ethical' depend on cultural value positions. In politics, value positions are further confounded by perceived interests. There has been a strong tendency in international politics to use different ethical standards towards other countries.

A case study which should encourage modesty about ethics in politics is the international drug trade. Western countries are presently involved in a virtual war to prevent the importation of drugs. Not so long ago, from 1839–1842, a Western country (UK) fought an 'Opium War' with Imperial China. The Chinese Emperor took the position Western governments are taking now, trying to keep drugs out of his country. The British, however, had strong economic interests in a Chinese market for the opium they imported from India, and through an active sales promotion they had large numbers of Chinese addicted. The British won the war, and in the peace treaty they not only won the right to continue importing opium but they also acquired the island of Hong Kong as a permanent foothold on the Chinese coast. The returning of Hong Kong to China in 1997 is therefore, ironically, a belated victory of the Chinese in their war against drugs.[3]

From a values point of view it is difficult to defend that the trade in arms is less unethical than the trade in drugs. One difference is that in the drugs traffic the poor countries tend to be the sellers, in the arms traffic the rich countries. The latter make more money on selling arms to Third World countries than they spend on development assistance to these countries. Of course, in this case the buyers and the sellers are both to blame, but the rich countries are in a better position to break the vicious circle. The 1990–1991 Gulf War has again stressed the urgency of controlling the arms trade.

Reducing the trade in arms would reduce civil wars, terrorism, and murder. It would improve the chances of respect for human rights in the world: these arms are often used to crush human rights. While at present it is unrealistic to expect all countries of the world to become Western-style democracies, a more feasible goal is to strive for more respect for human rights even in autocratically led states.

The Universal Declaration of Human Rights adopted in 1948 is based on universalist, individualist Western values which very clearly are not shared by the political leaders or by the populations of all other parts of the world. On the other hand, the Declaration is a fact, and international organizations as well as individuals will undoubtedly continue to signal infringements, regardless of the country in which these take place. No government is powerful enough to silence, for example, Amnesty International. All but the most ruthless governments try to maintain an appearance of international respectability. The fact that the world has become one interdependent whole leads to the public being informed about more suffering than ever before, but it also offers more opportunities to protest against this suffering. Many people are prepared to testify that suffering should not be a normal situation. Increasing the respect for human rights is a worthwhile goal for a multicultural world.

Notes

[1] 'The Ballad of Lake Laloo and Other Rhymes', quoted by Renier (1931).

[2] Margaret Mead's film 'Four Families' showing the relationship between parents and small children in India, France, Japan, and Canada, produced by the National Film Board of Canada, dates from 1959 and is still extremely instructive. To my knowledge a similar effort has never been repeated. See also Chapter 2, note 7.

[3] The war of 1839–1842 was only the First Opium War. After a Second Opium War, in 1860, the British also acquired Kowloon on the Chinese mainland opposite Hong Kong island, and in 1898 they leased the 'New Territories' adjacent to Kowloon. This lease was concluded for 99 years and therefore will expire in 1997; at that moment, the entire colony will be returned to China.

Appendix: Reading mental programs

The manner in which animals learn has been much studied in recent years, with a great deal of patient observation and experiment. Certain results have been obtained as regards the kinds of problems that have been investigated, but on general principles there is still much controversy. One may say broadly that all the animals that have been carefully observed have behaved so as to confirm the philosophy in which the observer believed before his observations began. Nay, more, they have all displayed the national characteristics of the observer. Animals studied by Americans rush about frantically, with an incredible display of hustle and pep, and at last achieve the desired result by chance. Animals observed by Germans sit still and think, and at last evolve the solution out of their inner consciousness. To the plain man, such as the present writer, this situation is discouraging. I observe, however, that the type of problem which a man naturally sets to an animal depends upon his own philosophy, and that this probably accounts for the differences in the results. The animal responds to one type of problem in one way and to another in another; therefore the results obtained by different investigators, though different, are not incompatible. But it remains necessary to remember that no one investigator is to be trusted to give a survey of the whole field.

(Bertrand Russell, *Outline of Philosophy*)

The controversial nature of research into national culture differences

Bertrand Russell was a great British philosopher. The above quote from his work, written more than half a century ago, is a warning that results of scientific research depend on the researcher in ways which may not even be conscious to him or her. The same theme returns in a different way in the work of the American Thomas Kuhn who in 1962 published a famous little book *The Structure of Scientific Revolutions* in which he illustrates with examples from various sciences how scientific innovation is brought about. In a given period certain common assumptions called 'paradigms' dominate a scientific field and constrain the thinking of the scientists in this field. Kuhn labels the work done within these paradigms 'normal' science. Every now and then, normal science runs into limits: it is unable to explain new facts, or unable to meet new challenges. Then, a paradigm change is initiated, but those who start the change are, at first, rejected and ridiculed by those involved in normal science. The new paradigm is seen as a threat. Gradually, however, more and more people move to the new paradigm, which then becomes part of a new type of normal science.

Kuhn's examples are from the natural sciences. The social sciences, dealing with individual and collective human behavior, have their paradigms too, but in their case there is less consensus at a given time about which paradigms dominate. The social sciences have always shown many paradigms in competition. Human behavior is an immensely complex subject. Moreover, even more strongly than in the case reported by Bertrand Russell, the researcher is part of the phenomenon studied. Social science research is like trying to watch a drama in which one is an actor oneself.[1]

In the face of the complexity of their subject the social sciences have over the past 150 years developed a division of labor. Psychology deals with the behavior of individuals, social psychology with face-to-face groups. Sociology deals with larger collectivities and categories of people. Political science is concerned with states and other political entities. Economics studies the allocation of scarce resources, that is the production, distribution, and consumption of goods and services. Cultural anthropology deals with entire societies or parts thereof, often with relatively isolated societies of the preliterate type. Within all these disciplines many different paradigms exist which have led to the creation of subdisciplines and subsubdisciplines. Quite a few social scientists communicate almost exclusively with colleague specialists in their subsubdiscipline. The way social scientists work has been compared to the Indian fable of the blind men studying the elephant: the one who gets hold of a leg thinks it is a tree, the one who gets the tail thinks it is a rope, but they will only be able to appreciate what the whole animal is like by pooling their opinions—which they are unlikely to do.

Cultural anthropology, too, is a multi-paradigmatic discipline (Kloos, 1984, pp. 145ff). The study of national culture differences corresponded to a popular paradigm in anthropology during the 1930s and 1940s. Later, other paradigms gained more popularity. Mainstream anthropology in recent decades has constrained itself to marginal groups and to problems which for society as a whole are fairly trivial. It has avoided touching areas where it could be relevant to other disciplines and to practitioners. Claude Lévi-Strauss said in an interview:

'Many anthropologists including myself may have chosen their profession as an escape from a civilization and from a century in which they did not feel at ease. Not all: Margaret Mead, for example, felt solidarity with her society and with her time. She wanted to serve her generation. If I have sometimes defended a similar position, I must confess this was only lip service.'[2]

National and intranational culture differences represent an area in which insights from anthropology *can* serve society. Because such differences were already studied decades ago, some present-day anthropologists consider them as belonging to an outdated paradigm. However, the fact that a problem received attention in the past does not necessarily condemn it in the present. Acquiring insight into the differences in dominant ways of thinking, feeling, and behaving across and within nations has become a more urgent issue than ever.

Sources of valid data on national culture
In daily life many statements are made by someone from one society about people from another. When a person X makes a statement about a population or population group Y (his or her own or another) this statement always contains information about X, but whether it also contains valid information about Y remains to be proven. In order to be considered valid, information about a population should meet four criteria:

1. It should be descriptive and not judgmental (otherwise it contains more information about the value system of the informant than about the particular population).
2. It should be verifiable from more than one independent source (otherwise it reflects only one subjective perception).
3. It should apply, if not to all members of the population, at least to a statistical majority (otherwise it is a false generalization).
4. It should discriminate, i.e., it should indicate those characteristics which apply to this population but not to others (otherwise it is trivial).

Mainstream cultural anthropology collects its data almost entirely through participant observation. Anthropological reports are basically statements by an observer from one society about people from another, and the four above criteria apply to them. In particular, the element of subjectivity in anthropological reports is unavoidable (criterion 2).

A quarrel within the anthropological profession based upon this subjectivity was brought to the attention of the American public in 1983. An Australian anthropologist called Derek Freeman had attacked Margaret Mead's study of young girls at Samoa, done in 1925. Freeman had worked in and on Samoa for 40 years but only published his critique after Mead's death. He basically stated that Mead's findings about the sexual liberty of Samoan girls were a myth, and that his own research had shown considerable sexual violence and puritanism (Freeman, 1983). Since Margaret Mead had by then become a national and international personality, Freeman's criticisms, which were framed as accusations, raised quite a stir. Mary Catherine Bateson, Margaret Mead's daughter and herself an anthropologist, was asked to have a discussion with Freeman on a popular television program. Bateson argued that the criticisms on Mead's work at Samoa apply equally to Freeman's: they are rooted in the subjectivity of anthropological observations. A young woman talking to young women produced a sunny view of a society; a grumpy old man who collected his data from male chiefs, a world war later, produced a grim view (Bateson, 1984; Howard, 1984). Every human being perceives selectively, and this also holds for anthropologists who are not exempt from humanity.

Cultural anthropology has resorted to the participant observation method because this is the only way of collecting information about isolated and preliterate societies. Curiously, many anthropologists have converted this necessity into a dogma, a major part of their paradigm: other ways of collecting data, such as are being used by other social sciences, have nothing to teach them. 'This thing has the antique flavor of the anthropology of the 1940s and 1950s, when we seemed to think that sociological systems-builders had answers for us . . .': this rather sneering remark was written down by an anonymous reviewer of a paper I submitted to an anthropological journal. (Fortunately, not all his or her colleagues agreed.)

Valid information on national culture differences between literate and easily accessible societies can more readily be collected from indirect sources—like national statistics and the results of comparative surveys—than from statements by individual observers. Statements by observers remain useful as sources of inspiration on what indirect sources to look for, and for providing depth to interpretations of differences found. In historical research they are often the only source available. One can find remarkable agreement among foreign observers of the same country centuries apart in history, testifying to the stability of culture differences over long time periods.

A Frenchman wrote about the USA:

> 'The American ministers of the Gospel do not attempt to draw or to fix all the thoughts of man upon the life to come; they are willing to surrender a portion of his heart to the cares of the present . . . . If they take no part themselves in productive labor, they are at least interested in its progress, and they applaud its results; and whilst they never cease to point to the other world as the great object of the hopes and fears of the believer, they do not forbid him honestly to court prosperity in this. Far from attempting to show that these things are distinct and contrary to one another, they study rather to find out on what point they are most nearly and closely connected.'

A comment on US television evangelists? No, Alexis de Tocqueville (1805–1859) in his book *Democracy in America* from 1835 (de Tocqueville, 1956, p. 155).

National statistics as sources of comparative information have their own pitfalls. The data may not have been collected in the same way in different countries, or governments may have an interest in presenting a particular picture through their statistics. Again, the use of more than one source and more than one statistic is imperative. Indices calculated from a number of statistics have a smaller margin of error than single items.

Survey and similar data collected from individuals pose the question of functional equivalence. As one can never reach an entire population, surveys are based on samples. Functional equivalence means that the sample drawn from the population in country A is equivalent to the sample from country B in all respects except nationality. One should not collect data from policemen in country A and from nurses in country B. Comparative studies are done on broad samples or on narrow samples. Broad samples are used in public opinion polls. They are expensive, the respondents and paid data collectors are often unmotivated,[3] and poll data are usually only available for developed countries. Narrow samples are taken from groups within easy reach of researchers, like university students or business managers attending development courses. They may or may not be functionally equivalent.

IBM subsidiaries as a source of cross-cultural data

As this book showed, the initial material for my own cross-national study consisted of the answers of employees from subsidiaries of the IBM corporation in different countries, on the same paper-and-pencil questions. These questions dealt mainly with the employees' personal *values* related to the work situation, and they had been collected as part of a larger survey material on employee attitudes. The database was unusually extensive, covering employees in 72 national subsidiaries, 38 occupations, 20 languages, and at two points in time: around 1968 and around 1972. Altogether, there were more than 116 000 questionnaires with over 100 standardized questions each.

In Chapter 1 I referred to the amazement of some people about how employees of a very specific corporation like IBM can serve as a sample for discovering something about the culture of their countries at large. 'We know IBMers,' they say, 'they are very special people, always in a white shirt and tie, and not at all representative for our country.' The people who say this are quite right: IBMers do not form representative samples from national populations. As argued in the previous section, however, samples for cross-national comparison need not be representative, as long as they are functionally equivalent. IBM employees are a narrow sample, but very well matched. Employees of multinational companies in general and of IBM in particular form attractive sources of information for comparing national traits, because they are so similar in respects other than nationality: their employer (with its common corporate culture), their kind of work, and—for matched occupations—their level of education. The only thing that can account for systematic and consistent differences between national groups *within* such a homogeneous multinational population is nationality itself— the national environment in which people were brought up *before* they joined this employer. Comparing IBM subsidiaries therefore shows national culture differences with unusual clarity.

The initial analysis of the IBM data was done on the 40 largest subsidiaries, as I was afraid of using data from samples smaller than about 50 people. The number of countries studied was afterwards extended by another 10, while 14 more countries were grouped into 3 regions (East Africa, West Africa and Arab-speaking countries), raising the number of units to 53. Eight of the subsidiaries had too few native employees to be included in the analysis.

Statistical handling of the data (a factor analysis of country mean scores for 32 values questions which had proven stable from the first to the second survey round) produced the four dimensions described in the Chapters 2 through 5: power distance, individualism versus collectivism, masculinity versus femininity, and uncertainty avoidance. Actually, power distance and collectivism at first formed one factor together (Chapter 3 shows they are rather closely associated), but after the influence of national wealth was eliminated, they became two separate dimensions. The four together account for 49 percent of the country differences in the data, just about half. The remaining half is country specific: it cannot be associated with any worldwide factor, at least not in the data I had. Whether explaining half of the differences is a lot or not depends on one's degree of optimism. An optimist will call a bottle half full while a pessimist will call it half empty.

The country scores derived from the IBM data acquired their real meaning only after having been tested against data about the same countries deriving from other sources. I described the IBM samples as functionally equivalent but their equivalence is based on an assumption which should still be proven: that the company had used similar recruiting policies in different countries. The proof is delivered if IBM dimension scores explain differences among countries known from other sources. Testing against independent outside data is called *validation*: and the validation of the IBM dimension scores against other information receives extensive attention in my book *Culture's Consequences* (1980, pp. 326–331). The validation process shows that scores on many conceptually related measures from other sources are correlated sufficiently strongly with the IBM dimension scores to eliminate a chance explanation.

Relating the IBM results to those of various other cross-national studies also led to relating these other studies among themselves; and sometimes parallels appeared among studies which their authors had not yet noticed.

Social scientists are often so much in a hurry to get their work published that they do not attempt to compare their results systematically with the findings of others. Maybe some feel that such comparison would threaten their scientific independence. Universities in rich countries nowadays have excellent bibliographical tools available for tracking related research. Overlooking relationships with other findings leads to the same wheels being reinvented many times over: it limits the synergy in the social sciences. Secondary analysis, that is combining and comparing data collected by others rather than collecting one's own, has a low status at most universities. I think it should be encouraged much more and students should win their spurs at secondary analysis before being asked to collect data of their own.

Statements about culture are not statements about individuals: a caution against stereotyping

Survey data like those from the IBM studies are collected from individuals, but for the study of cultures they have to be compared at the level of countries. This implies that mean values are calculated from the scores on each question for the respondents from each country. We do not compare individuals, but we compare what is called *central tendencies* in the answers from each country. There is hardly an individual who answers each question exactly by the mean score of his or her group: the 'average person' from a country does not exist, only an average tendency to respond among the members of the group of respondents.

For example, on the questions used to calculate the scores for the dimension individualism–collectivism, American IBM respondents tended to score much more individualist than Japanese respondents. However, some Japanese respondents gave quite individualist answers: they scored more individualist than the average for the Americans. Some Americans scored quite collectivist, more collectivist than the average for the Japanese IBMers.

This should be a caution against using the country scores obtained from the IBM research for the purpose of stereotyping. Stereotyping occurs when assumptions about collective properties of a group are applied to a particular individual from that group. 'Mr Suzuki is Japanese, therefore he holds collectivist values; Ms Smith is American, therefore she holds individualist values.' These are stereotypes, and they are unwarranted. Chances are that Mr Suzuki and Ms Smith are exceptional in this respect. Stereotypes are half-truths, and as such they are undesirable in intercultural communication: half the truth is not enough. If we want to find out about Mr Suzuki and Ms Smith we had better make our judgment after meeting and getting to know them.

The usefulness of the country scores is not for describing individuals, but for describing the social systems these individuals are likely to have built. Social systems are not made for the exceptional individual, but they have to take account of the dominant values of the majority from the people involved. So if we prepare to do business with the Suzuki Corporation we had better assume their organization to be built on collectivist values; if we approach the Smith Corporation, we had better assume individualist values.

A note to those considering replications

The state of the art in cross-cultural research suffers from ill-advised replications. A common approach is for a masters or doctoral student to take an instrument (normally a paper-and-pencil questionnaire) developed in one country, usually in the USA by a US scholar who tested it on US respondents, and to have it administered to respondents in one or more other countries. Sometimes the instrument is translated; this is done (or claimed to be done) by a translation–backtranslation process involving two different people.

The fundamental flaw in this approach is that such instruments cover only issues considered relevant in the society in which they were developed, but exclude questions unrecognized by the designer because they do not occur in his or her society. They could, however, be highly relevant in other societies. Such questions are precisely the ones most interesting from a cultural point of view. There is a hidden ethnocentrism in this type of replication and it has produced many quite trivial cross-cultural studies.

Cross-cultural research should only be done with cross-culturally designed instruments, that is, instruments for which the content was collected in a number of different countries, culturally as different as possible. In this respect the questionnaire used in the IBM studies is all right because it was developed after interviews in seven countries and pretested in four, although the countries in which it was developed were all Western, which was a weakness (see Chapter 7).

Yet even such an internationally developed questionnaire presents its pitfalls in replication. Some readers of *Culture's Consequences* have been sufficiently turned on by the book's message to want to replicate the research in some way. Partly I am guilty of this myself, because the book contains as an appendix a Values Survey Module, recommended for future cross-cultural survey studies.[4] To date, reports have come in of about 30 replications. Not all of them have been equally meaningful or flawless, and the following is meant to caution future replicators against the most common pitfalls (see Bosland, 1985b).

First, and in line with the previous section, as the dimensions from the 4-D model were designed for discriminating among national cultures, they are not suitable for discriminating among individuals. The structure of national (and also of other) cultures differs from the structure of individual personalities. An error which psychologists sometimes make when looking at a culture is to treat it as a kind of common personality: 'personality writ large', as anthropologist Ruth Benedict suggested in the 1930s. This, however, overlooks the fact that cultures are formed by the interaction of different personalities, both conflicting and complementary, forming a whole which is more than the sum of its parts.

The national culture questionnaire is no personality test and should not be used as such (see Bosland, 1985a). For training purposes a trainer may give the questionnaire to classroom participants for answering, as an illustration of the kind of issues on which opinions depend on national value systems. However, he or she should not suggest that, for example, a personal power distance index score or individualism score has any meaning in predicting a person's effectiveness in another culture.[5] It is quite possible that personality tests can be developed that could serve for selecting future expatriates. The design and validation of such tests, however, will need a special research project.

Second, the dimensions were chosen so as to discriminate among national and maybe regional and ethnic cultures, but, as was already argued in Chapter 1, not for discriminating according to other (sub)cultural distinctions like gender, generation, social class, or organization (see Hofstede and Spangenberg, 1987, pp. 113–122) (power distance, exceptionally, is also relevant for social classes, occupation and education levels; masculinity is relevant for distinguishing occupations). One replication study used the Values Survey Module to discriminate between normal and orthopedically handicapped workers within the same factory in one country. The logic of this replication has escaped me.

Third, the scores on a question obtained for a group of respondents will very likely be affected by other factors besides nationality: for example, depending on the question, by education, gender, age, type of work organization, or when the survey was held. It is for these reasons that this chapter has stressed the need for doing research on *matched samples* only, that is, samples similar in all respects except nationality. It is meaningless to use the questionnaires for one single sample of respondents from one country and to compare the scores against those in this book which were based on matched IBM populations. This is only allowed if it can be argued that the new sample is a match for the original IBM population in all important respects. Such a match is virtually impossible to make, if only because the IBM studies were done around 1970 and the point in time of the survey is one of the matching characteristics.[6]

The national culture scores in this book, it should be emphasized again, only describe *differences* between countries: their absolute value has no meaning.

If one wants to replicate the study, one should have at least two matched samples of respondents from different countries, regions, or ethnic groups. Preferably at least one of these should also be covered in the IBM studies, so as to supply an anchoring point.

A sound although rather trivial replication covered small samples (20 and 21) of foreign graduate students in the USA from two countries/regions also represented in the IBM research: Iran and Arab countries. The two groups of foreign students can be considered matched samples. Both in the IBM data and in the student data the two countries/regions scored rather similar; for two dimensions the differences between Iran and the Arab countries were in the same direction as in the IBM study, for the two other they were not, which was to be expected given the small size of the samples. In the same replication, scores by 33 US graduate students were also included. In this case the matching is more doubtful (a foreign student is not in the same situation as a domestic student; in this case the Americans were also much older). Nevertheless, the differences in dimension scores between the Americans and the two groups of foreign students were in the predicted direction for all four dimensions.[7]

A more interesting replication was undertaken with the purpose of obtaining scores for Surinam, a former Dutch colony in South America not represented in the IBM research. The researcher sought a company having similar operations in both Surinam and the Netherlands and had access to a sample of about 25 employees in each operation, matched as closely as possible in all respects except nationality. The Values Survey Module was administered and the dimension scores were calculated for the two countries. The difference between Surinam and the Netherlands found in the new study was then used to compute scores for Surinam on the IBM table, by adding or subtracting the differences found from the scores for the Netherlands within IBM.[8]

In general, replications become more informative, the larger the number of countries or ethnic groups covered. Unfortunately, the logistic problems of doing research on more than two groups are insurmountable for most master's or doctoral researchers, the ones responsible for most replications. An exception is a project by Michael Hoppe of the University of North Carolina at Chapel Hill, USA, reference to which was made in Chapter 4. Hoppe obtained scores on the values survey module for the alumni of the Salzburg Seminar, a US sponsored institute in Austria which invites to its courses élites (political leaders, employers' representatives, and labor leaders) from mainly European countries. Michael Hoppe, a former German citizen, and his American wife had earlier been employed by the seminar themselves. The project supplied VSM scores for reasonably well-matched samples from 19 countries, 18 of them also on the IBM list. It is the most extensive replication carried out to date (see Hoppe, 1990).

The experiences with the Hoppe replication may enable a better version of the Values Survey Module to be issued. The VSM is by no means an ideal instrument for its purpose. The IBM surveys were held for reasons internal to the corporation, not for studying culture differences. Only after the data had been collected did I decide to use them as a basis for a cross-cultural study. The process could be labeled 'survey archaeology': digging for information in an existing database, without the possibility of adding questions not covered in the IBM questionnaire. The questions used to compute the four dimensions are the best from this questionnaire (according to statistical criteria) but not the best that could have been designed if comparing cultures had been the original purpose of the exercise. Michael Hoppe used an improved version of the VSM which I developed in 1982. As well as the original questions this version contains a number of items borrowed from other sources (for example, from my French colleague André Laurent) or newly made up. The new questions, however, should still be validated, and Hoppe's results are the first which are extensive enough for such a validation.

The fact that IBM has a strong corporate culture does not mean that IBM data cannot be used for comparing countries; I have argued that the opposite is the case. It does, however, limit the usefulness of a questionnaire written for use inside IBM for replications on other populations. As was demonstrated in Chapter 8, organizational cultures affect the symbols recognized by the organization's members: part of these symbols is the jargon used inside the corporation, including the emotional meaning of certain words. As soon as the IBM questions were given to non-IBMers it became clear, for example, that the importance of 'having training opportunities' and 'having good fringe benefits' for people inside IBM meant something else than for outsiders. These two items were therefore already omitted from the VSM as presented in *Culture's Consequences*, although they had been used in computing the dimension scores for the IBM samples. Comparing the results of the IBM study with Hoppe's 19-country study suggests that other items, too, may have a meaning to IBMers not shared by others.

The ideal questions for a cross-cultural survey instrument are those for which answers depend as much as possible on nationality and as little as possible on anything else, and which carry the same meaning for widely different respondents: from academics to semiliterates, from politicians to artists, from children to senior citizens. Whether such questions exist is doubtful. As data on replications accumulate I will try to select the best questions for a new VSM.

Conclusion

In the meantime, my advice to prospective researchers on national and ethnic culture differences is to develop their own survey instruments aimed at the particular kind of people they want to study. Much more interesting than replications using the IBM questionnaire, which may not be very suitable for other populations, is to compare the dimensional structures obtained with different instruments on different populations, but across the same countries. For example, there is the study of student values in 10 Asian and Pacific countries using the Rokeach value survey referred to in Chapter 7, which produced five dimensions of which four were significantly correlated each with one of the four IBM dimensions (Hofstede and Bond, 1984). There are the results obtained with the Chinese value survey across 23 countries, also described in Chapter 7, which reproduced three of the IBM dimensions plus a new one. A similar analysis could be done on the results of the European value systems study which to date have been published for 10 countries but which in the meantime seem to have been collected in over 20 countries worldwide (Stoetzel, 1983; Harding and Phillips, 1986). As far as I know, nobody has yet analyzed the data of this survey for underlying cultural dimensions.

Of equal interest is what could be called a 'paradigmatic' use of dimensional frameworks of cultural differences. In the past few years authors in a variety of fields: management, political science, communications, cross-cultural psychology, development economics, organization sociology, and others have adopted the concept of cultural dimensions, often using the framework presented in this book. They use it to classify and explain the influence of culture on their particular object of study. In this way, otherwise seemingly unrelated phenomena can be shown to be linked together. Moreover, this approach makes social science disciplines less ethnocentric. We may have been accustomed to looking at the social reality in one way but as the song goes in Gershwin's opera *Porgy and Bess*: 'It ain't necessarily so.'

Notes

1 Physicists know the 'Heisenberg Principle' which means that a particle can only be observed by destroying it; in this way the physics researcher is also part of the phenomenon studied. While the Heisenberg effect in physics is a special case, researcher effects in the social sciences are a universal phenomenon.
2 Translation by GH from Lévi-Strauss and Eribon (1988, pp. 98–99).
3 For a testimony by a former data collector see Roth (1965). Also in Deutscher (1973, pp. 134–146).
4 This Values Survey Module is included both in the 1980 integral hardcover edition of *Culture's Consequences* and in the 1984 abridged paperback edition. In 1981 and 1982 experimental improved versions (VSM 81 and VSM 82) were issued by IRIC.
5 The scoring guide for the Values Survey Module contains no rules for computing dimension scores for a single respondent.

[6] Working Paper 85-2 by Nico Bosland (see Bosland, 1985b) contains tables derived from the IBM data and showing how much a country's scores on each of the four dimensions would be affected by changes in the respondents' education level.

[7] Mohammad G. A. Ashkanani, *A Cross-Cultural Perspective on Work-Related Values*. San Diego CA: Unpublished doctoral dissertation, School of Business and Management, US International University, 1984.

[8] Rita Nanhekhan, unpublished MA thesis, Free University of Amsterdam, 1990.

Glossary

For terms not mentioned in this Glossary see the Subject Index.

Anthropology   The science of man in his physical, social, and cultural variation. In this book 'anthropology' always stands for social or cultural anthropology which is the integrated study of human societies, in particular (although not only) traditional or preliterate ones.

Anxiety   A diffuse state of being uneasy or worried about what may happen.

Bureaucracy   A form of organization based on strict rules and competencies attached to positions.

Collectivism   The opposite of individualism; together, they form one of the dimensions of national cultures. Collectivism stands for a society in which people from birth onwards are integrated into strong, cohesive ingroups, which throughout people's lifetime continue to protect them in exchange for unquestioning loyalty.

Confucian dynamism   A dimension of national cultures found through research among student samples using the Chinese Value Survey. Rebaptized in this book Long-term versus Short-term orientation (see under these catchwords).

Correlation   A term from mathematical statistics expressing the degree of common variation of two sets of numbers. The coefficient of correlation can vary from a maximum of 1.00 (perfect agreement) via the value 0 (no relationship) to a minimum of -1.00 (perfect disagreement).

Culture   (1) The training or refining of the mind; civilization. In this book, this meaning is called 'culture one'. (2) The collective programming of the mind which distinguishes the members of one group or category of people from another. This meaning corresponds to the use of the term 'culture' in anthropology and is used throughout this book.

Culture Assimilator   A programmed learning tool for developing intercultural communication skills.

Culture shock   A state of distress following the transfer of a person to an unfamiliar cultural environment. It may be accompanied by physical symptoms.

260

Dimension   An aspect of a phenomenon that can be measured (expressed by a number).

Dimensional model   A set of dimensions used in combination in order to describe a phenomenon.

Ethnocentrism   Applying the standards of one's own society to people outside that society.

Extended family   A family group including relatives in the second and third degree (or beyond), like grandparents, uncles, aunts, and cousins.

Face   In collectivist societies, a quality attributed to someone who meets the essential requirements related to his or her social position.

Factor analysis   A technique from mathematical statistics designed to assist the researcher in explaining the variety in a set of observed phenomena by a minimum number of underlying common factors.

Femininity   The opposite of masculinity; together, they form one of the dimensions of national cultures. Femininity stands for a society in which social gender roles overlap: both men and women are supposed to be modest, tender, and concerned with the quality of life.

Fundamentalism   The belief that there is only one Truth and that one's own group is in possession of this Truth which is usually defined in great detail.

Gestalt   An integrated whole which should be studied as such and loses its meaning when divided into parts; from a German word meaning 'form'.

Gross national product (GNP)   A measure of the total flow of goods and services produced by the economy of a country over a year, including income from foreign investments by domestic residents, but excluding income from domestic investments by foreign residents.

Heroes   Persons, alive or dead, real or imaginary, assumed to possess characteristics highly prized in a culture, and who thus serve as models for behavior.

Individualism   The opposite of collectivism; together, they form one of the dimensions of national cultures. Individualism stands for a society in which the ties between individuals are loose: everyone is expected to look after himself or herself and his or her immediate family only.

Individualism index (IDV)   A measure of the degree of individualism in a country's culture, based on the IBM research project.

Ingroup   A cohesive group which offers protection in exchange for loyalty and provides its members with a sense of identity.

Long-term orientation   The opposite of short-term orientation; together they form a dimension of national cultures originally labeled 'Confucian dynamism'. Long-term orientation stands for the fostering of virtues oriented towards future rewards, in particular perseverance and thrift.

Long-term orientation (LTO) index   A measure for the degree of long-term orientation in a country's culture, based on the Chinese Value Survey research project among student samples.

Masculinity The opposite of femininity; together, they form one of the dimensions of national cultures. Masculinity stands for a society in which social gender roles are clearly distinct: men are supposed to be assertive, tough, and focused on material success; women are supposed to be more modest, tender, and concerned with the quality of life.

Masculinity index (MAS) A measure for the degree of masculinity in a country's culture, based on the IBM research project.

Matrix organization An organization structure in which a person can report to two or three superiors for different aspects of his or her work: for example, one for the task and one for the professional aspects, or one for the business line and one for the country.

Motivation An assumed force operating inside an individual inducing him or her to choose one action over another.

National character A term used in the past to describe what is called in this book 'national culture'. A disadvantage of the term 'character' is that it stresses the individual aspects at the expense of the social system.

National culture The collective programming of the mind acquired by growing up in a particular country.

Nuclear family A family group including only relatives in the first degree (parents and children).

Organizational culture The collective programming of the mind which distinguishes the members of one organization from another.

Paradigm A set of common assumptions which dominate a scientific field and constrain the thinking of the scientists in this field.

Particularism A way of thinking prevailing in collectivist societies, in which the standards for the way a person should be treated depend on the group to which this person belongs.

Power distance The extent to which the less powerful members of institutions and organizations within a country expect and accept that power is distributed unequally. One of the dimensions of national cultures (from small to large).

Power distance index (PDI) A measure for the degree of power distance in a country's culture, based on the IBM research project.

Relativism A willingness to consider other persons' or groups' theories and values as equally reasonable as one's own.

Risk The chance that an action will have an undesirable but known outcome.

Rituals Collective activities, technically superfluous in reaching desired ends, but which within a culture are considered as socially essential: they are therefore carried out for their own sake.

Short-term orientation The opposite of long-term orientation; together, they form a dimension of national cultures originally labeled 'Confucian dynamism'. Short-term orientation stands for the fostering of virtues related to the past and present, in particular respect for tradition, preservation of 'face', and fulfilling social obligations.

Statistically significant   A term indicating that the relationship between two measures is sufficiently strong to rule out the possibility that it is due to pure chance. The 'significance level', usually 0.05, 0.01 or 0.001, is the remaining risk that the relationship could still be accidental.

Socialization   The acquisition of the values and practices belonging to a culture, by participating in that culture.

Symbols   Words, pictures, gestures, or objects which carry a particular meaning only recognized as such by those who share a culture.

Typology   A set of ideal types used to describe a phenomenon.

Uncertainty avoidance   The extent to which the members of a culture feel threatened by uncertain or unknown situations. One of the dimensions of national cultures (from weak to strong).

Uncertainty avoidance index (UAI)   A measure for the degree of uncertainty avoidance in a country's culture, based on the IBM research project.

Universalism   A way of thinking prevailing in individualist societies, in which the standards for the way a person should be treated are the same for everybody.

Validation   Testing the conclusions from one piece of research against data from independent other sources.

Values   Broad tendencies to prefer certain states of affair over others.

Xenophilia   The feeling that persons and things from abroad must be superior.

Xenophobia   The feeling that foreign persons or things are dangerous.

Bibliography

Years in square brackets [ ] are years of first publication. Newspaper cuttings and unpublished documents have been listed within 'Notes' at end of each chapter.

Adler, Nancy J. (1986) *International Dimensions of Organizational Behavior*, Boston MA: Kent Publishing Company.

Albert, Rosita (1983) 'The intercultural sensitizer or culture assimilator: a cognitive approach' in *Handbook of Intercultural Training*, Vol.2., D. Landis and R. Brislin (eds), Elmsford NY: Pergamon Press.

Almond, Gabriel A. and Sidney Verba (1963) *The Civic Culture: Political Attitudes and Democracy in Five Nations*, Princeton NJ: Princeton University Press.

Andersson, L. and G. Hofstede (1984) *The Effectiveness of Expatriates—Report on a Feasibility Study*, Maastricht: IRIC.

Baena, Duke de (1968) *The Dutch Puzzle* The Hague: Boucher.

Baker, C. Richard (1976) 'An investigation of differences in values: accounting majors versus non-accounting majors', *The Accounting Review*, 51, 4, 886–893.

Bateson, Mary Catherine (1984) *With a Daughter's Eye*, New York: Pocket Books.

Berg, Per-Olof (ed.) (1986) 'Organizational symbolism', Special issue of *Organization Studies*, 7, 2.

Blake, Robert R. and Jane Srygley Mouton (1964) *The Managerial Grid*, Houston TX: Gulf Publishing Co.

Bloom, Allan (1988) *The Closing of the American Mind*, London: Penguin Books [1987].

Bosland, Nico (1985a) *The (Ab)use of the Values Survey Module as a Test of Individual Personality*. Working Paper 85-1, Maastricht: IRIC.

Bosland, Nico (1985b) *An Evaluation of Replication Studies Using the Values Survey Module*. Working Paper 85-2, Maastricht: IRIC.

Boulding, Elizabeth, S.A. Nuss, D.L. Carson and M.A. Greenstein (eds) (1976) *Handbook of International Data on Women*, Beverly Hills CA: Sage/Halstead Press.

Bourdieu, Pierre (1980) *Le sens pratique*, Paris: Editions de Minuit.

Brislin, Richard W., Kenneth Cushner, Craig Cherrie and Mahealani Yong (1986) *Intercultural Interactions: A Practical Guide*, Beverly Hills CA: Sage Publications.

Broms, Henry and Henrik Gahmberg (1983) 'Communication to self in organizations and cultures', *Administrative Science Quarterly*, 28, 482–495.

Brunsson, Nils (1985) *The Irrational Organization*, Chichester UK: Wiley.

Campbell, Joseph (1988) *Myths to Live By*, New York: Bantam Books [1972].

Carlzon, Jan (1987) *Moments of Truth*, Cambridge MA: Ballinger Publishing Company.

Chenery, Hollis B. and Alan M. Strout (1966) 'Foreign assistance and economic development'. *American Economic Review*, **56** 4/I, 679–733.

Cleverley, Graham (1971) *Managers and Magic*, London: Longman.

Cohen, Peter (1973) *The Gospel According to the Harvard Business School: The Education of America's Managerial Elite*, Garden City NY: Doubleday.

Crozier, Michel (1964) *The Bureaucratic Phenomenon*, Chicago IL: The University of Chicago Press.

Crozier, Michel and Erhard Friedberg (1977) *L'acteur et le système: les contraintes de l' action collective*, Paris: Editions du Seuil.

Cyert, Richard M. and James G. March (1963) *A Behavioral Theory of the Firm*, Englewood Cliffs NJ: Prentice-Hall.

Deal, Terrence E. and Allan A. Kennedy (1982) *Corporate Cultures: The Rites and Rituals of Corporate Life*, Reading MA: Addison-Wesley.

de Tocqueville, Alexis (1956) *Democracy in America*, edited and abridged by Richard D. Heffner. New York: Mentor Books.

Deutscher, Irwin (1973) *What We Say/What We Do: Sentiments and Acts*, Glenview IL: Scott, Foresman & Company.

d'Iribarne, Philippe (1989) *La logique de l' honneur: Gestion des entreprises et traditions nationales*, Paris: Éditions du Seuil.

Douglas, Mary (1966) *Purity and Danger*, London: Routledge and Kegan Paul.

Earley, P. Christopher (1989) 'Social loafing and collectivism: a comparison of the United States and the People's Republic of China', *Administrative Science Quarterly*, **34**, 565–581.

Fayol, Henri (1970) *Administration industrielle et générale*, Paris: Dunod [1916].

Fiedler, Fred E., Terence Mitchell and Harry C. Triandis (1971) 'The Culture Assimilator: an approach to cross-cultural training', *Journal of Applied Psychology*, **55**, 95–102.

Fisher, Glen (1988) *Mindsets: The Role of Culture and Perception in International Relations*, Yarmouth ME: Intercultural Press.

Forss, Kim, Johan Carlsen, Egil Frøyland, Taimi Sitari and Knud Vilby (1988) *Evaluation of the Effectiveness of Technical Assistance Personnel Financed by the Nordic Countries*, Stockholm: Swedish International Development Authority.

Freeman, Derek (1983) *Margaret Mead and Samoa: The Making and Unmaking of an Anthropological Myth*, Cambridge MA: Harvard University Press.

Furnham, Adrian and Stephen Bochner (1986) *Culture Shock: Psychological Reactions to Unfamiliar Environments*, London: Methuen.

Gambling, Trevor (1977) 'Magic, accounting and morale', *Accounting, Organizations and Society*, **2**, 141–151.

Gherardi, Silvia and Barry Turner (1987) *Real Men Don't Collect Soft Data*, Trento, Italy: Dipartimento di Politica Soziale, Università di Trento.

Gray, Sid J. (1988) 'Towards a theory of cultural influence on the development of accounting systems internationally', *Abacus*, **24**, 1, 1–15.

Gregory, Michael S., Anita Silvers and Diane Sutch (eds.) (1978) *Sociobiology and Human Nature*, San Francisco CA: Jossey-Bass.

Grunberg, Leon (1981) *Failed Multinational Ventures*, Lexington MA: Lexington Books.

Hall, Edward T. (1976) *Beyond Culture*, Garden City NY: Doubleday Anchor Books.

Harding, Stephen and David Phillips, with Michael Fogarty (1986) *Contrasting Values in Western Europe*, London: Macmillan.

Harrison, Lawrence E. (1985) *Underdevelopment is a State of Mind*, Lanham MD: Madison Books.

Hawes, Frank and Daniel J. Kealey (1979) *Canadians in Development: An Empirical Study of Adaptation and Effectiveness on Overseas Assignment*, Ottawa: Canadian International Development Agency.

Herzberg, Frederick (1966) *Work and the Nature of Man*, Boston MA: World Publishing Co.

Herzberg, Frederick, Bernard Mausner and Barbara Bloch Snyderman (1959) *The Motivation to Work*, New York: John Wiley & Sons.

Ho, David Yau-Fai (1976) 'On the concept of face', *American Journal of Sociology*, **81**, 867–884.

Hofstede, Geert (1968) *The Game of Budget Control: How to Live with Budgetary Standards and Yet be Motivated by Them*, London: Tavistock and Assen, Netherlands: Van Gorcum [1967].

Hofstede, Geert (1975) 'Predicting managers' career success in an international setting: the validity of ratings by training staff versus training peers', *Management International Review*, **15**, 43–50.

Hofstede, Geert (1978) 'The poverty of management control philosophy', *Academy of Management Review*, **3**, 450–461.

Hofstede, Geert (1980) *Culture's Consequences: International Differences in Work-Related Values*, Beverly Hills CA: Sage Publications.

Hofstede, Geert (1981) 'Management control of public and not-for-profit activities', *Accounting, Organizations and Society*, **6**, 3, 193–221.

Hofstede, Geert (1983) 'Dimensions of national cultures in fifty countries and three regions', in *Expiscations in Cross-Cultural Psychology*, J.B. Deregowski, S. Dziurawiec and R.C. Annis (eds), Lisse Netherlands: Swets and Zeitlinger.

Hofstede, Geert (1984) *Culture's Consequences: International Differences in Work-Related Values*, abridged edition, Beverly Hills CA: Sage Publications.

Hofstede, Geert (1986) 'Cultural differences in teaching and learning', *International Journal of Intercultural Relations*, **10**, 3, 301–320.

Hofstede, Geert (1987a) 'The cultural context of accounting', in *Accounting and Culture*, Barry E. Cushing (ed.), American Accounting Association, pp. 1–11.

Hofstede, Geert (1987b) *Dutch Culture's Consequences: Health, Law, and Economy*, Research Memorandum 87–037. Maastricht: Dept of Econ. and Bus.Admin., University of Limburg.

Hofstede, Geert (1989) 'Organising for cultural diversity', *European Management Journal*, **7**, 4, 390–397.

Hofstede, Geert and Michael Harris Bond (1984) 'Hofstede's culture dimensions: an independent validation using Rokeach's Value Survey', *J. of Cross-Cultural Psychology*, **15**, 4, 417–433.

Hofstede, Geert and Michael Harris Bond (1988) 'The Confucius connection: from cultural roots to economic growth', *Organizational Dynamics*, **16**, 4, 4–21.

Hofstede, Geert and John F.A. Spangenberg (1987) 'Measuring individualism and collectivism at occupational and organizational levels', in *Growth and Progress in Cross-Cultural Psychology*, C. Kagitcibasi (ed.), Lisse Netherlands: Swets & Zeitlinger, 113–122.

Hofstede, Geert, Bram Neuijen, Denise D. Ohayv and Geert Sanders (1990) 'Measuring organizational cultures', *Administrative Science Quarterly*, **35**, 286–316.

Hoppe, Michael H. (1990) *A Comparative Study of Country Elites: International Differences in Work-related Values and Learning and their Implications for*

International Management Training and Development. Ph.D thesis, University of North Carolina at Chapel Hill.

Horovitz, Jacques Henri (1980) *Top Management Control in Europe*, London: Macmillan.

Howard, Jane (1984) *Margaret Mead: A Life*, New York: Fawcett Crest.

Hsu, Francis L.K. (1971) 'Psychological homeostasis and jen: conceptual tools for advancing psychological anthropology', *American Anthropologist*, **73**, 23–44.

Hume, David (1964) *The Philosophical Works*, vol. 3, p. 252, T.H. Green and T.H. Grose, eds. [1882]. Reprinted by Scientia Verlag, Aalen.

Inkeles, Alex and Daniel J. Levinson (1969) 'National character: the study of modal personality and sociocultural systems', in *The Handbook of Social Psychology*, 2nd edn, vol. 4, G. Lindsey & E. Aronson (eds), Reading MA: Addison-Wesley [1954].

Kahn, Herman (1979) *World Economic Development: 1979 and Beyond*, London: Croom Helm.

Kelen, Betty (1983) *Confucius in Life and Legend*, Singapore: Graham Brash (Pte.) Ltd [1971].

Khandwalla, Pradip N. (1985) 'Pioneering innovative management: an Indian excellence', *Organization Studies*, **6**, 161–183.

Kieser, Alfred and Herbert Kubicek (1983) *Organisation*, Berlin: Walter de Gruyter.

Kloos, Peter (1984) *Antropologie als wetenschap*, Muiderberg Netherlands: Coutinho.

Kohn, Melvin L. (1969) *Class and Conformity: A Study in Values*, Homewood IL: Dorsey Press.

Kraemer, Alfred J. (1978). 'Cultural aspects of intercultural training', in *International Congress of Applied Psychology*, Munich, August 1978.

Kuhn, Thomas S. (1970) *The Structure of Scientific Revolutions*, 2nd edn, Chicago IL: University of Chicago Press.

Lammers, Cornelis J. (1988) 'Transience and persistence of ideal types in organization theory', *Research in the Sociology of Organizations*, **6**, 203–224.

Laurent, André (1981) 'Matrix organizations and Latin cultures', *International Studies of Management and Organization*, **10**, 4, 101–114.

Lawrence, Peter (1980) *Managers and Management in West Germany*, London: Croom Helm.

Lévi-Strauss, Claude and Didier Eribon (1988) *De près et de loin*, Paris: Editions Odile Jacob.

McClelland, David (1961) *The Achieving Society*, Princeton NJ: Van Nostrand.

Machiavelli, Niccolò (1955) *The Ruler*, translated by Peter Rodd, Los Angeles CA: Gateway Editions Inc. [1517].

March, James G. and Johan P. Olsen (1976) *Ambiguity and Choice in Organizations*, Bergen, Norway: Universitetsforlaget.

Maslow, Abraham H. (1970) *Motivation and Personality*, 2nd edn, New York: Harper & Row.

Mead, Margaret (1962) *Male and Female*, London: Penguin Books [1950].

Merton, Robert K. (1968) *Social Theory and Social Structure*, enlarged edition. New York: Free Press.

Metcalf, Henry C. and Lyndall Urwick (1940) *Dynamic Administration: The Collected Papers of Mary Parker Follett*, New York: Harper & Row.

Mintzberg, Henry (1979) *The Structure of Organizations*, Englewood Cliffs, New Jersey: Prentice-Hall.

Mintzberg, Henry (1983) *Structure in Fives: Designing Effective Organizations*, Englewood Cliffs NJ: Prentice-Hall.
Mintzberg, Henry (1989) *Mintzberg on Management: Inside our Strange World of Organizations*, New York: Free Press.
Morier, James J. (1923) *The Adventures of Hajji Baba of Ispahan*, edited with an introduction and notes by C.W. Stewart, London: Oxford University Press [1824].
Mulder, Mauk (1976) 'Reduction of power differences in practice: the power distance reduction theory and its applications', in *European Contributions to Organization Theory*, G. Hofstede and M.S. Kassem (eds), pp. 79–94, Assen Netherlands: Van Gorcum.
Mulder, Mauk (1977) *The Daily Power Game*, Leiden Netherlands: Martinus Nijhoff.
Negandhi, Anant R. and S. Benjamin Prasad (1971) *Comparative Management*, New York: Appleton-Century-Crofts.
Ng, Sik Hung *et al.* (1982) 'Human values in nine countries', in *Diversity and Unity in Cross-Cultural Psychology*, R. Rath *et al.* (eds), pp. 196–205. Lisse Netherlands: Swets & Zeitlinger.
Orwell, George (1945) *Animal Farm: A Fairy Story*, London: Secker & Warburg.
Otaki, Midori, Mary Ellen Durrett, Phyllis Richards, Linda Nyquist and James W. Pennebaker (1986) 'Maternal and infant behavior in Japan and America', *J. of Cross-Cultural Psychology*, **17**, 3, 251–268.
Ouchi, William G. (1980) 'Markets, Bureaucracies and Clans', *Administrative Science Quarterly*, **25**, 129–141.
Page, Martin (1972) *The Company Savage: Life in the Corporate Jungle*, London: Coronet.
Pagès, Max, Michel Bonetti, Vincent de Gaulejac and Daniel Descendre (1979) *L'emprise de l'organisation*, Paris: Presses Universitaires de France.
Peters, Thomas J. and Richard H. Waterman (1982) *In Search of Excellence: Lessons from America's Best-Run Companies*, New York: Harper & Row.
Pondy, Louis R., Peter J. Frost, Gareth Morgan and Thomas C. Dandridge (eds.) (1983) *Organizational Symbolism*, Greenwich CT: JAI Press.
Pugh, Derek S. and David J. Hickson (1976) *Organizational Structure in its Context: The Aston Programme I*, Westmead, Farnborough, Hants, UK: Saxon House.
Pümpin, Cuno (1984) 'Unternehmenskultur, Unternehmensstrategie und Unternehmenserfolg', *GDI Impuls*, no. 2, pp. 19–30. Bern Switzerland: Gottlieb Duttweiler Institut.
Pümpin, Cuno, J.M.Kobi and H.A.Wüthrich (1985) *La culture de l'entreprise: le profil stratégique qui conduit au succès*, Bern Switzerland: Banque Populaire Suisse.
Renier, G. J. (1931) *The English: Are They Human?* London: Williams & Norgate.
Rose, Reginald (1955) *Twelve Angry Men: A Play in Two Acts*, London: Samuel French.
Roth, Julius A. (1965) 'Hired hand research', *The American Sociologist*, **1**, 1, 190–6.
Russell, Bertrand (1979) *An Outline of Philosophy*, London: Unwin Paperbacks [1927], pp. 23–24.
Sadler, Philip J. and Geert Hofstede (1976) 'Leadership styles: preferences and perceptions of employees of an international company in different countries', *International Studies of Management and Organization*, **6**, 3, 87–113.
Schildhauer, Johannes (1985) *The Hansa: History and Culture*, Leipzig DDR: Edition Leipzig.
Schmitter, Philippe C. (1981) 'Interest intermediation and regime governability in contemporary Western Europe and North America', in *Organizing Interests in*

Western Europe, Suzanne Berger (ed.), Cambridge UK: Cambridge University Press.

Smircich, Linda (1983) 'Concepts of culture and organizational analysis', *Administrative Science Quarterly*, **28**, 339–358.

Soeters, Joseph and Hein Schreuder (1986) 'Nationale en organisatieculturen in accountantskantoren', *Sociologische Gids*, **33**, 2, 100–121.

Stoetzel, Jean (1983) *Les valeurs du temps présent*, Paris: Presses Universitaires de France.

Stroebe, Wolfgang (1976) 'Is social psychology really that complicated? A review of Martin Irle's Lehrbuch der Sozialpsychologie', *European Journal of Social Psychology*, **6**, 4, 509–511.

The Chinese Culture Connection (a team of 24 researchers) (1987) 'Chinese values and the search for culture-free dimensions of culture', *Journal of Cross-Cultural Psychology*, **18**, 2, 143–164.

Theroux, Paul (1988) *Riding the Iron Rooster: By Train through China*, London, Hamish Hamilton.

Todd, Emmanuel (1983) *La troisième planète: Structures familiales et systèmes idéologiques*, Paris: Editions du Seuil. English translation: *The Explanation of Ideology: Family Structures and Social Systems*, Oxford UK: Basil Blackwell, 1985.

Triandis, Harry C. (1972) *The Analysis of Subjective Culture*, New York: Wiley-Interscience.

Triandis, Harry C. (1973) 'Culture training, cognitive complexity and interpersonal attitudes', in *Readings in Intercultural Communication*, D.S. Hoopes (ed.), pp. 55–68, Pittsburgh PA: Regional Council for International Education.

Tung, Rosalie L. (1982) 'Selection and training procedures of US, European and Japanese multinationals', *California Management Review*, **25**, 1, 57–71.

Tylor, Edward B. (1924) *Primitive Culture*, Gloucester MA: Smith [1871].

Vroom, Cas W. (1981) *Indonesia and the West: An Essay on Cultural Differences in Organization and Management*, Jakarta: Catholic University.

Webber, Ross A. (ed.) (1969) *Culture and Management*, Homewood IL: Irwin.

Weber, Max (1970) *Essays in Sociology*, H.H. Gerth and C.W. Mills (eds), London: Routledge & Kegan Paul [1948].

Weber, Max (1976) *The Protestant Ethic and the Spirit of Capitalism*, London: George Allen & Unwin [1930].

Westerlund, Gunnar and Sven-Erik Sjöstrand (1975) *Organizational Myths*, London: Harper & Row.

Williamson, Oliver E. (1975) *Markets and Hierarchies: Analysis and Antitrust Implications*, New York: Free Press.

Wilson, Edward O. (1975) *Sociobiology: The New Synthesis*, Cambridge MA: Harvard University Press.

Witte, Eberhard (1973) *Organisation für Innovationsentscheidungen: Das Promotoren-Modell*, Göttingen FRG: Verlag Otto Schwarz & Co..

Witte, Eberhard (1977) 'Power and innovation: a two-center theory', *International Studies of Management and Organization*, **7**, 1, 47–70.

World Development Report, 1984. Oxford: Oxford University Press.

World Development Report, 1989. Oxford: Oxford University Press.

Name Index

Subject Index

Page numbers in italics refer to the Glossary.